Dewey

John Dewey (1859–1952) was the dominant voice in American philosophy through the world wars, the Great Depression, and the nascent years of the Cold War. With a professional career spanning three generations and a profile that no public intellectual has operated on in the US since, Dewey has been accurately described by his biographer, Robert Westbrook, as "the most important philosopher in modern American history."

In this superb and engaging introduction, Steven Fesmire begins with a chapter on Dewey's life and works, before discussing and assessing Dewey's key ideas across the major disciplines in philosophy, including metaphysics, epistemology, aesthetics, ethics, educational philosophy, social-political philosophy, and religious philosophy.

This is an invaluable introduction and guide to this deeply influential philosopher and his legacy, and essential reading for anyone coming to Dewey's work for the first time.

Steven Fesmire is Professor of Philosophy and Environmental Studies at Green Mountain College, Vermont, USA. He is the author of *John Dewey and Moral Imagination*, winner of a 2005 *Choice* Outstanding Academic Title award.

Routledge Philosophers

Edited by Brian Leiter

University of Chicago

Routledge Philosophers is a major series of introductions to the great Western philosophers. Each book places a major philosopher or thinker in historical context, explains and assesses their key arguments, and considers their legacy. Additional features include a chronology of major dates and events, chapter summaries, annotated suggestions for further reading and a glossary of technical terms.

An ideal starting point for those new to philosophy, they are also essential reading for those interested in the subject at any level.

Available:

Hobbes
A P Martinich

Leibniz
Nicholas Jolley

Locke
E J Lowe

Hegel
Frederick Beiser

Rousseau
Nicholas Dent

Schopenhauer
Julian Young

Freud
Jonathan Lear

Darwin
Tim Lewens

Rawls
Samuel Freeman

Spinoza
Michael Della Rocca

Merleau-Ponty
Taylor Carman

Russell
Gregory Landini

Wittgenstein
William Child

Heidegger
John Richardson

Adorno
Brian O'Connor

Husserl, second edition
David Woodruff Smith

Aristotle, second edition
Christopher Shields

Kant, second edition
Paul Guyer

Hume
Don Garrett

Dewey
Steven Fesmire

Forthcoming:

Freud, second edition
Jonathan Lear

Habermas
Kenneth Baynes

Nietzsche
Maudemarie Clark

Plato
Constance Meinwald

Einstein
Thomas Ryckman and Arthur Fine

Mill
Daniel Jacobson

Berkeley
Lisa Downing and David Hilbert

Plotinus
Eyjólfur Emilsson

Levinas
Michael Morgan

Cassirer
Samantha Matherne

Kierkegaard
Paul Muench

Steven Fesmire

Dewey

Routledge
Taylor & Francis Group

LONDON AND NEW YORK

First published 2015
by Routledge
2 Park Square, Milton Park, Abingdon, Oxon OX14 4RN
and by Routledge
711 Third Avenue, New York, NY 10017

Routledge is an imprint of the Taylor & Francis Group, an informa business

© 2015 Steven Fesmire

The right of Steven Fesmire to be identified as the author of this work has been asserted by him in accordance with sections 77 and 78 of the Copyright, Designs and Patents Act 1988.

British Library Cataloguing in Publication Data
A catalogue record for this book is available from the British Library

Library of Congress Cataloging in Publication Data
Fesmire, Steven, 1967–
Dewey / by Steven Fesmire.
pages cm. – (The Routledge philosophers)
Includes bibliographical references and index.
1. Dewey, John, 1859–1952. I. Title.
B945.D44F43 2014
191–dc23
2014023953

ISBN: 978-0-415-78274-6 (hbk)
ISBN: 978-0-415-78275-3 (pbk)
ISBN: 978-0-203-81689-9 (ebk)

Typeset in Joanna MT and Din
by Cenveo Publisher Services

Printed and bound in the United States of America
By Edwards Brothers Malloy on sustainably sourced paper.

For Jamie

Contents

Acknowledgments

Many friends, colleagues, and students helped to hone this manuscript. I am especially grateful to Kenneth Keith and Jim Garrison for reviewing and offering critical feedback on multiple chapters of the draft. My research assistant at Green Mountain College, Ryann Collins, did Herculean labors reading and responding to the draft. The manuscript was much improved through the diligence of Larry Hickman, David Hildebrand, Brian Leiter, and anonymous reviewers for Routledge. Portions of the manuscript also benefited directly from the critical feedback of Thomas Alexander, Mark Johnson, Philip Kitcher, Erin McKenna, Raymond Boisvert, Nobuo Kazashi, Todd Lekan, Heather Keith, Gregory Pappas, William Myers, William Throop, Thomas Mauhs-Pugh, Neil Conklin, Andrew Light, Trevor Pearce, Phillip Deen, John Van Hoesen, Meriel Brooks, and John Shook. The Society for the Advancement of American Philosophy continues to be a primary source for my intellectual rejuvenation. I extend a warm thank you to numerous Green Mountain College undergraduate and graduate students who read portions of the manuscript, and to Blake Kyler, who served as my student research assistant as the project began. Tony Bruce and Adam Johnson at Routledge were extraordinarily supportive, thoughtful, and collegial. The staff of the Center for Dewey Studies, and Special Collections at Morris Library, Southern Illinois University at Carbondale, were warmly hospitable and accommodating during a 2013 research visit. Paul Millette and Rachel Pusateri at Green Mountain College's Griswold Library were generous, supportive, and professional, as were William Fontaine and the staff of Baker-Berry

Library, Dartmouth College. A portion of this research was supported by a Fulbright grant, which allowed me to teach and conduct research at Kyoto University and Kobe University in 2009. I extend a warm thank you to the Japan–United States Educational Commission in Tokyo for very generous support. I am forever grateful to Michael Mitias for putting me on the scent of Dewey's wisdom long ago at Millsaps College. To Heather Keith and James Kenneth Fesmire-Keith, my gratitude is beyond words.

Abbreviations

Citations of John Dewey's works are to the thirty-seven-volume critical edition published by Southern Illinois University Press under the editorship of Jo Ann Boydston. In-text citations give text abbreviation (for selected books), series abbreviation, followed by volume number and page number. For example: (AE, LW 10:12) is page 12 of *Art as Experience*, which is published as volume 10 of *The Later Works*.

Series abbreviations for *The Collected Works*

EW	*The Early Works* (1882–98)
MW	*The Middle Works* (1899–1924)
LW	*The Later Works* (1925–53)

Abbreviations for selected books

1908 E	*Ethics*, 1978 (1908), MW 5
1932 E	*Ethics*, 1985 (1932), LW 7
ACF	*A Common Faith*, 1986 (1933), LW 9
AE	*Art as Experience*, 1987 (1934), LW 10
CC	*The Child and the Curriculum*, 1976 (1902), MW 2
DE	*Democracy and Education*, 1980 (1916), MW 9
EE	*Experience and Education*, 1988 (1938), LW 13
EEL	Introduction to *Essays in Experimental Logic*, 1985 (1916), MW 10
EN	*Experience and Nature*, 1981 (1925), LW 1
FC	*Freedom and Culture*, 1988 (1939), LW 13
HNC	*Human Nature and Conduct*, 1983 (1922), MW 14

HWT   *How We Think*, 1986 (1933), LW 8
ION   *Individualism, Old and New*, 1984 (1930), LW 5
KK   *Knowing and the Known*, 1989 (1949), LW 16
LSA   *Liberalism and Social Action*, 1987 (1935), LW 11
LTI   *Logic: The Theory of Inquiry*, 1986 (1938), LW 12
PP   *The Public and Its Problems*, 1984 (1927), LW 2
QC   *The Quest for Certainty*, 1984 (1929), LW 4
RP   *Reconstruction in Philosophy*, 1982 (1920), MW 12
TV   *Theory of Valuation*, 1988 (1939), LW 13
UPMP *Unmodern Philosophy and Modern Philosophy*, 2012 (1941–42)

Citations of Dewey's correspondence are to the *The Correspondence of John Dewey, 1871–2007*, published by Southern Illinois University Press under the editorship of Larry Hickman. Citations give the date, reference number for the letter, and author followed by recipient. For example: 1973.02.13 (22053): Herbert W. Schneider to H. S. Thayer. All citations to the *Correspondence* are found in the endnotes.

Chronology

1859	John Dewey born in Burlington, Vermont, on October 20.
1864	Lucina Dewey moves the family to Virginia to be near John's father Archibald, who had enlisted in 1861 as quartermaster in the First Vermont Cavalry during the American Civil War (1861–65).
1865	Lucina and the children return to Burlington.
1875	Enters the University of Vermont in September.
1879	Graduates from the University of Vermont, Phi Beta Kappa.
1879	Teaches High School in Oil City, Pennsylvania.
1880	On a worry-filled evening in Oil City, he has a serene, readjustive experience.
1881	Sole teacher at a small seminary in Charlotte, Vermont for the winter term; pursues private philosophical study with H. A. P. Torrey.
1881	Submits article critiquing materialistic metaphysics to W. T. Harris, editor of the *Journal of Speculative Philosophy* in St. Louis, with a letter requesting Harris's opinion on Dewey's ability.
1882	Enters graduate studies at the Johns Hopkins University in Baltimore; studies philosophy with George S. Morris; studies psychology with G. Stanley Hall; takes a logic course with Charles S. Peirce.
1884	PhD from Johns Hopkins University with a dissertation in Kant's psychology; accepts position in the Department of Philosophy at the University of Michigan.
1886	On July 28 marries Alice Chipman, who had been his student at the University of Michigan.

1887	Birth of their first child, Frederick Archibald.
1887	Publishes *Psychology*, his first book, replete with Hegelian religious apologetics which Dewey would later recall as a "youthful indiscretion."
1888	Publishes *Leibniz's New Essays concerning the Human Understanding*, his second book and a culminating statement of his early metaphysical idealism.
1888	Brief stint as head of the Department of Philosophy at the University of Minnesota.
1889	Birth of daughter Evelyn Riggs.
1889	Upon death of George S. Morris, accepts position as head of the Department of Philosophy at the University of Michigan.
1892	Birth of son Morris, named for George S. Morris.
1894	Accepts position as head of the Department of Philosophy, Psychology, and Education at the University of Chicago and becomes the central figure in what would become known as the Chicago School of Pragmatism, including among others George Herbert Mead, James Tufts, James Angell, and Jane Addams.
1894	Joins the Board of Trustees of Hull House; his most significant education in democracy and social reform begins under the guidance of Jane Addams.
1894	Death of son Morris in Italy from diphtheria at age two and a half; daughter Jane described this as "a blow from which neither of his parents ever fully recovered."
1895	Birth of son Gordon.
1896	Founds the Laboratory School, University of Chicago, known as the "Dewey School."
1896	"Interest in Relation to Training of the Will."
1896	"The Reflex Arc Concept in Psychology."
1897	Birth of daughter Lucy Alice.
1899	President of the American Psychological Association, 1899–1900.
1900	*The School and Society* (revised 1915).
1900	Birth of daughter Jane, named for Jane Addams.
1902	*The Child and the Curriculum.*
1903	*Studies in Logical Theory* becomes a birth announcement of the Chicago School of Pragmatism.

1904   Resigns on April 11 from all appointments at the University of Chicago.

1904   Accepts professorship in the Department of Philosophy at Columbia University, to begin spring semester 1905.

1904   Death of son Gordon in Ireland of typhoid fever at age eight.

1904   Adoption of son Sabino in Italy.

1905   Assumes new position at Columbia University in February.

1905   President of the American Philosophical Association, 1905–6.

1905   "The Postulate of Immediate Empiricism."

1908   Ethics (1st edition), with James H. Tufts.

1908   "Does Reality Possess Practical Character?"

1909   Founding member of the National Association for the Advancement of Colored People.

1909   "The Influence of Darwinism on Philosophy."

1910   How We Think (1st edition).

1910   Charter member of the Men's League for Women's Suffrage.

1915   Cofounder and first president of the American Association of University Professors.

1915   German Philosophy and Politics.

1916   Democracy and Education.

1916   Essays in Experimental Logic.

1916   Begins working on his posture with F. Matthias Alexander, innovator of the "Alexander technique," which effectively relieved him of neck pain, eye strain, and general fatigue.

1917   US enters the First World War; to his later dismay and regret, Dewey controversially supports the national ideal of making the world "safe for democracy."

1917   "The Need for a Recovery of Philosophy," in Creative Intelligence: Essays in the Pragmatic Attitude.

1918   The Polish Experiment funded by the Barnes Foundation; Dewey critical of immigrant assimilation programs.

1918   Relationship from 1917 to 1918 with the novelist Anzia Yezierska. The chaste relationship inspired Dewey to write personal poems which were discarded, salvaged, preserved, and eventually published along with other poems in 1977 as The Poems of John Dewey.

1919   Cofounder of the New School for Social Research in New York City.

1919   Embarks with Alice for a short vacation in Japan, which would extend to more than two years in China and add cross-cultural depth to his subsequent work.

1919   Delivers lectures at Tokyo Imperial University (Tokyo University) on the topic of reconstruction in philosophy.

1919   On May 1 arrives in China, where he would live for over two years. His visit coincides with the historic "May Fourth movement."

1920   The American Civil Liberties Union is founded, with Dewey as an early member.

1920   *Reconstruction in Philosophy.*

1920   Cited as a "second Confucius" in October in an honorary doctoral degree from the National University in Peking (Beijing University).

1921   The Sacco–Vanzetti murder trial incites international protests and divides Americans. Dewey believed they were innocent.

1921   Returns from China in July.

1922   *Human Nature and Conduct.*

1922   Delivers the first series of Paul Carus Lectures, which would form the core of *Experience and Nature.*

1924   Visits Turkey in summer to survey its educational system.

1925   *Experience and Nature.*

1926   School visits in Mexico; lectures at the National Autonomous University of Mexico.

1927   Death of Alice Chipman Dewey.

1927   *The Public and Its Problems.*

1928   Travels to the Soviet Union as a delegate with other American educators and reports somewhat glowingly on the USSR's possible trajectory, a prophecy he very soon revised.

1929   Revised edition of *Experience and Nature.*

1929   Delivers the Gifford Lectures at the University of Edinburgh in April and May.

1929   *The Quest for Certainty.*

1929   October 18–19, seventieth birthday celebration in New York City, with a luncheon attended by 2,300.

1929	October 29 "Black Tuesday" stock market crash ushers in the Great Depression.
1930	*Individualism, Old and New.*
1930	"From Absolutism to Experimentalism."
1930	Retires from Columbia University as Professor Emeritus on July 1.
1930	Honorary degree awarded in November by the Sorbonne; travels in Europe with Albert Barnes, preparing lectures on aesthetics.
1930	"Qualitative Thought."
1930	"Three Independent Factors in Morals."
1931	Gives the William James Lectures at Harvard, the basis for *Art as Experience.*
1931	Jane Addams awarded the Nobel Peace Prize.
1932	*Ethics* (2nd edition), with James H. Tufts.
1932	Honorary degree, Harvard University.
1933	*How We Think* (2nd edition).
1934	Delivers the Terry Lectures at Yale University in January.
1934	*A Common Faith.*
1934	Travels to South Africa with his daughter Jane to participate in an education conference.
1934	*Art as Experience.*
1934	Warns that Hitler and Hitlerism are "the greatest threat to world peace today."
1935	*Liberalism and Social Action.*
1935	The John Dewey Society is founded by educators.
1937	In Mexico City, heads the Commission of Inquiry into the Charges Made against Leon Trotsky in the Moscow Trials, the "Dewey Commission."
1938	China confers on Dewey the Order of the Jade for his contributions to education in China.
1938	*Logic: The Theory of Inquiry.*
1938	*Experience and Education.*
1939	*Freedom and Culture.*
1939	*Theory of Valuation.*
1939	Vacates office at Columbia University.
1939	The first volume of the Library of Living Philosophers, *John Dewey*, is published. The volume, edited by Paul Arthur

Schilpp, contains a biographical essay penned by Jane Dewey in collaboration with her father.

1940 "Time and Individuality."

1940 Defends Bertrand Russell, who had been dismissed from the City University of New York due to nontraditional views of God, marriage, and sexuality.

1941 US enters the Second World War.

1942 J. Edgar Hoover initiates FBI investigation of Dewey for possible subversive activities.

1942 Between summer 1941 and late 1942 works with intense concentration on a book summing up his cultural naturalism. This incomplete manuscript was lost in 1947, recovered sixty years later, and finally published as *Unmodern Philosophy and Modern Philosophy*.

1944 Member of Educators-for-Roosevelt Committee for reelection of Franklin D. Roosevelt.

1946 Marries Roberta Lowitz Grant on December 11.

1946 Supports the People's Party in the election; supports third-party politics.

1949 *Knowing and the Known* with Arthur Bentley.

1949 Ninetieth birthday celebration in New York City.

1951 Honorary degree, Yale University.

1952 Dies in New York City on June 1.

Introduction

John Dewey (1859–1952) was the dominant voice in early to mid-twentieth-century American philosophy through war and depression. His professional career spanned three generations, principally at the University of Chicago (1894–1904) and Columbia University (from 1905). If "there could be such an office as that of national philosopher" in the way of some European nations, Morris Cohen wrote, "no one else could be properly mentioned for it."[1] Indeed *The New York Times* hailed him on his ninetieth birthday as "America's Philosopher." The historian Henry Steele Commager sized up Dewey's impact in his 1950 classic *The American Mind*: "So faithfully did Dewey live up to his own philosophical creed that he became the guide, the mentor, and the conscience of the American people; it is scarcely an exaggeration to say that for a generation no issue was clarified until Dewey had spoken."[2] No public intellectual has operated on this scale in the US since Dewey. In this respect, biographer Robert Westbrook describes him as "the most important philosopher in modern American history."[3]

Such superlatives identify Dewey as a critical precedent for contemporary philosophic work, which may surprise anyone taking a survey of university philosophy curricula. Dewey and other classical pragmatists were by the 1960s dismissed among most mainstream professional philosophers as an "inert fragment of intellectual history."[4] Two generations of Anglophone philosophers taught their students that Charles S. Peirce, William James, and Dewey were, as Philip Kitcher succinctly frames the prejudice in *Preludes to Pragmatism*, "well-intentioned but benighted, laboring with crude tools to develop ideas that were far more rigorously and exactly shaped by the immigrants from Central Europe whose work generated" the Anglo-American or "analytic" tradition in philosophy.[5] Yet a resurgence of interest in Dewey during the past three decades is producing a highly articulated framework for clarifying and extending the achievements of contemporary philosophy while urging at the same time that the future of philosophy "should be unlike (most of) the recent past."[6]

As the most celebrated achievement of the "golden age" of American intellectual ferment in the opening decades of the twentieth century, the philosophical movement of Peirce (1839–1914), James (1842–1910), Dewey, Jane Addams (1860–1935), and George Herbert Mead (1863–1931) paralleled the eighteenth-century Enlightenment in the application of experimental inquiry to humane ends. They were called *pragmatists*, despite their shared discomfort with this label, nowadays co-opted as a synonym for self-serving expediency and realpolitik. Dewey wrote in a 1940 letter: "The word 'pragmatism' I have used very little, and then with reserves."[7]

The classical American pragmatists destabilized the popular perception that, to paraphrase Henry David Thoreau, philosophers are builders of luxurious conceptual castles that nowhere touch the Earth. The "laboratory-minded" logician Peirce fathered pragmatism in 1878 as a means for clarifying the general meaning of concepts by tracing their implied experimental consequences. The humanistic and individualistic James reinterpreted Peirce's principle for clarifying concepts, extended it to the term "truth," and launched the pragmatic movement with his 1898 essay "Philosophical Conceptions and Practical Results."

James's principal aim was to highlight the concrete practical import of differing philosophical beliefs (see LW 2:3–21). He was not staking out a familiar or predecessor position within twentieth-century philosophy of language or philosophy of mind, such as problems of linguistic or cognitive significance. He was insisting that the important philosophical questions are those that make a difference in our lives, and by implication that some nominally philosophical questions are unimportant. He wrote in *Pragmatism* in 1907: "There can be no difference anywhere that doesn't *make* a difference elsewhere—no difference in abstract truth that doesn't express itself in a difference in concrete fact and in conduct consequent upon that fact, imposed on somebody, somehow, somewhere and somewhen."[8]

Over the next half-century, the democratic Dewey expanded and rigorously systematized pragmatism as a means for regenerating philosophy and intelligently redirecting culture to meet life's evolving difficulties. He envisioned resilient communities, at all scales, guided in pursuit of social goods by a citizenry educated in the methods of organized cooperative intelligence.

In terms of both cultural and professional influence, Dewey and his elder contemporary James are the preeminent voices speaking to us from what is now dubbed the "classical" period of American philosophy. In addition to the aforementioned pragmatists, philosophers of the classical period included (among others) skeptical materialist George Santayana, idealist and "Absolute pragmatist" Josiah Royce, philosophical social scientist W. E. B. Dubois, and English-born "process" philosopher and logician Alfred North Whitehead.

As Kitcher observes, some recent scholarship on Dewey has sought, as a sort of re-domestication project, to bring him back into "the pantheon of respectable philosophers." Yet the point for Dewey "is not to continue philosophy-as-usual, but to change it."[9] Anglophone philosophers in the main have given the lion's share of philosophical attention—and in Aesop's fable the lion did not actually share—to the meaning of abstract concepts or the representational content of thought. This overriding focus, not shared by the classical pragmatists, has tended to isolate philosophers from contemporary conflicts, disparities, divisions, and drift. Meanwhile, philosophers who do deal with urgent and widely shared problems have too often reached for outworn intellectual tools which have not, in Dewey's view, been reformed to meet the jobs at hand.

Dewey viewed philosophy as "a criticism of criticisms" (EN, LW 1:298), a critique of the comfortable assumptions that color, shape, and prejudice our thinking. Well-conceived in the main as "an organized attitude of outlook, interpretation, and construction" (LW 5:278), philosophy is also a practice of generalizing judgments that can only be developed and renewed "through the discipline of severe thought" (EN, LW 1:40). In Stanley Cavell's idiom, philosophy is the education of grown-ups. It is a critique of the formative influences on our fundamental intellectual and emotional dispositions (DE, MW 9:338).[10] One's philosophic outlook is not mere assent to one set of intellectual propositions over another. It is a tendency to perceive, think, and *act* one way rather than another. Its trial and test, for Dewey, is in this active, prospective tendency (LW 5:278). The greatest problems of philosophy are those that are emerging before us. Whatever the merits of a work's schematic form and its scholarly chewing of a "historic cud" (MW 10:47), by Dewey's own standards it is *philosophically* valuable only insofar as it sheds light "upon what philosophy should now engage in" (LW 16:361).[11]

Philosophic criticism is pertinent when it extends and deepens our most worthwhile experiences, that is, when it perpetuates goods that are justified by open reflection or helps us to mediate shared difficulties (EN, LW 1:299–302). Philosophy is impertinent when it degenerates into a form of theater or a complacent professional identity, or worse, when it devolves into a form of verbal conquest and scholasticism confined to "timeless" core problems manufactured by a small esoteric class of symbolic technicians (see DE, MW 9:338).[12]

Dewey daily bet his life out of a trust that we can intelligently deal with problems and direct ourselves toward desirable goals, both individually and collectively, without transcendental standards that hide from inspection even as they pretend to guarantee the validity of judgments. Dewey's philosophic trust in natural intelligence is his greatest legacy, more than any specific conclusion he arrived at.

Much published writing about Dewey's work is piecemeal and appropriative. Epistemologists tend to mine Dewey's compelling critique of the presumed gap between a knowing subject and known objects, yet ignore or dismiss his reconstruction of metaphysics. Richard Rorty, for example, offers a Jekyll-and-Hyde interpretation of Dewey's *Experience and Nature* as an ill-begotten foray into metaphysics by a "bad" Hegelian Dewey who was otherwise a "good" naturalistic epistemologist.[13] Meanwhile, philosophers of education tap Dewey's theories of inquiry and democratic citizenship but often ignore his aesthetics, despite Dewey's contention that both education *and* art are testing grounds for the adequacy of any philosophy.

Partial treatments of Dewey have contributed to uncritical devotion and offhanded dismissals by those who either ignore or exaggerate tendencies, such as Dewey's at times overstated faith in the humanizing arts of technological control. Neither reverential apologetics nor self-confident dismissal is compatible with a philosophical appraisal. As a result of such partialities, the newcomer is too rarely offered an opportunity to see beneath Dewey's veneer to anticipate his moves across the philosophic spectrum. Consequently, the general coherence of his philosophy often escapes notice.

Having shed an early commitment to Hegelian idealism by his late thirties, Dewey retained a lifelong distrust of the construction of closed, all-inclusive philosophical systems. *All philosophies are transitional.* No philosophic problem is placeless or timeless. Yet he was a systematic thinker in his elaboration of a comprehensive philosophy of ameliorative experience (and imaginative experimentation) in its intellectual, practical, and affective dimensions. I accordingly take Dewey's philosophy of experience as the key to interpreting his principal writings. This offers a standpoint from which to see the integrity of his philosophy.

This book does not emphasize arcane debates of yesteryear. Instead, in the spirit of Dewey, it engages perennial problems along with ideas that are players on today's philosophic stage, or that hold promise but have not yet "made it" beyond specialist circles. I give special attention to theories attracting interest beyond Dewey aficionados, such as his naturalistic theory of knowing among philosophers of science, his critique of mind/body dualism and the cognitive/emotive split among cognitive scientists, his pluralism and conception of moral imagination among ethicists, and his work to achieve a deliberative democratic community educated in the ways of open inquiry among social-political philosophers and advocates.

The first chapter introduces the essentials of Dewey's life and writings. The second chapter introduces his theory of interactive, embodied experience. The spotlight is on *Experience and Nature,* his most rigorous analysis and defense of a naturalistic and experimental "metaphysics" that is answerable to experience. Subsequent chapters explore Dewey's philosophy of experience in its intellectual (epistemology), practical (ethics), and affective (aesthetics) dimensions, all of which play a role in his democratic social-political, educational, technological, and religious philosophies. The final chapter describes and appraises Dewey's influence, legacy, and prospects in some of these areas.

Dewey was arguably the twentieth century's most prolific first-tier philosopher, so to be both synoptic and substantive I have avoided extremes of telescopic inclusion and microscopic parsing that would frustrate newcomers. To accomplish this, I have foreshortened the thirty-seven-volume *Collected Works of John Dewey* and the four-volume *Correspondence of John Dewey* by viewing traditional topical areas (e.g., metaphysics, epistemology, ethics, aesthetics, political philosophy) from the standpoint of concepts central to Dewey's reconstruction of those areas (e.g., experience, inquiry, imagination, consummatory experience, democracy). I have retained traditional philosophical signposts in chapter and section headings. Dewey's favored theme of "reconstruction" gives continuity across chapters, and its appearance in chapter titles signals his reframing of a philosophical tradition from which he parted company.

Where specialized vocabulary is unavoidable (as with Chapters Two and Three), or where Dewey employed ordinary English words in technical ways, readers can count on definitions in the glossary. In his technical writings Dewey presupposed considerable knowledge of ancient Greek and seventeenth- to nineteenth-century European philosophy, as well as a background in biology and physics, so I have included brief synopses and endnote references where essential.

I have sought a sympathetic but not uncritical tone, along with a style that is concrete, accessible, and engaging. Dewey's questions are framed to become the reader's own questions. To avoid the un-Deweyan impression that philosophers work in a detached universe of timeless problems, I present Dewey in the historical context of problematic situations to which he was responding. But I also invite the reader to join me as we sort through generalized twenty-first-century problems with Dewey's help and critique him in turn. I will give some special emphasis to what we narrowly refer to as environmental problems—there is some poetic symmetry here, as Dewey's address, at 2880 Broadway near Columbia University, is home to the NASA Goddard Institute for Space Studies directed by climate scientist James Hansen.[14] The result, I hope, is a selective overview that is constructive rather than simply summative.

The text grows out of my twenty-five years of engagement with contemporary scholarship on Dewey. It incorporates a major recovered book manuscript from the 1940s, presumed lost for sixty years and at last published in 2012.[15] Specific scholarly references and documentation have been mostly relegated to endnotes. Scholarly debates among specialists are reviewed when pertinent to introducing Dewey to a twenty-first-century audience, but otherwise I silently take positions. I bypass philosophical problems that absorbed Dewey but that are overly technical or that we have since, in his words, gotten over. For example, only passing attention is given to British neo-Hegelian idealist Thomas Hill Green, despite the profound importance of British idealism as an inspiration and foil in the development of classical American pragmatism. Instead, I clarify Dewey's arguments by referencing more persistent and familiar forms of metaphysical idealism. In general I follow Dewey's own lead, emphasizing his ideas more than their historical origins and development (e.g., see LW 5:179).

Be cautioned throughout this book that Dewey does not follow a linear style of argumentation in which each link in a chain of reasoning is fatally vulnerable. He made many formal arguments with conclusions supported by tightly constructed premises, but his analyses were more often like cables with many intertwining strands, as Peirce counseled for experimental methods in his 1868 essay "Some Consequences of Four Incapacities." Consequently, a volume limited solely to reconstructing Dewey's formal arguments would fail to give the reader Dewey, and it would fail to make his philosophy intuitive for the reader.

Dewey sought to advance philosophy's project of "intellectual disrobing," enabling us to critically inspect intellectual habits to see "what they are made of and what wearing them does to us" (EN, LW 1:40). His philosophy came of age during the first half of the twentieth century, and it requires the ongoing tempering and criticism of subsequent experience. We and not our predecessors are more in the know about the problems with which we must now deal and the questions we must now ask. Yet we are entangled in the hazy assumptions of our own day and the uninspected doctrines of bygone days. Economist Paul Krugman has lately called such bygone doctrines "zombie ideas," creeds of the living dead.[16] If this book conveys something of Dewey's wisdom in critiquing prevailing assumptions and thereby inspires some readers to carefully study his own writings, it will have well repaid the writing.

Notes

1 In George Dykhuizen, *The Life and Mind of John Dewey* (Carbondale, IL: Southern Illinois University Press, 1973), 324.
2 In Robert B. Westbrook, *John Dewey and American Democracy* (Ithaca, NY: Cornell University Press, 1991), xiv.
3 Westbrook, *John Dewey and American Democracy*, ix.
4 Philip Kitcher, *Preludes to Pragmatism: Toward a Reconstruction of Philosophy* (Oxford: Oxford University Press, 2012), 1.
5 Kitcher, *Preludes to Pragmatism*, xi.
6 Kitcher, *Preludes to Pragmatism*, xiv. One of the best general elaborations of Dewey's pragmatism is Ralph Sleeper's *The Necessity of Pragmatism* (New Haven, CT: Yale University Press, 1986).
7 1940.09.06 (13667): Dewey to Corliss Lamont. Cf. Thomas M. Alexander, "John Dewey's Uncommon Faith: Understanding 'Religious Experience,'" *American Catholic Philosophical Quarterly* 87, no. 2 (2013): 347–62, at 351. In 1908 Arthur Lovejoy influentially identified thirteen conflicting senses of pragmatism then in vogue among philosophers (Arthur O. Lovejoy, *The Thirteen Pragmatisms and Other Essays* [Baltimore: Johns Hopkins University Press, 1963]). The word pragmatism in colloquial English is a bit more definite, with arguably two principal meanings. It primarily suggests the tempering of ideologies with practicality, the balancing of principles with achievable outcomes, or simply flexibility amid contingencies. The word secondarily means, again outside of academic philosophy, pursuit of the most expedient means to satisfy a self-interested desire. If we shave off any antiintellectual connotation, the first popular sense above may capture something of the "Yankee pragmatism" Dewey imbibed as a Vermonter. But Dewey's philosophical reconstructions cut much deeper than the "pragmatism" of common parlance. To call someone a pragmatist popularly suggests a counterweight to compensate for the unworldliness of pie-in-the-sky ideals or dogmatic ideology. The worldly pragmatist ensures that some portion of our ideals may be realized, which we presume is better than none at all. Yet Dewey rejected the fixed ideals that are usually presupposed in such machinations. Pragmatism in the colloquial sense, no matter how valuable, could be no more than a small part of an adequate philosophy. A pragmatism whose sole role is to compensate for excesses would lack legs of its own.
8 William James, *Pragmatism*, in *Writings 1902–1910* (New York: Library of America, 1988 [1907]), 508. Cf. Kitcher, *Preludes to Pragmatism*, 3–5. For an analysis of differences between Peirce's and James's versions of pragmatism, see Thomas Burke, *What Pragmatism Was* (Bloomington, IN: Indiana University Press, 2013).
9 Kitcher, *Preludes to Pragmatism*, xiv.

10 On Cavell's statement about philosophy in *The Claims of Reason*, see Naoko Saito and Paul Standish, eds., *Stanley Cavell and the Education of Grownups* (New York: Fordham University Press, 2012).

11 See John Stuhr, "Dewey's Social and Political Philosophy," in *Reading Dewey: Interpretations for a Postmodern Generation*, ed. Larry A. Hickman (Bloomington, IN: Indiana University Press, 1998), 82–84.

12 For a thoughtful book-length exploration of the implications of Dewey for contemporary analytic philosophy, see Philip Kitcher's collection of essays *Preludes to Pragmatism: Toward a Reconstruction of Philosophy* (cited above).

13 For the classic statement of the "two Deweys" view, see "Good Dewey, Bad Dewey," in Richard Rorty, *Consequences of Pragmatism* (Minneapolis, MN: University of Minnesota Press, 1982).

14 Hanson retired in 2014. Dewey's address is better known to locals as the home of Tom's Restaurant, made famous by singer Suzanne Vega and the television sitcom *Seinfeld*.

15 John Dewey, *Unmodern Philosophy and Modern Philosophy*, ed. Phillip Deen (Carbondale, IL: Southern Illinois University Press, 2012).

16 Paul Krugman, "Rubio and the Zombies," *The New York Times*, February 14, 2013, http://www.nytimes.com/2013/02/15/opinion/krugman-rubio-and-the-zombies.html?_r=0; accessed September 26, 2014.

Further reading

For a range of helpful online articles on John Dewey's philosophy, consult the *Stanford Encyclopedia of Philosophy*. Readers seeking further introductory works on Dewey may wish to consult (in alphabetical order):

Raymond D. Boisvert, *John Dewey: Rethinking Our Time* (Albany, NY: SUNY Press, 1998).
James Campbell, *Understanding John Dewey* (LaSalle, IL: Open Court, 1995).
David L. Hildebrand, *Dewey: A Beginner's Guide* (Oxford: Oneworld Publications, 2008).

For scholarly essays ranging over much of Dewey's philosophy, see:

Molly Cochran, ed., *The Cambridge Companion to Dewey* (Cambridge, UK: Cambridge University Press, 2010).
Larry A. Hickman, ed., *Reading Dewey: Interpretations for a Postmodern Generation* (Bloomington, IN: Indiana University Press, 1998).
John R. Shook and Paul Kurtz, eds., *Dewey's Enduring Impact* (Amherst, NY: Prometheus Books, 2011).

For general collections of Dewey's works, see:

Larry A. Hickman and Thomas M. Alexander, *The Essential Dewey*, 2 vols. (Bloomington, IN: Indiana University Press, 1998).
John J. McDermott, *The Philosophy of John Dewey* (Chicago: University of Chicago Press, 1981).

One
Life and works

The things in civilization we most prize are not of ourselves. They exist by grace of the doings and sufferings of the continuous human community in which we are a link. Ours is the responsibility of conserving, transmitting, rectifying and expanding the heritage of values we have received that those who come after us may receive it more solid and secure, more widely accessible and more generously shared than we have received it.

(ACF, LW 9:57–58)

Dewey published 32 books in his lifetime (11 after his 1929 retirement), over 600 articles and essays, and 135 reviews. The 37-volume critical edition of his writings, *The Collected Works of John Dewey*, is organized into early, middle, and late works, and consists of around 8 million words.[1] This chapter provides a selective chronological narrative of Dewey's personal and intellectual biography. Priority is given to themes, concepts, events, and writings that set the biographical and historical context for later analysis of his key writings.[2]

Are you right with Jesus, John?

Burlington rises above the eastern shore of Lake Champlain in a wide valley between Vermont's Green Mountains and New York's Adirondack Mountains. By the time of John's birth to Archibald and Lucina Rich Dewey on October 20, 1859, Burlington was Vermont's cultural and commercial hub. Vermont was, and to some degree remains, a hub of "town meeting" participatory democracy. It is tempting to imagine young John weaned on a wholesome diet of earnest "town meeting days" in a sleepy, homogeneous New England village, white steeples rising unassumingly from a thickly forested landscape. But this is tempting fiction. Burlington's rapidly growing waterfront, where Dewey worked in the lumber yards as a youth, was the third busiest lumber port in the United States. The port attracted a relatively diverse working class, over 40 percent Irish or French-Canadian. Lakeside tenement houses and distant mountains shorn of trees bore witness to the social and environmental costs of the rise of industrial capitalism.

John's father Archibald was a grocer and tobacconist from an old farming family. His humor and love of wordplay shone through his store ads, one of which read "Hams and Cigars—Smoked and Unsmoked."[3] Another touted his cigars as "a good excuse for a bad habit." He had an impressive memory and a penchant for quoting classical British literature, along with distaste for Ralph Waldo Emerson's unconventional theology. He was easygoing in both religious and business matters, and was reputed to be better at selling goods than collecting payments.[4] Vermont was a stronghold in the temperance movement, and Archibald ran Burlington's sole licensed medical liquor dispensary. John would have fond recollections of what he called his father's "sympathetic stories about this branch of the business."[5]

Lucina was of bourgeois Vermont stock. She was religiously pious, philanthropic, strict, and ambitiously committed to the education of her sons. With the outbreak of the American Civil War in 1861, Archibald served as quartermaster for a regiment of Vermont cavalry in Virginia. Weary of the prolonged separation of her family, Lucina boldly moved her children to Archibald's northern Virginia headquarters for the winter of 1864, where they witnessed the war's devastation of the region. This experience deeply affected the children.

The third of four sons, the first of whom died in infancy, John attended the public school with his brothers. Unsurprisingly, the father of progressive pedagogy in the United States found his formulaic grade school to be boring. Thankfully there were occasional off-topic deviations from the rote curriculum, during which his teachers accidentally happened upon some connection to life. Aside from such episodic learning, Dewey's enduring early education occurred spontaneously through interpersonal contacts and occupational responsibilities. As the Dewey boys grew older they outfitted rowboats and joined friends for trips around Lake Champlain and Quebec, by and by learning enough French to read novels before studying the language in school.[6] The boys also regularly visited and did chores on their grandfather's farm. Dewey later lamented that such occupational supplements to formal education were mostly eclipsed by urbanization and mechanization.[7]

Self-conscious and shy as a youth, his introverted passion for ideas grew in the long shadow of his mother's evangelical intensity. She would sporadically ask John and his brothers "Are you right with Jesus? Have you prayed to God for forgiveness?"[8] Due in part to this fervent inspection and religious pressure by Lucina, John retained sympathy throughout his life for those suffering a personal religious crisis. In one of his first articles, Dewey wrote pointedly: "Religious feeling is unhealthy when it is watched and analyzed to see if it exists, if it is right, if it is growing. It is as fatal to be forever observing our own religious moods and experiences, as it is to pull up a seed from the ground to see if it is growing."[9]

Dewey identified himself as a Christian into his thirties, but he would never approach organized religion as a philosophical matter of universal import. His intellectual life was dedicated to social problems, and religious questions interested him only as a type of social question. Dewey wrote in his sole autobiographical essay, "From Absolutism to Experimentalism" (1930): "While the conflict of traditional religious beliefs with opinions that I could myself honestly entertain was the source of a trying personal crisis, it did not at any time constitute a leading philosophical problem" (LW 5:154).

With the help of scholarships and affordable tuition, at age fifteen John enrolled as a student at the University of Vermont. There were eight professors on the faculty. The first two years were dull, but during his junior year the broad evolutionary outlook of geology, zoology, and physiology stirred his interests.[10] Philosophical, psychological, and religious courses were finally taken up during the "finishing" process of senior year. Yet his philosophic interests were more piqued in the university's library, which subscribed to periodicals from England representing radical, moderate, and traditional perspectives on the blazing controversies between empirical findings of the natural sciences and long-cherished religious beliefs.[11] He graduated in 1879 at the age of nineteen, second in a class of eighteen.

Dewey was anxious about his vocation after graduating. He sought throughout the summer for a teaching position but was too young and green to secure one. Still unemployed in the fall, he received word of a job opening in Oil City, Pennsylvania, where a cousin served as high school principal. He taught there for two years and read philosophy all the while. He read Kant, Hegel (1770–1831), Leibniz, and the *Journal of Speculative Philosophy*, the only philosophy journal in the United States at that time. One worry-filled evening in Oil City in 1880, Dewey had a serene, readjustive experience. He described the feeling to his friend Max Eastman many years later: "What the hell are you worrying about, anyway? Everything that's here is here, and you can just lie back on it."[12] When his cousin resigned as principal, Dewey returned to Burlington. He became the sole teacher for a winter term at a small seminary in Charlotte, just south of Burlington.

During the 1881/82 academic year Dewey studied philosophical classics privately on long walks with his former philosophy professor at the University of Vermont, H. A. P. Torrey. The principal focus was metaphysics. For Torrey, as for almost all philosophers in American universities at this time, the bedrock of Protestant Christianity was never seriously questioned. Philosophy courses were offered for students seeking a more rigorous and contemplative expression of Christianity, those who were not fully content with simple faith that humans were central figures in the universe's drama of redemption as members of a species specially created in an instant by a word from God. To counter the mechanistic material universe presented by English empiricism without thereby rejecting science, nineteenth-century philosophers like Torrey found allies in Scottish "common sense" philosophers who extolled the free mind's timeless intuitions. Torrey was averse to philosophies that ran against the grain of religious faith. Dewey later said that Torrey "was a man of genuinely sensitive and cultivated mind. ... He was, however, constitutionally timid, and never really let his mind go" (LW 5:148).

About Vermont Dewey was ambivalent. His Columbia University colleagues Herbert Schneider and John Herman Randall, who had summer homes in Peacham, Vermont, report him exclaiming he "left that God-foresaken country as soon as he could."[13] By way of explanation, Vermont is today one of the most politically progressive states in the US, but in Dewey's youth it was a conservative stronghold, not congenial to "the development of a freer American philosophy" (LW 5:149). Moreover, Vermont was at the time among the most impoverished of the United States, and Dewey's departure was part of a massive outmigration from the state. The adventure of urban life awaited him, but he would retain the deep imprint of a rural life in which people in closer contact with natural cycles occupied themselves with producing their sustenance rather than just consuming it.

The novelist George Eliot, whose great sympathy for characters and events was an enduring influence on Dewey's moral imagination, observed in *Scenes of Clerical Life* that our faith in ourselves is for the most part due to faith that others believe in us. Dewey was now envisioning philosophy as a professional vocation, and he sought a looking-glass for his talents. In 1881 he submitted a critique of materialistic metaphysics to the Hegelian philosopher and educational reformer W. T. Harris, editor of the *Journal of Speculative Philosophy* in St. Louis. In "fear and trembling" he included a letter: "An opinion as to whether you considered it to show ability enough of any kind to warrant my putting much of my time on that sort of subject would be thankfully received." Harris eventually responded that "the essay showed a philosophical mind of high rank."[14] Harris published the piece and two subsequent articles. Dewey's faith in his philosophical abilities was buoyed by both Torrey and Harris, and he set out in 1882 for Johns Hopkins University with the help of a $500 loan from an aunt.

From absolutism to experimentalism

Johns Hopkins University had been founded six years previously as a center for research and graduate education. It attracted nonclergy philosophers such as the Hegelian George S. Morris, a fellow Vermonter. A popular and kind professor, Morris at that time taught fall terms at Johns Hopkins while also heading the University of Michigan's philosophy department. Charles S. Peirce taught logic, though the influence on Dewey of Peirce's pragmatism would come much later.[15] G. Stanley Hall, who studied with William James at Harvard, where Hall received the first psychology PhD granted in the US, tugged at Dewey from the empiricist side while the more traditional Morris reinforced the supremacy of the theological. It was the latter who confirmed Dewey as a Hegelian.

By the 1880s religious apologists were replacing the Scottish intuitionism expounded by Torrey with the "Absolute idealism" of Hegel, Fichte, and Schelling. These giants of nineteenth-century German idealism were interpreted by American and English philosophers through a selective reading of the English Romantic poet Samuel Taylor Coleridge's writings on imaginative creativity. Like all other forms of metaphysical idealism, Coleridge's *Aids to Reflection* analyzed existence, value, and knowledge from the standpoint of mind or spirit. Such a worldview harmonizes better than empiricism with popular religious conviction. It celebrates a world forged with purpose and inscribed with value, and it more readily subordinates science to theology. Later nineteenth-century Hegelian idealists, such as the influential Oxford don Thomas Hill Green (1836–82), conceived such a purposeful universe as an essential condition for the possibility of liberating human life.

In sharp contrast with the necessity of bloody conflict and all-encompassing state control described by Hegel and Marx, Green's idealism supported radical liberal reform to maximize individual freedom while countering the great inequalities of laissez-faire industrial capitalism. As a young man Dewey was inspired by the idealistic conception that the fabric of the world is ultimately congenial to being grasped as a perfect unity by our minds and warmly appraised as purposeful and benevolent by our judgments. The mature Dewey would not share Green's metaphysical faith, but the latter's radical liberalism and emphasis on local problem-solving did find in Dewey a voice for twentieth-century reforms.

In 1884 Dewey completed his PhD at Johns Hopkins University with a dissertation in Kant's psychology. Morris offered, and Dewey accepted, a position in the Department of Philosophy at the University of Michigan. Dewey became a member of Ann Arbor's Congregational Church and a leader of classes in the university's Student Christian Association, where in the mid-1880s he spoke on the duty of religious faith.[16] His reputation as a teacher at this time was captured in a student publication's satirical dictionary: "Dew(e)y. Adj. Cold, impersonal, psychological, sphinx-like, anomalous and petrifying to flunkers."[17]

In the summer of 1886 Dewey married Alice Chipman (1859–1927), who had been his student at the University of Michigan. Their early social life revolved around the Morris home. Their first child, Frederick Archibald, was born in 1887. Alice had a profound influence on the introverted John, not least in their mutual advocacy for women. She was among six women of the thirteen students who graduated in philosophy from the University of Michigan in 1886, making that department especially progressive for its time.[18] Many years later Dewey would tell his friend Max Eastman that "no two people were ever more in love." The affection between John and Alice is apparent to any scholar who has eavesdropped on their early letters. They esteemed each other both morally and intellectually.[19]

Alice's parents died in her early childhood, and she was raised by her unorthodox grandparents Frederick and Evalina Riggs. The staunchly independent Fred Riggs worked as a surveyor and trader for the Hudson Bay Company, and eventually joined, defended, and became proficient in the language of the Chippewa tribe.[20] Imbibing her grandfather's independent spirit, Alice was the most significant, if unsung, influence on Dewey's shift away from religious orthodoxy. John and Alice's daughter Jane wrote that her mother "had a deeply religious nature but had never accepted any church dogma. Her husband acquired from her the belief that a religious attitude was indigenous in natural experience, and that theology and ecclesiastic institutions had benumbed rather than promoted it."[21]

Dewey's first book, *Psychology* (1887), was an influential attempt by a twenty-eight-year-old Hegelian idealist to reconcile the emerging experimental psychology with the tradition-friendly metaphysics to which he still clung. The book's style was the target of satirical "grinds" by University of Michigan students who jokingly advertised the availability of an authorized English translation. Dewey's seminal insight was that human consciousness must be studied empirically via psychology, not by means of armchair speculation in the style of Descartes. On the strength of this insight Dewey was launched to fame as author of the leading psychology text for students of philosophy. While students packed his classes to explore cutting-edge ideas, his former Johns Hopkins professor G. Stanley Hall tellingly criticized the book's evidence-free assertions about the necessity of God. Hall pithily wrote: "That the absolute idealism of Hegel could be so cleverly adapted to be 'read into' such a range of facts, new and old, is indeed a surprise as great as when geology and zoology are ingeniously subjected to the rubrics of the six days of creation."[22] William James reportedly sighed "poor Dewey" after reading the book.

His second book, *Leibniz's New Essays concerning the Human Understanding* (1888), was commissioned for a book series on German Philosophical Classics edited by Morris. The technical proficiency and clarity of this book on Leibniz, whom Dewey regarded as "the greatest intellectual genius since Aristotle" (EW 1:267), solidified Dewey's reputation as a historical scholar.

In 1888 Dewey accepted a position as head of the Department of Philosophy at the University of Minnesota. Upon the death of his beloved professor and former colleague Morris in 1889, he returned to the University of Michigan to head its Department of Philosophy. When James's two-volume masterpiece *The Principles of Psychology* appeared in 1890, Dewey had been poised to use his own *Psychology* as the text for a course. He shelved it after reading James. It later pained him to recall his Hegel-steeped *Psychology*. Despite remaining his best-selling book through the 1890s, Dewey relegated it to "a kind of youthful indiscretion."[23] In James's *Principles*, according to Herbert Schneider, Dewey "not only found the 'instrumental theory of concepts' on which Dewey's logic was based, but also experienced that contagious mental 'loosening up' with which James influenced his generation and which made him the father of American philosophy."[24]

As his engagement in educational and political problems grew in the coming years, he abandoned Hegelian Absolute idealism. The influence of German thought on Dewey's subsequent work was more subdued than for his Berlin-educated contemporaries Mead and DuBois. Yet Dewey acknowledged that Hegelian idealism "left a permanent deposit" in his thinking.[25] As Kwame Anthony Appiah says of Mead and DuBois, Dewey sought to steal the fire of German thought without getting burned by its parochialism.[26] Indeed, in his seventies Dewey would say "there is greater richness and greater variety of insight in Hegel than in any other single systematic philosopher" with the exception of Plato (LW 5:154).

At his seventieth birthday celebration, Dewey characterized himself in the third person as "somewhat sensitive to the movements of things about him. He had a certain appreciation of what things were passing away and dying and of what things were being born and growing."[27] In part due to James's *Principles* "loosening" him up in the 1890s, Dewey demonstrated this sensitivity to historical movements by seizing on the revolutionary philosophical implications of the evolutionary outlook. Charles Darwin's *On the Origin of Species* was published in 1859, the year of Dewey's birth, and from the 1890s Dewey devoted his career to developing an evolution-steeped naturalistic philosophy that conceived mind, value, and existence in terms of coordinated interactions between biological organisms and their environments. If Hume aspired in the eighteenth century to be the Newton of the mind, Dewey aspired in the twentieth century to be its Darwin.[28]

Educator, educated

Dewey had been working all the while on pedagogy and educational reform. If so-called knowledge quickly evaporates or cannot be put to work in circumstances that differ from the context in which it was learned, it can hardly be said that a student has learned anything. Better to learn through concrete and specific activities, such as mastering the basics of math through cooking or calculating distances on excursions, rather than beginning in a fog of abstractions. Abstraction, precision, and generalization can and must be grafted in due course.

In 1894 Dewey became head of the Department of Philosophy, Psychology, and Education at the new University of Chicago. He remained for a decade, building the "Chicago School of pragmatism" alongside Mead, Jane Addams, James Tufts, James Angell, and others.

Soon after arriving in Chicago the educator was educated in democracy and social reform with the help of Addams. The philosopher, social worker, international peace advocate, and community organizer Addams cofounded Hull House on the West Side of Chicago as a settlement house for European immigrant women in 1889, and Dewey joined its Board of Trustees in 1894.[29] Addams, who was later honored with the 1931 Nobel Peace Prize, helped

Dewey learn to habitually check the prejudices and conventions that lead us to mentally resist lives and conceptions that are alien and unfamiliar (LW 5:421). Addams and Hull House also underscored for Dewey the ever-growing happiness to be "found simply in this broadening of intellectual curiosity and sympathy in all the concerns of life" (LW 5:422).[30]

He and Alice, who in 1900 named their third daughter after Jane Addams, had great need for such enduring satisfactions during their Chicago years. John and Alice would eventually have seven children, one adopted. It is by no means incidental to the development of Dewey's philosophy that two of his children died in childhood. Morris Dewey was born in 1892, named for George S. Morris. Dewey wrote to Alice in 1894 that Morris is "the most perfect work of art in his attitude to the world that I have ever seen."[31] After a long journey later that year, the two-and-a half-year-old Morris died of diphtheria in Italy. This was, according to their daughter, "a blow from which neither of his parents ever fully recovered." Fifty years later Dewey could not speak of his son Morris without a hitch in his throat. A year after Morris's death, Gordon Dewey was born. A gifted child, he died in Ireland of typhoid fever at age eight, leaving his parents inconsolable. Alice experienced severe bouts of depression for the remainder of her life.

Dewey was shaken by these losses. In his ethical and political writings he would come to highlight the need to see beyond confused conditions so that we may eventually construct more desirable circumstances. Yet he and Alice understood, painfully, that some conditions do not yield readily to reconstruction and that wresting meaning from tragic situations does not in all cases better prepare one to deal with similar situations in the future. Commentators who pay too little heed to Dewey's life often fail to note the attention he gave throughout his mature writings to the tragic dimension of experience.[32] The mediation of intelligence cannot avert tragedy, but it is, after all, "the sole alternative to luck" (EN, LW 1:279). "Nature is the mother and the habitat of man," Dewey wrote in *Art as Experience*, "even if sometimes a stepmother and an unfriendly home" (AE, LW 10:34).[33]

In 1896, in addition to publishing his watershed article "The Reflex Arc Concept in Psychology," Dewey founded an experimental school affiliated with the University of Chicago. The Laboratory School, which became known as the "Dewey School" despite its founder's disdain for despotic rule, provided the testing grounds for his theories of education and for his philosophy more generally. The school was genuinely experimental, with ideas tested, judged to be failures, and set aside even in the middle of a term. Alice served as principal of the school from 1896 to 1904. In 1903 the school merged with another elementary school (the Chicago Institute), with Alice as principal. Alice had publicly criticized the Chicago Institute, and her position as principal led to resignation threats from Chicago Institute teachers who distrusted her. William Harper, the university's president, dealt with the unrest by refusing to renew Alice's appointment.[34] This prompted both Deweys to resign all appointments at the University of Chicago. Despite their founder's departure, the "Laboratory Schools" remain prominent in progressive education in the United States, drawing about one-half of their students from the children of University of Chicago faculty, including at one time the children of Barack and Michelle Obama.

The philosopher of the progressive era

In 1904 Dewey accepted a professorship in the Department of Philosophy at Columbia University, which he began spring semester 1905. He enjoyed thoroughgoing academic freedom at Columbia, in contrast with pressures he encountered at the University of Chicago. Academic honors continued to build. Having already served as president of the American Psychological Association, in the coming years Dewey was president of the American Philosophical Association, and cofounder and first president of the American Association of University Professors.

The father of progressive pedagogy had a droning lecturing style in university courses that bore little resemblance to the interest-sparking methods he influentially prescribed for secondary education. To paraphrase Dewey's student and later Columbia colleague Irwin Edman, it remains "one of the sociological paradoxes of American culture" why a man who "by all conventional criteria" was a poor classroom teacher "should have so deeply inspired and remade the thinking of crucial individuals in all the professions, teaching above all."[35] Still, his classes were well attended and painstakingly well-prepared. The most attentive students uniformly reported their amazement, particularly upon reviewing their notes, with Dewey's capacity to rethink ideas in class. Ideas were always real for Dewey, and he was expert at tracking their consequences.

Dewey's Columbia colleague and former student John Herman Randall Jr. observed that different professors evoke different sentiments such as admiration, respect, or affection. "For Dewey," he reported, "it was unashamed love."[36] He was mild and courteous in manner. His Yankee diffidence and shrewdness combined with careful speech, good-humored seriousness, and a lack of vanity. He was fearless yet unpretentious in discourse. His mind was as persistent as the natural force he believed all of our minds to be.

Several pivotal essays and books appeared during his first few years at Columbia, including "The Postulate of Immediate Empiricism" (1905), a best-selling textbook titled *Ethics* coauthored with James Tufts (1908), "The Influence of Darwinism on Philosophy" (1909), and the first edition of *How We Think* (1910). In 1916 Dewey published *Democracy and Education*, often pointed to as the best overall expression of his general philosophy. He typed it all with the two-finger method.

In 1916 he was experiencing neck pain, eye strain, and general fatigue, and he began working on his posture with F. Matthias Alexander, innovator of the "Alexander technique." The experience enhanced Dewey's well-being, and he subsequently wrote glowing introductions to three of Alexander's books. Alexander's method became a touchstone for Dewey's analysis of will and habit in *Human Nature and Conduct*. It is commonly believed, Dewey observed, that standing up straight is simply a function of will power. Alexander "pointed out that this belief is on a par with primitive magic in its neglect of attention to the means which are involved in reaching an end. And he went on to say that the prevalence of this belief, starting with false notions about the control of the body and extending to control of mind and character, is the greatest bar to intelligent social progress" (HNC, MW 14:23).[37]

Much to his later dismay and regret, Dewey supported President Woodrow Wilson's 1917 decision for the United States to join the First World War as the war that would end war and make the world "safe for democracy." Dewey's 1915 book *German Philosophy and Politics* attacked German thought as inherently antidemocratic and helped to substantiate American involvement in the war. His support for US entry into the war deepened the divide between prowar and antiwar progressives, and he was taken to task by former admirers, most astutely Randolph Bourne in his 1917 essay "Twilight of Idols." Bourne wrote antiwar editorials for *The Dial* magazine, which were eventually muzzled—sadly, with Dewey's collusion.[38] After the war Dewey quickly tempered his wartime writings. In an essay on "The Post-war Mind," he warned that "the embittered missionaries of a permanent vengeful punishment and cultivated hatred of Germany should be compelled to retire and undergo a period of historical study" (MW 11:114).

By fall 1918 Dewey was advocating a much more radical vision of freedom and equality for the budding postwar "League of Nations" than was President Wilson, a vision that would carry over to his leading role in the Outlawry of War movement in the 1920s. In "The League of Nations and the New Diplomacy" (1918), Dewey made what would later become his trademark distinction between a freedom that is merely *formal* and legally vouchsafed, on the one hand, and *effective* freedom and equality that checks "immense inequality of power," on the other hand (MW 11:133).[39] His proposal anticipated the now-common economic distinction between free trade and fair trade. It became evident within a few months that even Wilson's proposed formal equality among nations would be bargained away, resulting in a hollow and ineffective international peace agreement. Dewey's coeditor Thorstein Veblen wrote for *The Dial* in May 1919: "America has won the war; America has lost the peace, the object for which she fought."

Dewey was the principal advisor in 1918 for an ill-advised and poorly managed study of the Polish immigrant community in Philadelphia, funded by his new friend Albert Barnes of the Barnes Foundation. The novelist Anzia Yezierska, whose family emigrated from Poland in the 1880s, was retained as translator and typist. The confusing details of "The Polish Experiment" are beyond this book's scope, but it is relevant to spotlight Dewey's views in the 1910s on immigration and cultural pluralism. Dewey still tended in the 1910s toward a somewhat Hegelian emphasis on social harmony, but like fellow progressives such as Horace Kallen, he rejected the metaphor of America as a "melting pot" if this is taken to mean assimilation of other ethnic groups to Anglo-Saxon culture or assimilation that dissolves distinctive cultural traditions. What is required instead, Dewey argued, is that cultural groups in America each contribute to one another. Just as the horn section and the flute section in an orchestra ideally contribute to a harmonic symphony, so ideally cultural sections in America are symphonic and not a jumble of "different instruments playing simultaneously."[40] But instead of democratic conditions that promote crossfertilization and open communicative channels for dealing with conflicts, Dewey lamented, what we find instead in America is a great deal of xenophobic prejudice coupled with an antidemocratic infrastructure propped up by business interests, churches, and politicians who reap a harvest by keeping immigrant groups "isolated and therefore in easy subjection." Dewey argued that assimilating immigrants to existing conditions is not the problem. If one were to accept "Americanization" as a legitimate aim, then the problem of Americanization is "almost wholly one of reforming the environment of America" into which immigrants come.[41]

In 1917–18 Dewey had a brief relationship with Yezierska. The emotionally charged yet chaste romance inspired Dewey to write personal poems, several of which suggest that he concurred with her typecast of him as the quintessential cool, suppressed Yankee.[42] In his poems Dewey lamented "the woes of fresh made hells" that arise when one has to be satisfied not with romantic fulfillment, but with bittersweet memories. Yezierska apparently mistook his reticence about deepening the relationship as a selfish concern for his reputation, to which Dewey tellingly responded: "Not rightly have you guessed / The things that block the way, / Nor into what ties I've slowly grown / By which I am possessed."[43] He discarded one batch of poems in the late 1920s, but they were salvaged from his wastebasket by a librarian. Another "mess of loose scraps of poetry" was discovered in 1939 by his colleague Schneider, who had inherited Dewey's office and roll-top desk. This batch was also salvaged and preserved, and both batches were eventually published in 1977 with several other poems as The Poems of John Dewey.[44]

Of the political tensions inherent in daily life as a university professor, a former president of Columbia University said that

Dewey "has been a conscience, not always soothing."[45] His correspondence reveals him dealing with and irritated by day-to-day institutional politics, and he considered leaving Columbia in 1919 for the New School for Social Research, which he had just cofounded. While mulling over that decision, he wrote of his wife: "She [Alice] is certainly fonder of Columbia than I am, and I think than she would be if she had to stand it herself."[46]

The philosopher of democracy at home and abroad

Instead of leaving Columbia, Dewey embarked with Alice for what was to be a short vacation in Japan to deliver lectures at Tokyo Imperial University (Tokyo University) on the topic of reconstruction in philosophy. He found Japan to be aesthetically rich yet politically dispiriting. He wrote a series of essays exploring and critiquing Japan's feudal communitarianism, a social system in which individuals were subordinated to the emperor as the symbol of communal life so that the state became the ultimate moral standard.[47] He politely declined the emperor's offer to confer on him the Order of the Rising Sun.[48]

While in Japan, he was invited to visit China by several of his former Columbia University students, including Hu Shih, who sought to spread Dewey's emphasis on the child rather than the lesson as education's focus. He arrived in China on May 1, 1919, for a visit that would extend to over two years. His visit coincided with the historic "May Fourth movement," a pivotal prelude to the Maoist revolution of 1949. The May Fourth movement refers specifically to a mass demonstration of students in Beijing on May 4, 1919. The demonstration was sparked by the Treaty of Versailles, which, with President Wilson's support, ceded to Japan the Chinese territory of Manchuria that had been held by Germany prior to the war. From his vantage point in China, Dewey was angered and disillusioned by the Treaty of Versailles, and he deeply regretted his earlier support of Wilson and the "war to end war."[49] More generally, the May Fourth movement refers to the radicalization of China from around 1917 to 1921. In "The Student Revolt in China," which Dewey published in the New Republic magazine a month after the Beijing demonstration, he declared with some prescience that "the fourth of May, nineteen hundred and nineteen, will be marked as the dawn of a new day" (MW 11:191).

Dewey found these political events invigorating, an effect amplified by standing-room-only crowds everywhere he lectured. In October 1920 he was cited as a "second Confucius" in an honorary doctoral degree from the National University in Peking (Beijing University). Deeply moved by experiences in China, he wrote to a friend in January 1920: "Nothing western looks quite the same anymore, and this is as near to a renewal of youth as can be hoped for in this world."[50] The influence on Dewey was enduring. His experiences in China offered an East–West comparative standpoint to examine Euro-American presuppositions (e.g., see MW 12:217–27).[51] "China remains the country nearest his heart after his own," his daughter Jane wrote in 1939. "The change from the United States to an environment of the oldest culture in the world struggling to adjust itself to new conditions was so great as to act as a rebirth of intellectual enthusiasms."[52]

Dewey's influence in China fizzled as Maoism ignited, though his work is currently undergoing a renaissance with the recent completion of the Chinese translation of the Collected Works of John Dewey. His reputation in China was still sufficiently strong by 1942 that, in an unusual nod to the power of a philosopher's pen, during the Second World War Dewey wrote a "Message to the Chinese People" that was translated into Mandarin "and scattered as a leaflet by the US Army Air Force over Chinese cities."[53] "Your country and my country," Dewey wrote, "are alike in having been attacked without reason and without warning by a rapacious and treacherous enemy. ... The coming victory will restore to China her old and proper leadership in all that makes for the development of the human spirit" (LW 15:369–70).

Upon returning to the United States in 1921, Dewey threw himself into professional and political life. In 1922 he delivered the Paul Carus Lectures, which would form the core of arguably his greatest work, Experience and Nature (1925/1929). He visited Turkey in summer 1924 to survey its educational system at the request of the secularizing Turkish government, and in 1926 he visited schools in Mexico while giving lectures at the National Autonomous University of Mexico. In these trips, his daughter Jane recounted,

Dewey witnessed "the power and necessity of education to secure revolutionary changes" that are not merely external rearrangements of culture but genuinely benefit individuals.[54]

Alice joined her husband for the Mexico trip, but heart problems forced her to return home. Dewey went on leave from Columbia in spring 1927 to care for her as she became weaker. She died in July 1927. Dewey responded to a condolence letter from George Herbert and Helen Mead: "Over forty years we were together and Alice has made my life more than anything else."[55] Alice was the greatest influence on her husband's work as a social and educational reformer, and he reflected on the occasion of his seventieth birthday that his life with her, their children, and their grandchildren had been the greatest blessing of his life.[56]

In *Public Opinion* (1922) and *The Phantom Public* (1925), journalist Walter Lippmann influentially criticized participatory democracy. Susceptible as public opinion is to propaganda and manufactured consent, and consumed as we all are with affairs of family, career, and finances, Lippmann argued that it is impossible for us to be "sovereign and omnicompetent" citizens who "know what is going on" and "have an opinion worth expressing on every question which confronts a self-governing community."[57] Lippmann's books remain the classic sources for those favoring elite, expert-driven deliberative processes over participatory ones. Dewey's public responses to Lippmann culminated in 1927 with *The Public and Its Problems*, the classic argument for participatory democracy. In a 1939 letter to his former student Hu Shih, Dewey said that he had meant to emphasize in *The Public and Its Problems* the "absolute importance of democratic action in determining the policies of the government— for only by means of 'government by the people' can government for the people be made secure" (in LW 2:430).

Fresh from his debates with Lippmann, Dewey traveled to the Soviet Union in 1928 as a delegate with other American educators. He reported somewhat glowingly on the possible Soviet trajectory for cooperative life and experimental education, but he was soon to alter this bright prophecy as the Stalinist faction's "revolution from above" began its murderous purge. He later wrote that "the Russians are and will be a great people—when they get the chance."[58] Dewey remained prosocialist yet anti-Marxist.

Retirement?

The most productive decade of Dewey's career was 1929–39. In his final year before retiring as a full-time professor from Columbia, Dewey revised *Experience and Nature*, and in April and May 1929 delivered the Gifford Lectures at the University of Edinburgh which were promptly published as *The Quest for Certainty*. The book is a relentless attack on traditional epistemology from the revolutionary standpoint of knowing as acting. One reviewer observed that "the cumulative impression is one of stupendous destruction."[59] One strength of this widely read book was Dewey's cutting-edge grasp of developments in quantum physics, such as Werner Heisenberg's 1927 "uncertainty principle." This command of theoretical physics was due in part to conversations with his daughter Jane, who earned her PhD in physics at MIT in 1925, worked with Niels Bohr in Copenhagen, and in 1932 became chair of the Physics Department at Bryn Mawr.[60]

Dewey retired from Columbia University as Professor Emeritus on July 1, 1930. In the same year he was awarded an honorary degree by the University of Paris (the Sorbonne), delivered a watershed paper on ethical theory to the French Philosophical Society titled "Three Independent Factors in Morals," and published "Qualitative Thought," one of his most important essays.

In late 1930 he traveled in Europe with his friend Albert Barnes, the Philadelphia art collector and critic, preparing lectures on aesthetics which he presented as the William James Lectures at Harvard University in 1931. These lectures formed the basis for one of his best and most celebrated works, *Art as Experience* (1934). The private, eccentric, rough-tempered, and brilliant Barnes made his fortune as a physician–chemist and businessman. Before the days of antibiotics, he developed an antiseptic to treat gonorrhea and to prevent gonorrheal blindness in newborns. Dewey's correspondence with Barnes ran from 1917—when Barnes wrote an enthusiastic letter to Dewey after the appearance of *Democracy and Education*—until Barnes's 1951 death. Their correspondence comprises more than 1,500 letters, the later ones signed affectionately Jack and Al.

Dewey wrote Barnes in 1920 that he had long eschewed aesthetics in order to "reserve one region from somewhat devastating analysis."[61] The deferral paid off. Dewey's engaging prose in *Art as*

Experience reveals the freshness and vitality with which he approached the subject. His interactions with Barnes and the world-class Barnes Collection in Philadelphia prepared him to approach art in a nurturing and respectful rather than devastatingly analytical way. Dewey said of Barnes that he "is a man from whom one can learn a lot but apparently only the opposite kind of a crank like myself is capable of learning from him."[62] He dedicated *Art as Experience* to Barnes "in gratitude."

In 1932, as Dewey was penning his crowning achievement in aesthetics, he and Tufts finally completed a major revision of their 1908 *Ethics*, a process they had begun a decade earlier. Shifting between aesthetics and ethics came easily to Dewey. Indeed, in his view separating imagination and the aesthetic from our moral philosophies contributes to "the bleakness and harshness often associated with morals" (1932 E, LW 7:271). In *Reconstruction in Philosophy* Dewey argued that ethicists have dispassionately quested for "a single, fixed and final good," but what is needed is to "transfer the weight and burden of morality to intelligence" (RP, MW 12:172–73). His ethics textbooks sought to do just that. These books were bestsellers in their day; indeed, the 1908 *Ethics* was one of Dewey's bestselling books well into the 1920s.[63]

In 1934 he delivered the Terry Lectures at Yale University, published the same year as *A Common Faith*. This was Dewey's only book on the philosophy of religion. He argued for a secular democratic faith independent of creeds. "One of the few experiments in the attachment of emotion to ends that mankind has not tried," he urged, "is that of devotion, so intense as to be religious, to intelligence as a force in social action" (ACF, LW 9:53).

Political and economic struggles were never far from his mind. Months after the October 29, 1929, "Black Tuesday" stock market crash that ushered in the Great Depression, Dewey produced *Individualism, Old and New*, now a classic in political philosophy. In opposition to Marxism, Stalinism, Trotskyism, and Maoism, Dewey argued in his 1930s political writings that although violent revolution may sometimes be justified, violent class conflicts are not *inevitable* as a means to desired social changes. In fact, he argued, evidence favors the contrary view: violent revolutions no longer lead to sought-after revolutionary social consequences, particularly not to genuine democracy. "Russia has shown that the days of [violent] revolution with resulting good are over," he said.[64] In *Liberalism and Social Action* (1935) he argued against the growing Depression-era dogma among those on the political left that violent force is a political necessity for securing freedom and equality. "I know of no greater fallacy than the claim" that brute force "will be the method of calling genuine democracy into existence" (LSA, LW 11:60).

Dewey's analyses of violent class struggle remind more recent readers of debates between Martin Luther King Jr. and Malcolm X, and there is a connection. In 1933 Myles Horton acknowledged his indebtedness in a letter to Dewey. Horton was director of the Highlander Folk School in Tennessee, which in the 1950s became the training hub for key players in the American civil rights movement, such as Rosa Parks and Martin Luther King Jr. Horton expressed his gratitude to Dewey while adding that he did not see himself as a disciple. "I'm so delighted to find that you don't claim to be a disciple," Dewey promptly replied. "My enemies are bad enough, but my disciples are worse."[65]

In 1937, Dewey interacted with one of the twentieth century's master architects of violent revolution, when he traveled to Mexico City to head the Commission of Inquiry into the Charges Made against Leon Trotsky in the Moscow Trials, which became known as "The Dewey Commission." The Commission was organized to investigate spurious charges made by Joseph Stalin after ousting his brilliant Soviet corevolutionary Trotsky. The artist Diego Rivera, who was hosting the exiled Trotsky in Mexico, sketched Dewey during the proceedings. The Dewey Commission cleared Trotsky of all charges, angering apologists for Stalin on the American radical left. Dewey wrote to a friend: "It was the most interesting single intellectual experience in my life."[66]

In 1938, the seventy-nine-year-old Dewey published the monumental culminating tome of his instrumentalist theory of inquiry and knowing, *Logic: The Theory of Inquiry*. In the same exhausting year he wrote *Experience and Education*, which is today his most widely read, and his most lucid and concise, book in the philosophy of education. Before finally vacating his office at Columbia in 1939, he published two more major contributions to political philosophy and ethics: *Freedom and Culture* and *Theory of Valuation*.

In 1940 Dewey led a public defense of philosopher Bertrand Russell, who had been denied a proffered position at the City University of New York due to nontraditional views of God, marriage, and sexuality, which included advocacy for liberalizing British obscenity law. Dewey's only published discussion of homosexuality occurred in this context (LW 14:235–48). Even these two resolute progressives adhered to the then-prevailing "it's just a phase" view among psychologists that only heterosexuality is "normal" as an end-stage of sexual development. Dewey, for his part, understood the intertwining of science and values, and he took the long view that some amount of obtuseness is tragically unavoidable yet not thereby excusable. He and Russell may well have had a better philosophy of sexuality than their contemporaries in the 1940s, but in Dewey's view "the better is too often the enemy of the still better" (LSA, LW 11:50).

Dewey had warned in March 1934 in *The New York Times* that Hitler and Hitlerism were "the greatest threat to world peace today."[67] Nonetheless, his disillusionment and reflections after the First World War led him to oppose American military intervention in the late 1930s and early 1940s: let Europe sort out its own problems, since they keep causing them, while America charts a new course. After the Japanese attack on Pearl Harbor, he concluded alongside most other Americans that the country had no choice.[68]

Dewey spent many of his final years defending academic freedom against the "stupidity, intolerance, bullheadedness and bad education" (LW 2:219) that characterized the House Un-American Activities Committee and its Cold War demagogue Joseph McCarthy. From 1942 to 1943 the anti-Stalinist Dewey was, ironically, investigated as a communist subversive by J. Edgar Hoover's FBI as part of the Special Committee on un-American activities. The FBI in its files aptly described Dewey as having "carelessly combed gray hair," "disheveled attire," and a "monotonous drawl." The investigation exonerated Dewey, but the FBI continued to build its files. A 1957 FBI report on the late philosopher cautiously noted a warm birthday greeting from President Truman that Dewey had received on his ninetieth birthday.[69]

Dewey married Roberta Lowitz Grant in December 1946. He was eighty-seven; she was forty-two. He had become friends with the

Grant family in Oil City, Pennsylvania, about a quarter-century before the birth of his second wife, and when Roberta was a child he had interacted with the Lowitz family. They adopted two young sibling children, John Jr. and Adrienne.

Roberta and the children were present for his ninetieth birthday celebration in New York City in 1949, attended by 1,500 well-wishers, from close friends and colleagues to Prime Minister Jawaharlal Nehru of India. Dewey responded at the celebration that his work across the fields of "education, politics, social problems, even the fine arts and religion" had been an outgrowth of his "primary interest in philosophy." He saw himself as having been "first, last, and all the time, engaged in the vocation of philosophy," and his philosophical aim had been to get "a moderately clear and distinct idea of what the problems are that underlie the difficulties and evils which we experience in fact; that is to say, in practical life" (LW 17:84–85).[70]

Dewey died of pneumonia on June 1, 1952, in New York City. Just six blocks from his birthplace on Willard Street in Burlington, Dewey's ashes are interred beside the Ira Allen Chapel of his alma mater, the University of Vermont.[71] His epitaph, drawn from the close of A Common Faith, is the epigraph to this chapter.

Reading Dewey and the "lost" book

Dewey's prose at times rivals the greatest philosophic writers such as Hume and James, and his many popular writings on contemporary events are lively and accessible. Nonetheless, his overall reputation is deservedly that of a writer who repays hard work. US Supreme Court Chief Justice Oliver Wendell Holmes Jr. appraised Dewey's Experience and Nature "to have a feeling of intimacy with the inside of the cosmos that I found unequaled." It was what God might have said "had He been inarticulate but keenly desirous to tell you how it was."[72] In Dewey's early days as a Hegelian idealist, peers complimented his prose. He recalled: "During the time when [my] schematic interest predominated, writing was comparatively easy; there were even compliments upon the clearness of my style. Since then thinking and writing have been hard work" (LW 5:151). He did not seem to mind the criticisms. A writer may be reputed to be clear, he wrote, "merely because the meanings he expresses are so familiar as not to demand thought by the reader" (AE, LW 10:273).

Dewey struggled to see the world from the inside, but the traditional dualistic philosophical language he inherited was not up to this task. It was insufficient in both its rigor and its humanity. While most philosophers in his day still aspired to a disembodied standpoint to conceive the cosmos, what Thomas Nagel calls a "view from nowhere," Dewey strove to modify settled language in order to bridge the distance between the inadequacy of familiar notions and the vagaries of new ones. Yet he was far from a mere technical specialist writing on abstruse problems for an insular audience. As Schneider observed, *Experience and Nature* treats the most "common concerns of human existence" with "extraordinary directness, informality, and urbanity."[73] Dewey impressed Justice Holmes as "having more life and experience in his head than most writers. ... To my fancy he gets closer to the cosmic wiggle than anyone else that I know in these days."[74] US Supreme Court Justice Felix Frankfurter at Dewey's ninetieth birthday celebration hailed him as a philosopher who "transcends the bounds of his technical problems and fertilizes the thoughts of men to whom the terminology of philosophic inquiry may be a foreign language."[75]

Dewey continued to hone and develop his ideas throughout his life, and a portion of his most mature work has only recently become available to expand his philosophical legacy. In *Dialogue on Dewey*, which records a conversation several years after Dewey's death, his friend and former student Corliss Lamont lamented that Dewey never produced a single book summing up his philosophy. Between summer 1941 and late 1942 Dewey had worked with intense concentration on just such a book. He approached the work as a general historical critique of philosophy's lost opportunities, rooting out philosophical conceptions that had outlived their adaptiveness. "The working motto of one and all" modern philosophies, Dewey asserted, is to "get everything out into the open where it can be seen and examined" (UPMP:169). In 1945 Dewey wrote his friend Arthur Bentley, with whom he would coauthor *Knowing and the Known* (1949), that "I accumulated a lot of mss but it never would jell."[76]

This incomplete manuscript, or perhaps some less fragmented revision of it, was lost in 1947. There were conflicting reports about what happened. One story ran that Dewey absent-mindedly left the briefcase containing the manuscript in a cab; another that it had been left behind in the Deweys' summer cabin in Nova Scotia; another that it had been left on the sidewalk and disappeared. Regardless, *The New York Times* played up the loss by reporting the manuscript to have been complete (UPMP:xvii). Dewey's friend and former student Joseph Ratner urged him to begin anew in 1949, and Ratner agreed to join as coauthor, but the work never moved forward.[77]

Sixty years later the manuscript was recovered by a young scholar who was combing the Dewey Papers at Southern Illinois University. This scholar, Phillip Deen, edited and published the book in 2012 under Dewey's own working title, *Unmodern Philosophy and Modern Philosophy*.

Until publication of this "new book," the best picture scholars had of Dewey's most mature philosophy was an unfinished reintroduction he penned in the late 1940s for *Experience and Nature*, perhaps most notable for replacing Dewey's term experience with "culture." Now, over seventy years after it was typed, the recovered manuscript offers a cultural critique of still-persistent philosophical mistakes along with vital entry points into Dewey's works for a new generation.

Summary

Dewey was born in Vermont in 1859, the same year in which Darwin's *On the Origin of Species* was published, and he died in New York in 1952, the year in which the first hydrogen bomb was detonated. He became a liberal Hegelian during his PhD studies at Johns Hopkins, but influenced in part by James in the 1890s he began developing an evolution-steeped naturalistic philosophy. His professional home from 1894–1904 was the University of Chicago, after which he moved to Columbia University. Dewey authored thirty-three books, from his early *Psychology* (1887) to the recently recovered *Unmodern Philosophy and Modern Philosophy* (2012). Commager sized up the scale of Dewey's influence as a public intellectual: "So faithfully did Dewey live up to his own philosophical creed that he became the guide, the mentor, and the conscience of the American people; it is scarcely an exaggeration to say that for a generation no issue was clarified until Dewey had spoken."

Notes

1 Personal communication, Larry A. Hickman, The Center for Dewey Studies, Southern Illinois University at Carbondale. The word estimate includes introductions, appendices, and back matter.

2 I will emphasize the following key writings: "The Reflex Arc Concept in Psychology," "The Postulate of Immediate Empiricism," "The Influence of Darwinism on Philosophy," Democracy and Education, Introduction to Essays in Experimental Logic, "The Need for a Recovery of Philosophy," Reconstruction in Philosophy, Human Nature and Conduct, Experience and Nature, The Public and Its Problems, The Quest for Certainty, Individualism, Old and New, "From Absolutism to Experimentalism," "Qualitative Thought," "Three Independent Factors in Morals," Ethics (2nd edition), How We Think, A Common Faith, Art as Experience, Liberalism and Social Action, Logic: The Theory of Inquiry, Experience and Education, Theory of Valuation, Freedom and Culture, "Time and Individuality," Knowing and the Known, and Unmodern Philosophy and Modern Philosophy.

3 Jane M. Dewey, "Biography of John Dewey," in The Philosophy of John Dewey, ed. Paul Arthur Schilpp and Lewis Edwin Hahn (Chicago: Open Court, 1989), 5.

4 Jane Dewey, "Biography of John Dewey," 6.

5 Jane Dewey, "Biography of John Dewey," 8.

6 Jane Dewey, "Biography of John Dewey," 8.

7 Jane Dewey, "Biography of John Dewey," 9.

8 Quoted in Sidney Hook, "Some Memories of John Dewey," Commentary 14, no. 3 (1952): 245–53.

9 In George Dykhuizen, The Life and Mind of John Dewey (Carbondale, IL: Southern Illinois University Press, 1973), 7.

10 Jane Dewey, "Biography of John Dewey," 10.

11 Jane Dewey, "Biography of John Dewey," 10–11.

12 1965.11.17 (21794): Arthur G. Wirth to John L. Childs. Reported by Max Eastman in "John Dewey," Atlantic Monthly 168 (1941): 673. Cf. Robert B. Westbrook, John Dewey and American Democracy (Ithaca, NY: Cornell University Press, 1991), 8.

13 From Corliss Lamont, ed., Dialogue on John Dewey (New York: Horizon Press, 1959). Cf. James A. Good, A Search for Unity in Diversity: The "Permanent Hegelian Deposit" in the Philosophy of John Dewey (Lanham, MD: Lexington Books, 2006).

14 Jane Dewey, "Biography of John Dewey," 13–14.

15 Dewey wrote in a 1949 letter: "The influence of Peirce upon me was late & was through James & his references to Peirce. ... Aside from James Peirce was disregarded for the most part in all academic circles until after the Hartshorne-Weiss publication of his Collected Papers 1930–35. There is no mystery accordingly in the lateness of my references to him & my indebtedness to him" (1949.04.26 [15129]: Dewey to Haskell Fain).

16 Linda Robinson Walker, "John Dewey at Michigan," Michigan Today (Fall 1997). Walker's article is also available at http://archive.is/Y23Xg; accessed June 10, 2014.

17 Walker, "John Dewey at Michigan."
18 Walker, "John Dewey at Michigan."
19 Walker, "John Dewey at Michigan."
20 Walker, "John Dewey at Michigan."
21 Jane Dewey, "Biography of John Dewey," 21.
22 In Dykhuizen, *The Life and Mind of John Dewey*, 85.
23 1915.07.05 (03542): Dewey to Scudder Klyce.
24 Obituary of John Dewey, *The New York Times*, June 2, 1952; https://www. nytimes.com/learning/general/onthisday/bday/1020.html; accessed June 10, 2014. It would be a mistake to interpret Dewey as a disciple of James. As Mead observed, Dewey's independence is apparent as early as his 1891 *Outlines of a Critical Theory of Ethics* (EW 3:237–388), which does not draw from James in its development of a holistic approach to human action. See George Herbert Mead, "The Philosophies of Royce, James, and Dewey in Their American Setting," in *Selected Writings*, ed. Andrew Reck (Chicago: University of Chicago Press, 1964), 387–88. John Shook argues that the German psychologist Wilhelm Wundt was also a significant and underappreciated influence on Dewey's instrumentalism. See John R. Shook's *Dewey's Empirical Theory of Knowledge and Reality* (Nashville, TN: Vanderbilt University Press, 2000).
25 On the enduring Hegelian influence, see John R. Shook and James A. Good, eds., *John Dewey's Philosophy of Spirit* (London: Fordham University Press, 2010). Richard Gale goes further to label Dewey a "Promethean mystic," "the Plotinus of Burlington," in Richard M. Gale, *John Dewey's Quest for Unity* (Amherst, NY: Prometheus Books, 2010).
26 Kwame Anthony Appiah, plenary session of the annual meeting of the Society for the Advancement of American Philosophy, March 2013.
27 In *John Dewey: The Man and His Philosophy*, Addresses Delivered in New York in Celebration of His Seventieth Birthday (Cambridge, MA: Harvard University Press, 1930), 174.
28 Also in 1859 Henri Bergson and Edmund Husserl were born, John Stuart Mill published *On Liberty*, and Karl Marx published *Critique of Political Economy*.
29 Sadly, Hull House filed for bankruptcy and ceased social work operations in January 2012. It is now a museum.
30 Cf. Steven C. Rockefeller, *John Dewey: Religious Faith and Democratic Humanism* (New York: Columbia University Press, 1991), 229.
31 1894.07.09 (00156): John Dewey to Alice Chipman Dewey.
32 In comparison, an informed reader of Ralph Waldo Emerson detects a dramatic shift in essays written before and after his beloved five-year-old son Waldo died of scarlet fever in 1842—compare "Nature" (1836) and "Experience" (1844).
33 Cf. Jay Martin, *The Education of John Dewey: A Biography* (New York: Columbia University Press, 2002). See also Thomas Dalton's *Becoming John Dewey* (Bloomington, IN: Indiana University Press, 2002).
34 Good, *A Search for Unity in Diversity*, 233.
35 Irwin Edman, *John Dewey* (New York: Bobbs-Merrill, 1955), 24. For a glimpse of Dewey's style, insofar as it can be revealed through the always-stiff films of

the era, readers can watch a November 23, 1929, short film of Dewey distinguishing going to college from getting an education, hosted online by the University of South Carolina's Museum of Education: http://www.ed.sc.edu/museum/dewey_movietone.html; accessed June 10, 2014.

36 Dykhuizen, The Life and Mind of John Dewey, 250.
37 See Dewey's glowing introduction to one of Alexander's books: F. Matthias Alexander, The Resurrection of the Body: The Writings of F. Matthias Alexander, ed. Edward Maisel (New York: Dell Publishing, 1969). Richard Shusterman discusses Alexander in Pragmatist Aesthetics: Living Beauty, Rethinking Art, 2nd ed. (Oxford: Blackwell, 2000). On Dewey and Alexander, see for example Rockefeller, John Dewey: Religious Faith and Democratic Humanism, 334ff.
38 Westbrook, John Dewey and American Democracy, 233–35.
39 Cf. Westbrook, John Dewey and American Democracy, 236–37.
40 1915.03.31 (03222): Dewey to Horace Kallen. Dewey expresses similar ideas in his 1916 essay "Nationalizing Education" (MW 10:202–10). See Westbrook, John Dewey and American Democracy, 213–14.
41 1919.01.04 (05012): Dewey to Raymond Moley.
42 Jay Martin bases a number of interesting speculations on this insight in The Education of John Dewey, 287ff.
43 In Martin, The Education of John Dewey, 291.
44 Jo Ann Boydston, Introduction to The Poems of John Dewey, ed. Jo Ann Boydston (Carbondale, IL: Southern Illinois University Press, 1977), 4.
45 Frank Fackenthal, at Dewey's ninetieth birthday celebration in 1949, in the pamphlet "John Dewey at Ninety"; http://deweycenter.siu.edu/about_birthday.html; accessed June 10, 2014.
46 1919.01.08 (03745): Dewey to Evelyn Dewey.
47 On Dewey in Japan, see Naoko Saito, "Education for Global Understanding: Learning from Dewey's Visit to Japan," Teachers College Record 105 (December 2003): 1758–73.
48 See Dykhuizen, The Life and Mind of John Dewey, 194, 374. Cf. 1919.07.25 (03564): Davis Rich Dewey to Frederick A. Dewey.
49 See Westbrook, John Dewey and American Democracy, 240.
50 1920.01.13 (04882): Dewey to John Jacob Coss.
51 See Jessica Ching-Sze Wang, John Dewey in China (Albany, NY: SUNY Press, 2007).
52 Jane Dewey, "Biography of John Dewey," 42.
53 Textual commentary, LW 15:555.
54 Jane Dewey, "Biography of John Dewey," 42.
55 1927.07.27 (05437): Dewey to George Herbert and Helen Mead.
56 "In Response," in John Dewey: The Man and His Philosophy, Addresses Delivered in New York in Celebration of His Seventieth Birthday (Cambridge, MA: Harvard University Press, 1930), 177.
57 Walter Lippman, The Phantom Public (New York: Harcourt, Brace & Co., 1925), 20–21.
58 See Westbrook, John Dewey and American Democracy, 479.
59 Max Otto, review of The Quest for Certainty, by John Dewey, Philosophical Review 40 (1931): 79.

60 Jane soon suffered a decade of physical and emotional debilitation.
61 1920.01.15 (04091): Dewey to Albert C. Barnes.
62 1920.02.20 (03587): Dewey to Dewey children.
63 1927.04.25 (05495): Henry Holt & Co. to Dewey.
64 "A Philosopher's Philosophy Interview," S. J. Woolf, interviewer, *The Collected Works of John Dewey*, Supplementary Volume 1, electronic edition, ed. Larry A. Hickman (InteLex, 1989–2013), 233.
65 1933.10.03? (17256): Myles Horton to John Dewey; 1933.10.05 (17257): Dewey to Myles Horton. Cf. Michael Eldridge, Introduction to *The Correspondence of John Dewey*, vol. 2 (1919–39), electronic edition, ed. Larry A. Hickman (InteLex, 1989–2013).
66 1937.05.12 (08424): Dewey to Max Eastman. In her novel *The Lacuna* (New York: HarperCollins, 2009), Barbara Kingsolver devotes a section to Dewey and the 1937 Dewey Commission in Mexico City.
67 *The New York Times*, March 21, 1934, 10.
68 See 1967.03.06 (13675): Lucy Dewey Brandauer to George Dykhuizen.
69 For details of the FBI report on Dewey, see 1957.12.13 (16488): Mr. Nease to M. A. Jones. Cf. 1942.10.20? (16481). Cf. John R. Shook, Introduction to *The Correspondence of John Dewey*, vol. 3: 1940–53. For Truman's letter to Dewey, see 1949.10.06 (11242): Harry S. Truman to Dewey.
70 Cf. Harold Taylor, in Dykhuizen, *The Life and Mind of John Dewey*, xiv.
71 Dewey was interred at the University of Vermont twenty years after his death. A memorial to inter his ashes was held on October 16, 1972.
72 In Herbert Wallace Schneider, *A History of American Philosophy* (New York: Columbia University Press, 1946), 552n18. The original source is Oliver Wendell Holmes, *Holmes–Pollock Letters*, vol. 2 (Cambridge, MA: Harvard University Press, 1941), 287.
73 Schneider, *A History of American Philosophy*, 552.
74 Pamphlet on Dewey's ninetieth birthday celebration, p. 10, Center for Dewey Studies website; http://deweycenter.siu.edu/about_birthday.html; accessed June 10, 2014.
75 Pamphlet on Dewey's ninetieth birthday celebration, p. 10, Dewey center website.
76 1945.02.14 (15410): Dewey to Arthur Bentley.
77 1949.07.11 (07254): Dewey to Joseph Ratner.

Further reading

Jane Dewey, ed., "Biography of John Dewey," in *The Philosophy of John Dewey*, vol. 1 of *The Library of Living Philosophers*, 3rd ed. (LaSalle, IL: Open Court Press, 1989).
George Dykhuizen, *The Life and Mind of John Dewey* (Carbondale, IL: Southern Illinois University Press, 1973).
Steven C. Rockefeller, *John Dewey: Religious Faith and Democratic Humanism* (New York: Columbia University Press, 1991).
Jessica Ching-Sze Wang, *John Dewey in China* (Albany, NY: SUNY Press, 2007).
Robert B. Westbrook, *John Dewey and American Democracy* (Ithaca, NY: Cornell University Press, 1991).

Two

Metaphysics reconstructed

Is there not reason for believing that the release of philosophy from its burden of sterile metaphysics and sterile epistemology instead of depriving philosophy of problems and subject-matter would open a way to questions of the most perplexing and the most significant sort?

(RP, MW 12:152).

After his early years as a Hegelian idealist, Dewey was wary of the hyperrationalist's quest for grand metaphysical theories. "I am dubious of my own ability to reach inclusive systematic unity," he confessed, "and in consequence, perhaps, of that fact also dubious about my contemporaries" (LW 5:155). Yet he realized that ignoring metaphysics gives uninspected assumptions free rein in our philosophies. A dismissive attitude toward metaphysical inquiry was among the many fatal errors of his younger contemporaries the logical positivists. Instead of ignoring and thereby giving a pass to outworn metaphysical assumptions, Dewey criticized traditional metaphysics as the study of something beyond experience and developed a naturalistic and empirical theory of the nature of nature.

Irwin Edman wrote of *Experience and Nature* that "with monumental care, detail and completeness, Professor Dewey has in this volume revealed the metaphysical heart that beats its unvarying alert tempo through all his writings, whatever their explicit themes."[1] Dewey developed a metaphysics in the classical sense only insofar as "metaphysics is cognizance of the generic traits of existence" (EN, LW 1:50). On his pragmatic and naturalistic reinterpretation, metaphysics aims to project a provisional "map"—a key notion for

Dewey, as will become clear—to be used as a navigational tool for inquiring into the general characteristics of our natural existence. He rejected the traditional view of metaphysical subject matter as supernatural or "beyond-the-physical" and instead approached metaphysics as "a statement of the generic traits manifested by existences of all kinds without regard to their differentiation into physical and mental" (EN, LW 1:308). Chief among these general traits, as will be discussed, are stability and precariousness.

Dewey did not have a system of metaphysics that can be laid out in a straight path on the rationalist model, but he did make constructive (in addition to many destructive) metaphysical assertions. In this chapter I introduce several features of Dewey's constructive metaphysical map, but my primary aim is to introduce his more general *approach* to metaphysics by showing him in critical conversation with the Western tradition.

There is discernment and artistry involved in metaphysical inquiry, but it would have little practical import if waxing metaphysical meant no more than intellectually noting in general terms how the world behaves. There is a practical, cultural upshot of our metaphysical outlook: we *live by* our inherited "common sense" view of the nature of nature. Metaphysics is of course not unique in this respect. It is simply the most general framework for our discoveries, constructions, and convictions about the world, and by virtue of its generality our metaphysical "map" plays a role in orienting (and prejudicing) the rest of our thinking.

Long before Thomas Kuhn's revolt in the 1960s against the standpoint of pure, unbiased rationality in *The Structure of Scientific Revolutions*, Dewey argued that language-conditioned symbols through which we map the world operate together as "conceptual frameworks" (LTI, LW 12:138). We implicitly place a great deal of confidence in our conceptual frameworks, and the more confident one is that, from the widest angle, the world hangs together one way rather than another, the more one tries "to direct the conduct of life, that of others as well as of himself, upon the basis of the character assigned to the world" (EN, LW 1:309).

Given the persistent tendency to sow discord and damn as outcasts those who claim that existence has different traits than the authorized ones, metaphysics was fertile ground for Dewey as a cultural critic.[2]

He held that it is possible, through education in experimental inquiry that cuts against the grain of easy answers and quick solutions, to act with a wiser eye to revising our unreliable traditional maps of the world's processes and behaviors. Ultimately what mattered to Dewey was for philosophy to contribute to wiser practices, and he believed it could not do this unless it became more naturalistic and empirical. A genuinely empirical philosophy, he asserted, is

a kind of intellectual disrobing. We cannot permanently divest ourselves of the intellectual habits we take on and wear when we assimilate the culture of our own time and place. But intelligent furthering of culture demands that we take some of them off, that we inspect them critically to see what they are made of and what wearing them does to us.

(EN, LW 1:40)

These intellectual habits that are in need of critical inspection inform our "common sense," a socialized setup of possibilities that, for good or ill, is a primary determinant of what will appear reasonable to us. Our common sense includes a default metaphysics, a traditional "map" of the nature of nature that we carry around with us. Dewey sought substitutes for this map. Before moving to a detailed analysis of his rich notion of maps, the first three sections of this chapter will highlight some troublesome features of the traditional one, along with several prominent features of Dewey's proposed replacement.

Metaphysics in a moving world

Consider the famous depiction of Plato and Aristotle in Raphael's *School of Athens*, exhibited (fittingly) in the Vatican Museum. They are debating the locus of our knowledge of form as the disclosure of a thing's essential, permanent being. Plato holds his *Timaeus* and points to the heavenly forms while Aristotle holds his *Ethics* and extends his open palm over earthly matters. Aristotle replanted Plato's forms in the matter of natural species, but they both assumed the ideal forms are changeless. The forms organize matter without themselves being moved. They do not evolve. Time is secondary.

"Man is not modern merely because he lives in 1930" (LW 5:269), Dewey observed. Nor are we modern or postmodern merely because we happen to live in the twenty-first century. Mistakes in metaphysics are largely new iterations of old mistakes, such as the ancient Greek assumption that the world is complete and systematically intelligible, that the essential categories of existence are fitted to each other as neatly as Russian nesting dolls, and that there is a correct all-encompassing philosophical system for organizing knowledge.

In Dewey's view, both the subject matter of metaphysics (the world) and our way of making sense of it are incomplete, perpetually in process, so there can be no completed metaphysics. The work of metaphysics cannot even in principle be finished in a generative world that is always in the process of becoming, and in which our own engagement is never free of context and purposes. The long-cherished pursuit of complete and closed metaphysical or theological systems was, and is, born of fervent desire for a safe harbor from the illusory and fleeting insecurities of living. In the traditional outlook, which Martin Heidegger and Jacques Derrida later cast as the "metaphysics of presence," reality is at bottom atemporal. Both traditional metaphysics and traditional epistemology, Dewey held, "have a single origin in the dogma which denies temporal quality to reality as such" (EN, LW 1:120). In the traditional view, temporal quality is not a fundamental feature of our natural existence. In that view, whatever is in the future can in principle be seen from a God's-eye view as past and determinate, the universal history book already prewritten.[3] Dewey's is instead a metaphysics of "the temporal continuum of life-activities" (UPMP:325).

Peirce wisely cautioned that "great errors of metaphysics are due to looking at the future as something that will have been past."[4] Belief in already-existing perfection does not square, Dewey argued, with the "common traits of all existence" disclosed by empirical scrutiny through the sciences and ordinary experience. What is revealed is a mix of precariousness and stability, chance and regularity, struggle and safety. Our values, along with whatever measure of transient security we attain, are born of "qualitative individuality and constant relations, contingency and need, movement and arrest" (EN, LW 1:308).

How, from Dewey's standpoint, did philosophy become engaged in a quest for everlasting security? How did we get "diverted into absurd search for an intellectual philosopher's stone" (EN, LW 1:32–33), a quest to turn base uncertainty into the gold of unshakeable knowledge?[5]

Thales and his fellow Milesian philosophers concluded in the 500s BCE that there can be a reasoned account (*logos*) of nature (*physis*), and subsequent Greek philosophers agreed. But "Eleatic" philosophers such as Parmenides laid down a gauntlet: knowledge must be of that which is changeless, that which does not come to be and pass away. Being stands "in need of nothing," Parmenides argued, so "Being is one," whole.[6] He concluded that *material* experience is fleeting, illusory, dark, and driven by thoughtless convention. Only that which is changeless is real, and only the logical forms of thought are changeless. History, growth, novelty, individuation, and fulfillment are not real.

The philosopher Anaxagoras rejected the Eleatic idea that "Being is one," but he retained the split between mind and matter, giving birth to "metaphysical idealism" in Western philosophy. Mind, Anaxagoras argued, is a creative force prior to and unmixed with matter.[7] Mind does not decay, or grow. "While other things have a share in the being of everything else, mind is unlimited, autonomous, and unmixed with anything, standing entirely by itself."[8]

Seeds are headline news today: GMO patent law, food labeling, seed saving. So it is easy enough to enter Aristotle's Lyceum in our imaginations, where we encounter discussions of successive stages of development from acorn to oak, wheat seed to stalk, chickpea to plant. Each developmental process contains its own native moving force, unlike the external pushes and pulls of cogs in a modern machine. Placed in congenial circumstances a seed perfects itself. Order a pack of seeds, spread them over time and space, and they proceed through the identical stages toward the same form. At any stage from sprout to maturity a knowledgeable person could say by the characteristic look of it (i.e., its form) "that's barley," "that's wheat." Save the seed, plant the following year, and the process duplicates itself. Individual plants come to be and pass away, but the form is not bound to space and time (see MW 4:5–6).

Inspired by such observations, Aristotle's notion of unchanging, regulative forms revealed in the growth of plants and animals rose to the challenge laid down by the Eleatics. Plants become compost, but not their ideal forms. The species themselves do not change. As with the growth and maturation of plants, so with the rest of matter. The developmental process by which matter is organized is regulated by immutable forms which transcend change. So also with forms of good conduct, which enable individuals to enact the good in the successive stages of their own lives and thereby flourish like the barley and bean. These are the universal human virtues.

This compelling Aristotelian world hypothesis was worth betting on prior to Darwinism and subsequent knowledge of genetic variation. It helpfully flags stability as an existential trait, it highlights that change does not cancel out ongoing patterns, and it insists that nutritive surroundings *matter*. But as an *overall* map of natural existence it has outworn its welcome.

In an influential essay written in 1909 to mark the fiftieth anniversary of Darwin's *On the Origin of Species*, "The Influence of Darwinism on Philosophy" (MW 4:3–14), Dewey began by noting that Darwin's theory of natural selection provoked an intellectual and scientific revolution that ran much deeper than mere conflicts with religious doctrines. *Species* is the Latin (scholastic) translation of the Greek word *eidos*, associated with Plato's forms and Aristotle's "formal cause." Darwin's theory of evolution through natural selection overturned the Aristotelian idea of unchanging formal causes that define the essences of objects.[9] Permanence was gone, but not durability.

Enter philosophy's Darwin. Dewey set out to redirect the misguided quest for immutable principles in morals, logic, religion, economics, and politics just as Darwin (and evolutionary thinking more generally) had done for fixed species in biology.[10] He argued that philosophy's classic quest for fixity is, and has always been, ill-suited to the world we actually inhabit (see QC, LW 4:21–39). This quest has created a drag all along.

A metaphysics that aims to describe the general characteristics of our existence in nature must minimally square with evolutionary biology, which reveals that "incompleteness and precariousness is a trait that must be given footing of the same rank as the finished and fixed" (EN, LW 1:50).[11] The precarious *and* the stable must both be included on any workable map of the world's existential traits. "The world is a scene of risk," Dewey wrote. "It is uncertain, unstable, uncannily unstable. Its dangers are irregular, inconstant, not to be counted upon as to their times and seasons" (EN, LW 1:43). Stability is equally real and perhaps more emotionally consoling, but philosophy must *also* grapple with instability and agitation as an existential trait if it is to help us make the practical best of each trait and orient us "for the conduct of life, in devotion to what is good" (EN, LW 1:50). An escapist philosophy that sidelines precariousness as an existential trait, or an equally escapist philosophy that shrugs off the hard work of inquiry altogether, attains neither the cognitive nor the practical ends befitting the love of wisdom.

Wherever we drop anchor, our anchorage inevitably moves. It is futile to exert effort trying to stay its movement once and for all. We are part of the ongoing processes of a world that is "a moving whole of interacting parts," and as such our existence does not afford any "single universal and necessary frame of reference" to be accessed by a spectatorial mind or soul (QC, LW 4:232). In an essay titled "What I Believe" Dewey notes that the instability, discordance, and flux of a moving world have made themselves at home in the natural sciences, but in "religion, morals, economics, and politics" it is still widely presumed we must choose between anarchy and immutability, confusion and fixity (LW 5:271). Coming chapters will explore Dewey's own constructive alternative in each of these areas.

We divert energy and effort from our quest to secure a better, truer, freer, and more beautiful world when we imagine human ideals as already-secured actualities existing in an ethereal realm.[12] Ideals of justice, democracy, equality of opportunity, and freedom "are indications of the possibilities of existences, and are, therefore, to be used as well as enjoyed; used to inspire action to procure and buttress their causal conditions" (EN, LW 1:311). Our most inspiring ideals, no less than our most sensuous meaning-making, are "generated by existences" and "sustained by events" (EN, LW 1:311). So they are fundamentally precarious and in need of stabilizing action. Indeed, ideals such as justice, and the goods these ideals help us to secure, are real existential possibilities that can be realized only through action. That ideals emerge at all is due to a precarious existence in which fulfillments come, attract us, and motivate our efforts to secure them anew. A world without resistance is a world without ideals to strive for, because good objects would never be in jeopardy. "A 'perfect' world would mean just an unchanging brute thing" (EN, LW 1:58).

We are not yet at home in a moving world. We pretend that our religion is the final one, our savior or prophet the final embodiment of divinity, the general principles of our economic regime the completion of economic evolution (in need of touch-up work), our view of marriage and family the irrevocable word (see LW 5:271). The quest for safe harbors will continue as part of our biopsychological constitution; it is moot to declare that it "should" continue. We should, however, steer intelligently between the extremes of an immoveable anchorage and relativistic drift.

Dewey proposed a philosophy of experience that charts an experimental course "to determine the character of changes that are going on and to give them in the affairs that concern us most some measure of intelligent direction" (LW 5:271). A cultural shift away from fixity and toward a philosophy of experience will not achieve a Utopia, Dewey cautioned. Unlike Marx's notion of a final state of social evolution, for Dewey the process of becoming has no perfected terminus. But the revolutionary changes already wrought by experimental methods warrant active confidence that we can do a better job of intelligently directing social change (LW 5:271).

In this way Dewey's metaphysics, to the extent that he may be said to have had one, spotlights the ways we concretely tap into "the possibilities of existence" (EN, LW 1:311). In contrast with Aristotle, when Dewey speaks of potentiality or possibility he does not mean something like a latent seed awaiting the right conditions of soil, water, and light to manifest a preexisting, eternally fixed form. Rather, possibilities for directed and durable change emerge historically through the here and now of interaction. In this respect the possibility for directed change over time is a fundamental trait of our natural existence, as is novelty. Time, change, and novelty are real.

Dewey's metaphysics maps the landscape of philosophical criticism so that philosophy may more effectively pursue the love of wisdom by orienting our inquiries. The remainder of this chapter will explore some ways in which this rather broad formulation is made distinctive in Dewey's reconstruction. "Any theory that detects and defines these traits," he asserted in the final chapter of *Experience and Nature*, "is therefore but a ground-map of the province of criticism, establishing base lines to be employed in more intricate triangulations" (EN, LW 1:308–9).[13] *Experience and Nature* pointed a way toward revealing and constructing more specific "base lines" to guide philosophical inquiries into knowing, valuing, and expressing, which I take up in subsequent chapters on epistemology, ethics, and aesthetics.

The revolt against dualism

A fellow philosopher told me of a recurring dream from her graduate student days. Poring over Dewey's *Experience and Nature* in anticipation of a preliminary exam for her PhD, she dreamed that her examiners issued a double-barreled shotgun with instructions to shoot pairs of clay pigeons. With each cry of "pull!" two clay pigeons sailed to the horizon, one inscribed with the word "subject" and the other "object," "mind" and "body," "theory" and "practice," "spiritual" and "material," "knower" and "known," "proposition" and "state of affairs," "culture" and "nature," "freedom" and "necessity." After blasting dualisms from the sky each night, she was primed to write about Dewey's metaphysics.

Dewey did not reject these sharp splits simply because they were dualisms, but because they oblige us to reach for antithetical principles to make sense of the world, and this has consequences. All the evidence we can muster points instead to a *principle of continuity* (discussed in greater detail below) and to "the inextricable intertwining of the physical and psychical" in our make-up (LW 13:337). The consequences of dualistic starting points within professional philosophy, he concedes, "are of no great import. But philosophical dualism is but a formulated recognition of an impasse in life; an impotence in interaction, inability to make effective transition, limitation of power to regulate and thereby to understand" (EN, LW 1:186).

In Dewey's telling, what is the historical story of the emergence of dualism and hence of discontinuity in philosophy? Plato and Aristotle put a "metaphysical discount" on matter, subordinating it to changeless forms that define the essences of particular beings. In Christianity this developed into the idea that "spirit is simple, one, permanent and indissoluble; matter is multiple, subject to change and dissolution" (EN, LW 1:192). Christians added a moral discount to the metaphysical one. The sin of Adam and the consequent fallenness of man weighed us down and oriented us toward what Augustine called the City of Man. Meanwhile, damnation or redemption would be determined by grace and/or works that reorient our moral compass toward the City of God (see EN, LW 1:192–93). Medieval Christendom followed Aristotle in conceiving the material body as a necessary substrate with the dynamic potential to receive a perfected form. So in the medieval view, human bodies occupied a preparatory position without which our essential humanity could not become actualized. Because of this intermediate relationship, Dewey observed, "there was in medieval thought no special problem attaching to the relation of mind and body" (EN, LW 1:193).

Yet the closed, hierarchically ordered cosmos of medieval geocentrism shattered, and the mechanistic universe of modern astronomy and physics emerged. As Copernicus, Galileo, Descartes, and Newton took center stage, moral disparagement of flesh as the occasion of sin and rebellion "persisted in full vigor, while the classical [Aristotelian] metaphysics of the potential and actual fell into disrepute" (EN, LW 1:193). The resulting mechanistic worldview no longer left intermediate space for gradual shading between body and spirit, physical and ethical. Only stark, binary oppositions remained (EN, LW 1:193).

Descartes crystallized these tendencies for modernity. He argued that our minds are separate from and superior to our bodies and brains, hence our minds are not subject to the same laws of physics as our bodies and brains. In contrast with the medieval view, there was nothing intermediate between Descartes' extended realm of physical nature (*res extensa*) and his cognitive realm of human values (*res cogitans*). They have nothing in common. The mind, Descartes asserted, is "merely a thing that thinks." Its immutable nature is to determine action without itself being transformed by interactions. In his personal copy of *The Philosophical Works of Descartes*, Dewey marked up a summary passage: "the *whole nature* [underlined] of the mind consists in thinking, while the *whole nature* [underlined] of the body consists in being an extended thing, and that there is nothing at all common to thought and extension. I have often also shown distinctly that mind can act independently of the brain; for certainly the brain can be of no use in *pure thought* [double underlined]: its only use is for imagining and perceiving."[14]

Descartes' wedge between mind and matter was driven deeper by Kant in the late eighteenth century. Newton's mechanistic world-view was by then the dominant physical worldview. In contrast with the Aristotelian idea that matter cannot be appealed to for principles of order, Newton thought he had found nature's laws inscribed in matter. In Newton's clockwork universe, if you know precisely the external forces acting on an object, then you can pinpoint its future behavior. Kant argued that our minds are exempt from this realm of tight, deterministic necessity. Our minds operate outside physical laws in a realm of freedom studied indirectly through *a priori* analysis rather than evidence-based scrutiny.

The Cartesian idea that Kant exhibited was, in sum, that minds are self-contained islands of consciousness stuffed in bodily sacks. The mind's highest and essential calling was to know, and it achieved knowledge through exercise of pure thought that is noncultural, nonhistorical, disembodied, and dispassionate. The consequence has not, alas, been a celebration of mind or freedom, but a mystification that still haunts philosophy and our wider culture. Consider the shadows and whispers surrounding a person's mental health, her presumed unchanging essence, compared to the casual worldliness with which we now commercialize physical health problems.

The long-standing assumption that there exists a realm of immutable Being outside the arena of living, and that this plane is discontinuous with the doings and sufferings of human existence, has compelled desperate attempts to carve out a space for human freedom and thought. As the dogma of unchanging Being dissipates, "the need for such a measure of desperation vanishes" (QC, LW 4:200).

For Dewey, in opposition to the form/matter, body/mind, and freedom/necessity dichotomies, our "body-minds" are permeable membranes capable of deliberately mediating troublesome situations (see EN, LW 1:191–225). Our skins mark off social boundaries, but we live and think across skins. The ontological lesson "forecast by the descriptive spadework of the ecologies," Dewey wrote in his final book *Knowing and the Known*, is that we will increasingly recognize experience as "transdermally transactional" (KK, LW 16:117).[15] This was prophetic up to a point. Children now learn in elementary school that organisms above or below a pond's surface exist in and through each other. Yet most Euro-Americans nevertheless persist in uncritically assuming an ontological exemption for a gaseous human mind. We increasingly recognize that our bodies are connected to environing conditions in a uterine way, but we still tend toward an impermeable, Cartesian view of our remarkable capacity for organizing, symbolizing, and giving meaning to these interactions.

Dewey conceived mind from a biological standpoint as interactive minding: exploring, navigating, reaching, grasping, making. Like William James, he preferred the verb or gerund (-ing) to the substantive noun. Dewey argued at least as early as his watershed 1896 critique of "The Reflex Arc Concept in Psychology" (EW 5:96–109) that we achieve integration and coordination through the feedback loop of our relationships, not despite our relationships through exertions emanating from the spectral inner space of mind. Take a child seeing and reaching for a lit candle. The accurate characterization of a child seeing a candle is active "looking, and not a sensation of light" (EW 5:97). It is noncontroversial to say that there exists a candle prior to its being perceived and reached for by the child. But as Hume understood, it is only by way of inferential hindsight that we can discuss the candle as "causing" (stimulating) the child to reach. The child does not directly perceive the so-called stimulus, the candle, and then respond to it by reaching. The candle enters the child's awareness as a consequence of purposeful sensorimotor activities in which the child was *already* engaged (see EN, LW 1:251ff.).[16] Instead of a duality of physical stimulus and mental response, there is a feedback loop.

Accordingly, when Dewey talked about intellectual and emotional life, he often substituted tactile metaphors for the conventional Platonic and Cartesian ones of pure mental vision. Herbert Schneider reported Dewey's comment at a dinner party: "I think this whole problem of understanding should be approached not from the point of view of the eyes, but from the point of view of the hands. It's what we grasp that matters."[17]

Ever inspired by biological metaphors, Dewey turned to invertebrates in a 1902 lecture for an image of the live creature actively reaching out for subject matter: "My image of the mind is a sort of biological thing with arms or tentacles reaching out everywhere, and when they get appropriate food, just fastening down upon it" (LW 17:334). We reach out for past and present materials to feed and creatively consummate our ongoing projects. Humans are native learners, but education will do little to help us become more alert and disciplined unless we replace the insular Cartesian model of pure thought with a model that understands the way our "mental tentacles," native biological impulses, and emotions reach out for, gradually assimilate, and creatively transform nourishing subject matter (see HNC MW 14:68; cf. AE, LW 10:73).

Cultural existence in nature as situated

Dewey was skilled in a form of imaginative inquiry often identified today as ecological. We have belatedly grown aware of the hazards—political, ethical, aesthetic, educational, environmental—of using tired old preecological, nonrelational, individualistic "maps" for navigating interactions with each other and the world of which we are part. With *Experience and Nature*, Dewey redrew the map of philosophical reflection. In the words of one commentator, it consists of 400 pages teaching you to think out of the corner of your eye.[18] Its central lesson is that the visible is always situated within the invisible. Dewey wrote:

> The visible is set in the invisible; and in the end what is unseen decides what happens in the seen; the tangible rests precariously upon the untouched and ungrasped. The contrast and the potential maladjustment of the immediate, the conspicuous and focal phase of things, with those indirect and hidden factors which determine the origin and career of what is present, are indestructible features of any and every experience.
>
> (EN, LW 1:44)

Dewey's general philosophy of experience—his "house of theory," in Iris Murdoch's coinage—is in step with the twenty-first-century demand for greater ecological responsibility. His notion of a situation is central to what might be called his ecological imagination.[19] Like experience (to be discussed below), *situation* was intended as what James called a "double-barreled" word. Dewey used it to refer simultaneously "to what is indicated by such terms as 'organism' and 'environment,' 'subject' and 'object,' 'persons' and 'things,' 'mind' and 'nature,' and so on" (EEL, MW 10:324). It is the transactive scene of any action (Greek *pragma*) or event (Latin *res*).

If Dewey could be said to have a theory of substance even remotely analogous to traditional metaphysics, then it was encompassed in his idea of the situation as basic. Situation refers to any experience at hand, from its brilliant focus—conspicuous and apparent—to its horizonal field or background, the obscured, concealed, enveloping, and felt context (EEL, MW 10:323). The locus of a particular act or event is not a reflex response to sensory input but the whole biosociocultural context of this or that experience, when experience is taken in its widest and deepest sense (see EN, LW 1:155ff.).[20] Each situation uniquely "offers its own challenge to thought and endeavor, and presents its own potential value" (LW 5:272).

Acts or events develop over time, as with the act of writing an essay or the event of childbirth, so situations are temporally spread out. From composing a musical score to negotiating a peace treaty, the situational "spread" includes the immediately felt echo of the prior flow of experience and the dawning sense of the future flow.[21] Dewey's emphasis on the pervasive qualitative or felt dimension of situations, to be discussed in Chapter Six, is the heart of his concept. As he defines it, the term situation signifies "the fact that the subject-matter ultimately referred to in existential propositions is a complex existence that is held together in spite of its internal complexity by the fact that it is dominated and characterized throughout by a single quality" (QT, LW 5:246). A unique qualitative horizon differentiates this kiss from that one, this composition from a prior one, that ball game from another.

We typically fail to see the visible in light of the invisible, to map what we are focusing on so as to include the constitutive, enveloping situation. For example, recent work by microbiologists sheds light on decades of scattershot warfare against microbial life, during which we have killed a small number of harmful species while also subduing many bacterial species we depend upon for good health. There are "hundreds of bacterial species that call me home," journalist Michael Pollan wrote of these microbial menageries. These bacteria form "a vast, largely uncharted interior wilderness that scientists are just beginning to map."[22] Like other ecological philosophies, Dewey's urges humility about haphazard attempts to manage tiny portions of our environments without experimental understanding of unintended consequences. But as will be shown, his approach to experimental method is distinctive in its ongoing mapping of the visible and the invisible. By looping from the thick situation to abstract symbolic formulations and then back to the concrete situation, a contextually sensitive "denotative method" aims at an "intellectual piety toward experience" that compensates for our excessive "will to impose" conceptual and practical schemes on experience (EN, LW 1:392).

In order to clarify Dewey's denotative method, it will help to introduce some terminology. Distinctions are "functional" or "teleological" when they occasionally tap us on the shoulder to remind us they were made for our purposes, not found. In *Experience and Nature* Dewey made a functional distinction between *primary* and *secondary* phases or levels of an experience. First, the primary phase or level is immediately given. It is raw, unprocessed—or at least only minimally and incidentally refined. Things are experienced before they are known (EN, LW 1:28), so primary experience is viscerally *had* but not intellectually *known*. Such primal "crude or macroscopic experience" (EN, LW 1:16) is the pretheoretical origin of our secondary cognitive "take" on any matter.

Second, the selective, mediated conceptions of "secondary or reflective experience"—such as the philosophy book you are reading, a scientific theory, or an equation—are cooked by our symbolic-conceptual frameworks (EN, LW 1:16). In order to operate as intelligent guides, such symbolic conceptions must be derived and refined with systematic rigor, and then traced back to the primary context from which they emerged and which they nourish (EN, LW 1:39). Unlike the *a priori* approach to philosophical theorizing that Dewey targets, work in the natural sciences refers conceptions back to primary experience as test (EN, LW 1:15). "The charge that is brought against the non-empirical method of philosophizing," Dewey wrote, "is not that it depends upon theorizing, but that it fails to use refined, secondary products as a path pointing and leading back to something in primary experience" (EN, LW 1:16–17).

Consider Dewey's distinction between primary and secondary experience in light of J. L. Austin's criticism of "etiolated philosophies." Etiolation is the bleaching of plants by blocking sunlight so they grow without chlorophyll. Austin argued that etiolated philosophies reduce the multifaceted business of linguistic utterances to mere truth or falsity, seizing upon one function of language and taking this to be the essential one.[23] Austin's point is more specific than Dewey's, but the metaphor nicely highlights the way an etiolated philosophy is pale and feeble because its starting point is a wispy abstraction, not a robust situation. Dewey's empirical method begins and ends with the "chlorophyll" of primary experience, so intellectual abstractions are always secondary and intermediate to concrete situations. The implications ripple through Dewey's writings and through this book.

The *denotative method* is Dewey's name for this methodological loop that moves from immediate to mediated and back to immediate experience (EN, LW 1:16ff.).[24] It is synonymous in this book with experimental method, but as coming chapters will make clear, it should not be identified solely with the sciences. Experimental method, for Dewey, is not only our best check on the etiolation of philosophy. Most importantly, it is our best check on the pronounced human tendency for our choices, advocacies, hunches, and conclusions to be driven unreflectively by reactive habits. When we follow an experimental method, our responses are conditioned by thought and directed through foresight of consequences instead of simply being released accidentally by environmental conditions.

Mapping our milieu

Dewey's conception of maps was central to his naturalistic reconstruction of metaphysics as a "ground-map of the province of criticism" (EN, LW 1:309). Focusing on maps brings his general philosophical outlook and ideals quickly into focus. As Raymond Boisvert observes, maps do not "occupy a detached, disinterested standpoint that provides the snapshot of the world."[25] For example, there is no "true" projection scheme, in the sense of a literal reproduction, for translating a three-dimensional sphere onto a two-dimensional plane surface. Instead, a map may be true operationally. It may function well, or poorly, given our ends (see LTI, LW 12:399).

A map's depiction of scale, shape, and area is a matter of selectivity and choice. Consider the rectangular maps of the world still found on most school walls. In Mercator's projection, Dewey observes, "there is a morphological enlargement of polar regions" (LTI, LW 12:399), a distortion of area, and a diminution of the southern hemisphere. These characteristics were useful for nautical purposes by European navigators in the ages of exploration and imperial expansion. They were not troubled, for instance, by Mercator's depiction of Greenland as equal in size to Africa, which has a land area fourteen times greater. On old stereographic maps, areas are correct but scale is inconstant. On the Peters projection, used by the United Nations Development Programme as a replacement for Mercator maps still popular in schools, areas are presented equally while shapes are in places grossly distorted.

What makes a map correct and successful is determined by whether it meets our aims for the map when we journey with it. Vying for the "right" projection in the absence of specified purposes for the map is unintelligible. There can be no true map as some fixed and final charting of territory. The chart is "defined by its function" (LTI, LW 12:138), not by abstract (vs. functional) correspondence between the map's symbols, on the one hand, and extralinguistic entities, properties, and relations, on the other hand. We may imagine a hyperrationalist map-quest for the grand projection that will systematically unify and preserve the best of all competing projections and measures, but this too is misguided and indeed mathematically inconceivable. Maps are always provisional, open to revision and improvement.[26] One could perhaps in principle craft a duplicate globe. Or to plunge even further down the rabbit hole, we might imagine with Josiah Royce an equally unworkable "map" so exact that it represents itself, and so on *ad infinitum*.[27] In addition to an object lesson on the absurdity of rationalistic exactitude, Dewey observes that "such a reproduction would be useless for the purpose representation fulfills. It would, in fact, only duplicate the problems of the original" (LTI, LW 12:399n4).

More will be said of maps, but let's pause first to take stock. Dewey is up to something far more encompassing than a

philosophy of cartography. Maps are exemplars of symbolic communication, and map drawing is a form of cultural inquiry. Many of
the lessons gleaned from an analysis of maps and mapping can be
generalized to other sorts of symbol-mediated inquiry, including
science and philosophy. The analysis thus far brings three of Dewey's
philosophic positions into view:

1. rejection of purely detached standpoints (and assertion of the
   inescapability of selectivity and choice at every level of inquiry),
2. a functional–operational sense of truth that requires action (and
   rejection of truths as preexisting correspondences between symbols and states of affairs), and
3. the provisional nature of symbolic constructions (and rejection
   of final truths and all-encompassing systems).

Dewey's conception of mapping as cultural inquiry pivots on his
analysis of maps as propositions. The analysis of propositions in
Logic: The Theory of Inquiry is highly technical, but the gist is that a
map is a set of propositions in the sense that it makes *proposals* to
us.[28] When we follow an online map to a friend's address, the
map proposes that when we proceed as prescribed, here are the
sorts of existential traits or conditions that we can anticipate. All
propositions are similarly defined by their functions (LTI, LW
12:139). As Hickman points out, Dewey used baseball jargon to
clarify this operational sense of propositions as proposals: "A pitched baseball is to the batter a 'proposition'; it states, or makes
explicit, what he has to deal with next amid all the surrounding
and momentarily irrelevant circumstance" (MW 10:356).[29]
Dewey added in a 1915 letter that all propositional understanding
is similarly performative: "Philosophical errors come from taking
propositional knowledge as referring to the world or 'corresponding' to it or 'representing' or 'presenting' it in some other
way than as being direction for the performance of acts."[30] The
popular notion that propositions have truth values (that they
are either true or false) misses their performative function: they
are either helpful or unhelpful in furthering the journey of
inquiry. One goal of coming chapters will be to add specificity to
these vague notions of helpfulness and unhelpfulness.

We symbolically represent subject matter through maps as cultural tools for directing journeys and investigations. Likewise, we use blueprints and design specifications as tools for directing a construction process. In any complicated undertaking, conceptual instruments describing the lay of the land are as requisite as material preparations (LTI, LW 12:139). When going on journeys maps are as important as backpacks.

The communicative symbols we use in charting the course are conditioned by "language, the tool of tools" (EN, LW 1:134).[31] The set of interdependent propositions in a map or blueprint is no different in this respect than the symbolic representations we systematically arrange into philosophical and scientific theories. "Maps and blueprints are propositions and they exemplify what it is to be propositional" (LTI, LW 12:138). Here's the rub: Because maps are exemplars of symbolic communication that involves propositions, analyzing them reveals the projective, provisional, and constructive nature of all propositional thinking.

A map is not the journey, nor is a blueprint the process of building a house (LTI, LW 12:138; cf. MW 2:284).[32] Zen teaches that one should not mistake the finger (the language that points) for the moon (the subject matter). Dewey adds the feedback loop of experimental method. A map's experimental test, and hence our opportunity to *judge* its propositions to ascertain whether they are warranted, comes through the journey itself as we navigate the actual territory hypothesized in the map.[33] Through enactment we gain evidence we need to make assertions about the existential terrain, not in order to verify a mentally cloistered propositional attitude, but so that we can revise or reject wayward propositional representations and more reliably symbolize our transactions. In Dewey's terminology, the map's *affirmations* are vital leads for the journey, but the *assertions* we most rely on are deliberative judgments based on subsequent evidence. These assertive judgments have "existential import" (LTI, LW 12:123) in that, unlike symbolic operations, they reconstitute the terrain through interacting with it.[34]

I recently enjoyed a woodland hike with a remarkable mycologist, who commented here and there about the way names help mushrooms to stand forth for us. "We see what we allow in," he said at one juncture. "We create our own reality," he contradicted himself at another. Note my guide's dual language of undergoing and doing, receiving and creating. Dewey sought a philosophical vocabulary to coherently articulate the reciprocal receptivity and activity that my woodland guide was taking a stab at. We are not detached spectators who use symbols to detect a terrain that is forever "out there." As cognitive mapmakers and map-users, we select features of a "total field or situation" that need to be singled out and identified for the sake of certain purposes. Strictly speaking these situational features are selectively "*taken* rather than given" (LTI, LW 12:127).[35] But not just taken: a map guides a journey that is interactive, like all living. We alter territory and are ourselves altered as we traverse it.

Maps have consequences when we engage the existential terrain they symbolically represent. These consequences may be monumental, as with a map used for territorial expansion and conquest, or relatively trivial, as with a map sketched to help a friend locate a restaurant. Through imagination we see situational possibilities represented by a map's symbols, we judge the map's symbolic formulations good or bad, and if a feedback loop for input and editing exists then we revise according to our ends. The maps of Omaha Beach were anticipatory tools for the plans enacted on June 6, 1944. Data from the Landsat satellites are today used to map and project climate change, with implications for politics and policy that may reform our volatile world-in-the-making. Through maps we envisage possibilities for transforming existence through action, and we actively reconstitute existence (see LTI, LW 12:138).[36]

The accidental and highly tentative paths on a trailblazer's map are used, judged, and appraised by others in order to more completely chart terrain. Dewey observed in *The Child and the Curriculum* that records of prior mapping "proposals" are generalized, made available, engaged, and judged so that efforts may be shared and progressively economized without having to repeat past wanderings (MW 2:283). Eventually, as the results of prior inquiries are arranged systematically, informal maps may become scientific objects and logical tools that are "deliberately constituted by critical inquiry intended to produce objects that will operate as effective and economical means when they are needed" (LTI, LW 12:139). Of course modern cartography is mostly expert-driven, without much solicitation of user feedback in the revision process, but so much the worse for the maps and the users.

Maps impart meaning to the terrain, an intermediate significance that may alter it for better or worse. From online mapping services and GIS to back-of-envelope diagrams, maps impart different intermediate meanings, and they are constructed and judged in light of different purposes. In experience more generally, the monistic quest for the all-encompassing meaning and purpose in the singular—the correct metaphysical map that allows us to sit on our hands and avoid revising—has been a distracting exercise in futility. Were the monistic journey toward invulnerability to give way to plural "interconnected meanings and purposes," then our active participation might be "a means to a fuller and more significant future experience" (LW 5:272).

Selectivity, choice, and intellectual standpoint are inevitable and inescapable in the reflective construction of conceptual frameworks, including all philosophical formulations about reality. We follow our philosophies into existential terrain that they only partially map. "Selective emphasis, choice, is inevitable whenever reflection occurs. This is not an evil. Deception comes only when the presence and operation of choice is concealed, disguised, denied" (EN, LW 1:34). Indeed far from an evil, selective biases can operate as a check on institutions and customs that "breed certain systematized predilections and aversions" (MW 11:45). For example, Dewey argued in 1918 that women's emerging voices in philosophy are vitally important for reconstituting its tone and tenor: "As far as what is loosely called reality figures in philosophies, we may be sure that it signifies those selected aspects of the world which are chosen because they lend themselves to the support of men's judgment of the worth-while life, and hence are most highly prized. In philosophy, 'reality' is a term of value or choice" (MW 11:45).

The potential for checking, compensating for, and benefiting from habituated selectivity so that we achieve our ends is mostly untapped when we journey cocksure on our own. The best check on inescapable selectivity in our conceptual constructions is an experimental method that operates as part of what Peirce called a "community of inquirers." An experimental method, Dewey wrote, "points out when and where and how things of a designated description have been arrived at. It places before others a map of the road that has been traveled; they may accordingly, if they will, retravel the road to inspect the landscape for themselves. Thus the findings of one may be rectified and extended by the findings of others" (EN, LW 1:34). Through open and cooperative inquiry, different (though always provisional) maps can be constructed, terrain resurveyed, inevitable biases revealed, mistakes debated, novel trails blazed, and new values and purposes incorporated.

Most adults have too little practice revising their conceptual maps and avoid situations that might destabilize their matrix of intellectual habits. As will become clear in subsequent chapters, grappling with this problem was at the heart of Dewey's philosophy. His chief concern with traditional metaphysical mapping was that we persist in using baselines and meridians that are ill-suited to the situations at hand. They do not operate well under contemporary conditions, because they are not inferred through an experimental method. He did not, of course, have in mind maps with GPS-level precision. But GPS navigation is an especially revealing metaphor for philosophical inquiry. One little-known fact is that Einstein's equations for special and general relativity are programmed into modern GPS satellites and mobile receivers. These equations compensate for the relative motion of satellites, along with diminished gravity at their altitudes. Absent Einstein's equations, we would rely by default on the Newtonian assumption that space and time are absolute. This would be troublesome. The problem is not simply that Newtonian assumptions about nature are sterile and their persistence proof of benighted intellectual habits. There would be a practical pinch of programming GPS units using Newtonian mechanics: The system is designed to pinpoint location within 1 meter, but absent Einstein's equations it would accumulate an error of 10 kilometers per day.[37]

Outworn metaphysical assumptions are equally troublesome, and our common-sense default position is far closer to Newton—or often to Aristotle—than to Einstein. If our philosophies are to help us navigate real-world perplexities, then they had better map the world's traits through an experimental method. The traditional metaphysical map, with its unreliable and obsolete assumptions about perfected reality and assured knowledge, denigrates human experience and quickly leaves us wide of our marks.

Experience as cultural inhabitation of nature

Experience and Nature does not contain a theory of nature per se. Dewey's naturalistic metaphysics was more an anthropology of nature. As Alexander observes, Dewey developed a theory of "our shared cultural inhabitation of the world," and he called our cultural existence in nature *experience*.[38] We tend to see culture and conventions as nonnatural, as for instance in the popular image of a prize fight between Nature vs. Nurture. But nurturing is a feature of nature. It is something nature *does*. Moreover, through the range of human interactions of love, art, and science, nurturance is something *human* nature can do sympathetically, expressively, and knowingly. Experience, Edman adds, "is nature come to consciousness in animal life which acts and undergoes, does and suffers, in the changes and chances of living."[39]

Experiencing for Dewey is consequently not reducible to knowing alone. The Western philosophical tradition has been "intellectualistic" in that it has arbitrarily singled out knowing as the quintessential human experience. We have reduced nature to the distinct and explicit traits by which things are *known*. Not only does this bad intellectual habit tend to reduce nature to an inert mechanism "out there"; it also excludes or obscures the primary characteristics through which things are used, enjoyed, loved, and shunned. Moreover, when we fail empirically to note that nature is charged with hidden potential, novelties and potentialities must take refuge in a subjective realm discontinuous with natural events. All that is implicit and noncognitive is relegated to a private and unnatural inner space of "mind" set over and against the "real" traits of nature.

In opposition, Dewey asserted that "what is really 'in' experience extends much further than that which at any time is known" (EN, LW 1:27). Things are dealt with, used, enjoyed, and endured even more than they are known (EN, LW 1:28). A *genuinely* empirical philosophy should not ignore the primary originating context that gives urgent import to what is known. This primary context makes knowledge itself biologically explicable as a way of enriching "action-undergoing" (EN, LW 1:28–30). Parting ways with the philosophical tradition, experience for Dewey meant "the complex of all which is distinctively human" (EN, LW 1:331).

The imaginative creativity of cultural existence, from industry to the fine arts, stretches beyond what is already distinctly disclosed to reveal nature's generative potential. Dancing, writing a haiku, and improvising a jazz solo are events as revelatory of nature as a double-blind scientific experiment. Each actively discloses nature's actualities and emergent potentialities. Each is "true to nature" (EN, LW 1:4). Hence nature is more than an assemblage of completed facts that can be known, catalogued, and exhibited in museums and encyclopedias.[40] In Alexander's words, for Dewey "nature is what nature does."[41]

Unfortunately the word "experience" has a subjective and passive ring in ordinary English, and for British empiricists in the tradition of Locke, Berkeley, Hume, and Reid the word meant inner receptivity to sensory impressions—the mind as moviegoer. But in Dewey's idiom the term "experience" designates not the subject side of an encounter with the world, but experiencing and experimenting as a trans-active whole. Dewey had in mind the active, engaged, practical, and artistic sense in which you hope your pilot or surgeon is experienced and not just a passive receptacle of sense-data.[42] Boisvert points out that Dewey's interactive and involved sense of experience as living fares better in French: "To say of people that they are 'making experiences,' *faire des expériences*, means engaging in experiments."[43]

A related key Deweyan term, "environment," also fares better in French, and here he consciously intended the French *milieu*. Unlike the English word environment, *milieu* wraps in cultural as well as physical conditions and suggests an interactive medium rather than mere external surroundings. Dewey ineffectually stipulated that he meant the French when he used the English: "What is called *environment* is that in which the conditions called physical are enmeshed in cultural conditions and thereby are more than 'physical' in its technical sense. 'Environment' is not something around and about human activities in an external sense; it is their *medium*, or *milieu*" (KK, LW 16:244).

Miscommunication was inevitable, and terminology dogged Dewey throughout his life.[44] Faced with the insurmountable problem that in English "experience" had become too busy meaning the opposite of what Dewey meant, he came to prefer the term "culture" as a replacement "to designate the inclusive subject-matter which characteristically 'modern' (post-medieval) philosophy breaks up into the dualisms of subject and object, mind and the world, psychological and physical" (EN, LW 1:361–62). In a new introduction to *Experience and Nature* left unfinished at his death, Dewey wrote: "Were I to write (or rewrite) *Experience and Nature* today I would entitle the book *Culture and Nature*" (EN, LW 1:362). *Experience* had come to connote psychical processes going forth in the inner space between one's ears. Consequently, Dewey's stubborn insistence that the word "also designates *what* is experienced ... made this use of 'experience' strange and incomprehensible" (EN, LW 1:362). He had written, for example: "Experience thus reaches down into nature; it has depth. It also has breadth and to an indefinitely elastic extent" (EN, LW 1:13). Due to advances in anthropology, he judged that "culture" now carried a meaning of living and inhabiting that better designated "both what is experienced and the ways of experiencing it" (EN, LW 1:362–63; see UPMP:293–94).

Immediate, unanalyzed (primary) experiences have a focus and an encompassing field, a foreground and a background. James had called this field the *horizon* or *penumbra* and denounced philosophy's historic neglect of the horizon as "a monstrous abridgment of human life."[45] James's influence on Dewey was due in no small measure to the profound sensitivity to context opened up by the former's focus-field or foreground-background model of experience. Prior to James and Peirce, sensitivity to immediate experience in the nineteenth century inevitably came wrapped with an idealistic metaphysics.

This emphasis on context-sensitivity enabled Dewey to develop one of the overriding themes of his philosophy: Immediate (primary) experiences are pervaded with a quality that we feel rather than know (see QT, LW 5:243). This belongs on our metaphysical map as a general characteristic of our natural existence. When we come around to seeing that all inquiry—whether moral, scientific, or aesthetic—begins and ends in primary experience, the fruits of inquiry may serve to expand and enrich the quality of immediate experience (see Chapter Six).

Experience, no less than a mountain peak, emerges from nature, and it is as amenable to investigation as Earth's geologic processes that uplift and erode mountains. Consequently a theory of experience can be mistaken. A great deal of provisional charting of territory, and nonsense, marks the history of both geology and philosophical reflection on experience. Philosophers, however, are still struggling to internalize the experimental morale that aids natural scientists in "the growing progressive self-disclosure of nature itself" (EN, LW 1:5). Dewey's works aimed to rectify past mistakes by restoring continuity between experience and nature, and past and future.

In order to characterize traits in the field of human interaction (EN, LW 1:208), the naturalist in metaphysics must analyze art, science, values, and religious life as among nature's possibilities. Conscious experience, ideas, language, freedom, culture, education, hope, valuation, imagination, aesthetic experience, progress—these must be analyzed as continuous with nonconscious physical interactions. The naturalist must make sense of mind, "the body of organized meanings by means of which events of the present have significance for us" (AE, LW 10:276), and she must do this in terms not of some outside causal force but instead in terms of biological organisms interacting with environments. Dewey's naturalism took the postulate of physical and temporal continuity as its guiding assumption. In the 1938 *Logic*, Dewey explained:

> The primary postulate of a naturalistic theory of logic is continuity of the lower (less complex) and the higher (more complex) activities and forms. The idea of continuity is not self-explanatory. But its meaning excludes complete rupture on one side and mere repetition of identities on the other; it precludes reduction of the "higher" to the "lower" just as it precludes complete breaks and gaps.
>
> (LTI, LW 12:30–31)[46]

To see how the principle or postulate of continuity guided Dewey's metaphysical mapping, consider his functional treatment of ideas. He avoided casting them as either relativistically subjective or universally objective. For Dewey ideas, ideals, signs, symbols, and signals are real and objective in the limited sense that they have immediate or untried consequences for coordinating and transforming human affairs and discourse. Or in the case of abstract sorts of experimentation that we pursue via mathematics, logic, and theoretical science, ideas can creatively surprise experts who have "a sensitive ear for detecting resultant harmonies and discords" (EN, LW 1:152). Such abstract ideas, Dewey wrote in one of his lighter moments penning *Experience and Nature*, "copulate and breed new meanings" (EN, LW 1:152).[47] Many mathematicians are still old-fashioned Platonists, giving mathematical forms a reality wholly independent of material existence and thereby violating the principle of continuity.[48] Abstract mathematical and logical ideas are mistakenly conceived in the main as a nonnatural "order of entities independent of human invention and use" (EN, LW 1:153). But even highly abstract mathematical and logical ideas have dynamic "consequences with respect to one another" (EN, LW 1:149). These theoretical consequences may later become starting points for reflections that eventuate in hitherto unknown meanings, uses, and consequences (EN, LW 1:151). Just as philosophical thought experiments cultivate the skill of introducing familiar notions into unfamiliar contexts with an ear for what jives or jars, so the highest flights of deductive thought, excepting those performed by a computer, are "a series of trials, observations and selections" (EN, LW 1:152). The logician's or mathematician's abstract experimentation has consequences for subsequent interactions. Logic and mathematics are not independent of human intercourse and natural interactions. They are "demonstrably dependent" (EN, LW 1:153).

Hypostatization: the philosophical fallacy

Dualism is rooted in what Dewey called the *fallacy of hypostatization*. Dewey's critique of this fallacy, which will be referenced throughout this book, is at the heart of his philosophy of experience and is among his most enduring contributions to philosophy. For Dewey, as Paul Thompson observes, "hypostatization often carries the connotation of *hypostasis* in the medical sense: a blockage caused by a slowing down of blood flow."[49] Keep this image in mind. Functional distinctions and generalizations regarding mind and body, mental and physical, subjective and objective, knower and known, self and world, can help us zoom in on features of situations so we can investigate difficulties. There is no blockage here. But if we then read back these useful distinctions into the world as though they were preexisting features that we happened upon, we end up with dysfunctional dualisms. This is where we get the blockage. Whitehead accordingly admonished philosophers to "Seek for simplicity and then distrust it."[50]

Dewey defines the fallacy of hypostatization as "conversion of eventual functions into antecedent existence" (EN, LW 1:34). Hypostatization occurs when we abstractly configure a substance—like Descartes' *res cogitans*, Plato's Forms, God, or Soul—out of the flow of processes, events, or concepts, and then treat "it" as an "it." That is, we treat the abstraction as a self-existing basic entity and forget its genesis as a result of analysis.

More generally, hypostatization is Dewey's name for a range of fallacies of reification in which we get taken in by our own abstract clarities. In addition to proliferating intangible substances, the fallacy blocks the path of inquiry when we convert what was selectively taken from a situation into the whole of what may be found there. We ignore the rest. James dubbed such reification the "psychologist's fallacy," Dewey recognized it as "the philosophical fallacy" (see EN, LW 1:27–29), and Whitehead analyzed it in terms of the fallacy of "misplaced concreteness."[51] Many distracting pseudo-problems arise when we mistake, conceal, or disguise our selective emphases by privileging agents over situations, static forms over processes, actualities over potentialities.

There are specific contexts in which we properly search for as much invariance as possible, as with functions in mathematics. Our practical ability to deal with troubling instability is similarly enhanced when we can isolate and rely on something as "stable and constant." In particular contexts, relative invariance "answers genuine emotional, practical and intellectual requirements" in a precarious world (EN, LW 1:32–33). We commit the fallacy of selective emphasis only when we generalize these sorts of functional stabilities, then convert them "into the intrinsically eternal, conceived either (as Aristotle conceived it) as that which is the same at all times, or as that which is indifferent to time, out of time" (EN, LW 1:32). In lieu of this ancient quest, a reconstructed philosophy should clarify, critique, and redirect culture as we struggle with problems and search for security and peace "by practical means in place of quest of absolute certainty by cognitive means" (QC, LW 4:20).

Dewey was a nuanced observer of the mutualism between concrete particulars—this frog, that pond—and spatiotemporal relationships. He allied himself with Whitehead's 1925 critique in *Science and the Modern World* of the fallacy of "simple location," which gives rise to the aforementioned fallacy of "misplaced concreteness" (LW 2:223; cf. LW 11:149). The fallacy of simple location stems from a "generalized abstraction regarding space" (LW 2:223–24) that inclines us to forget the relationships incorporated into any object. It also inclines us to confuse fragments with wholes. In Bashō's most famous haiku (an old pond / a frog jumps in / plop!), the words "frog" and "pond" signify not only objects one can point to at a simple location, but also a complex network or field of relationships and events.[52] Mechanistic materialism in the natural sciences had attempted "to build up wholes out of simple, independent units" or atomic parts (LW 2:224). But modern science, Whitehead and Dewey agreed, was trending in a more holistic direction that uses mechanical-reductive techniques instead of superimposing them onto reality. The fallacy occurs when we suppose our reduction is all that the situation affords.

Like many contemporary environmental philosophies and East Asian philosophies, Dewey's metaphysical map emphasized intrinsic and constitutive relations over extrinsic ones.[53] Any map of the general characteristics of our experience will lead us astray if it treats "things" or individuals as ultimate existences that bear solely an extrinsic relation to other things (see LW 14:98–114). We have been habituated over centuries to think of things as static entities instead of in the context of situated energies, events, processes, and behaviors. Our metaphysics should cohere with developments in physics and ecology by displacing, except as a term of common discourse, "the categories of *substance* and *things* as entities" (UPMP:215).

In contemporary ecology the holistic trend that Whitehead and Dewey saw themselves furthering is expressed in the concept of "emergent properties," in which properties of the system emerge through relationships and cannot be inferred from complete knowledge of individual parts. For example, although above ground we see trees as individuals, they form network communities in which individuals are root-grafted to each other and share energy through mycorrhizal fungi. These communities have properties not found in individual trees. One practical implication is that logging has consequences for nontargeted trees.

The human mind is no less root-grafted and emergent. When I pay attention to a tree, who or what is doing the attending? We are mostly a culture of Cartesians who conceive the attending "I" as a unified center of consciousness who authors experience. This conception of the "I" as a single, alert inner sentinel was challenged by James's radical empiricism, and it was rejected throughout Dewey's mature work. I emerge historically as a differentiated locus of activity through organism-environment interactivity (UPMP:325). I am not an antecedently existing mind or soul. Accordingly Dewey's philosophy of mind criticized philosophies based on radical autonomy, and like James he rejected the Kantian transcendental subject—the "I" that lies behind the seemingly infinite regress of knowing that I know that I know.[54]

Far from deemphasizing the singular pulse of the individual, according to Dewey individuals co-constitute their horizonal field. Social and natural relationships are popularly conceived as discovered, found, *given*. Dewey recognized that we individually and collectively create relationships as well as selectively observe them, and we thereby change reality. We do not create from outside or above or even inside an already-completed whole. Instead, our relational constructions are possibilities or potentialities of situations that we actualize through ongoing interactivities. This is apparent in Dewey's analysis of maps, but it is most clearly exhibited for him through the interactive emergence of form in the arts, our source of renewal and redirection (see Chapter Six).

Dewey's arguments against hypostatization often relied on premises drawn from modern physics. To give a physical description of light, James Clerk Maxwell recognized in the 1860s that electromagnetic fields *between* particles are as real as the particles. This suggests that the relations between things are as real as the individuals they reflexively constitute. In 1915, Einstein demonstrated in the general theory of relativity that there is no such independently existing thing as space or gravity or mass. Gravity is the geometric pattern of spacetime (warp and weft of the same fabric) in the presence of massive bodies, and these bodies are themselves not ultimate individuals independent of velocity and time. Einstein showed that, contrary to the common-sense Newtonian view, gravity is not a "force" that reaches out to instantaneously attract distant objects. So in modern physics spacetime is a relational *event*, not a substantive thing that contains bodies in motion (see QC, LW 4:115–16).

To Dewey the new physics of fields and relations suggested as a postulate, to closely paraphrase a central thesis of James's radical empiricism, that the parts of existence are held together by relations that are themselves parts of existence. There is no need, in James's words, for any "extraneous ... connective support."[55] Reflecting on the revolutionary insights of modern physics in his late essay "William James and the World Today," Dewey proposed "temporal relationism" as another name for his own naturalistic philosophical framework in opposition to "the absolutism of a block-universe" (LW 15:3).

On the basis of such lessons from the natural sciences, Dewey postulated in "Time and Individuality" that scientific objects *are* relational (LW 14:98–114). Scientists are not detached subjects penetrating the intrinsic natures of self-contained individual existences. A search for intrinsic natures is, Dewey argued, epistemically on a par with espousing a belief in Locke's "primary qualities." Locke inferred the existence of qualities like mass and size that, unlike relational "secondary qualities" such as colors and sounds, are concealed forever beyond the veil of our sense perceptions. However, as noted, Einstein revealed that mass and size exist only in relation to time and velocity. They are not primary qualities of self-contained objects, and they are measured differently from equally valid observational frames of reference.

Any physicist knows this, but relational thinking proceeds slowly as a cultural force. Again, even the best scientists still casually write as though belief in extrarelational primary qualities is unproblematic. This confused and obsolete metaphysical map becomes relevant to practical navigation when it hinders attention to relationships. Such inattention obstructed the development of physical theories in the nineteenth century, and it also underwrote a dualistic philosophy of mind from Locke through Kant.

Having finally overturned the old Eleatic identity of reality with the static and permanent, in Dewey's view modern biology and physics also pulled the intellectual foundations from beneath the construction of any timeless metaphysical superstructure. This includes traditional formulations of the soul and God. Knowledge, beauty, goodness, and wisdom are imagined by the theologically inclined dualist to be qualities descending from "a super-gaseous spiritual force" (UPMP:292). Instead they emerge from, are embodied in, and exist through human activities. Life does not have to "testify to a reality beyond itself" to secure "organizing principles and directive ends" (LW 5:268).

There is, for Dewey, no philosophic need for some inaccessible essence "behind" personal identity to make a self cohere in all of its many attributes. Nor is an ethereal Being required to originate and cement the cosmos or to conscript human attention toward what is best in ourselves. We reach for such determinative, hypostatized notions because of outworn and misleading assumptions: One behind the many, Being over becoming, substance over process, permanence over change, certainty over fallibility. These dysfunctional dualisms are like the "ether wind" of nineteenth-century Newtonian physics, which Einstein showed was unnecessary as a pervasive medium for light to move in. In Dewey's view it is at best superfluous to postulate something extrarelational like Kant's reason-ruled will to explain and support personal identity and behavior. We achieve coherence and integration, and we coordinate our behaviors, through our embodied interactions with social, cultural, and physical environments.

Insofar as we persist in attending in our public policies and personal choices only to individuals in isolation, or pretend to hold in our hands a universal compass set changelessly to true metaphysical north, we will stay lost. As we navigate today's ecological and economic problems—from habitat depletion and climate change to radical income inequality and an unsustainable food system—our map of existential traits should help us to perceive and respond to events and relationships instead of concealing them.

Critique of Dewey's map: the animal plane

The beauty of what Dewey called his cultural naturalism or naturalistic empiricism is that all perspectives, including his own, must be run through its threshing machine separating the nutritious wheat from the worthless husks: "Only chaff goes, though perhaps the chaff had once been treasured. An empirical method which remains true to nature does not 'save'; it is not an insurance device nor a mechanical antiseptic. But it inspires the mind with courage and vitality to create new ideals and values in the face of the perplexities of a new world" (EN, LW 1:4).

As with any map, Dewey's metaphysical map was provisional and biased. It was a product of values and purposes of the first half of the twentieth century. When a map makes mistakes in charting territory, it leads to practical navigational problems. Hence Dewey argued that *if metaphysical inquiry is to be experimental it must retravel, inspect, and resurvey the ever-changing experiential terrain and revise past symbolic formulations* accordingly. It must reveal past biases from the vantage point of current values, purposes, and problems.

I close this chapter by analyzing a small portion of Dewey's map in light of developments, during the decades since his death, in scientific evidence and cultural attitudes regarding nonhuman animals. I will focus on Dewey's texts rather than recent developments. In Dewey's spirit, all assertions in this book should be similarly retraveled and reappraised, and I hope that this section serves as a model and a reminder that my own generally sympathetic treatment of Dewey in the coming chapters is far from the last word.

Dewey did not overly romanticize nature or parrot assumptions of a providential natural order. Instead he urged an existential attitude of "piety" toward nature.[56] *Natural piety*, Dewey asserted in *A Common Faith*, requires a sense of our dependence on infinite natural relations that precede us and are affected by us. We exist, and our lives are imbued with meaning, by grace of these relations. The attitude (and virtue) of natural piety extends beyond humans and other living organisms to the greater "imaginative totality we call the Universe" (ACF, LW 9:14). It rests "on a just sense of nature as the whole of which we are parts, while it also recognizes that we are parts that are marked by intelligence and purpose" (ACF, LW 9:18).

Dewey accordingly took our shared ancestry and continuity with nonhumans seriously, and he urged a deep perception of the kinship and differences between ourselves and other animals. Human, in the age of evolutionary biology and ecology, is an adjective for our specific animal nature, not the pinnacle of a hierarchy of who was made for whom.[57] But unreconstructed, Dewey's own natural piety fell short of a "full perceptual realization" (AE, LW 10:182) of the extent to which parts of nonhuman nature are looking back at us with awareness. Analysis of Dewey's view of animals across his published work reveals residual traces of philosophies he elsewhere discredited, such as a vestige of Cartesianism in which animals are mindless automatons (e.g., QC, LW 4:80–82).[58] The irony of this from the typewriter of arguably the twentieth century's most anti-Cartesian philosopher buttresses Dewey's position on the inescapably cultural and historical nature of inquiry.

Driven by the inertia of habit and impulse, nonhuman animal life is in Dewey's view marked by mechanical recurrence and uniformity. The reflex responses of other animals are blind yet well suited to survival because their responses are wholly triggered by environmental conditions. The body is in the mind (i.e., mental processes piggyback on sensorimotor processes), but only human bodies have minds. Humans have enduring "goods" such as love that are the results of thought and culture. All other animals are limited to "pleasures," which are accidental (HNC, MW 14:146).[59] Such views informed an article Dewey's wrote in 1926 on the "Ethics of Animal Experimentation," in which he expressed unqualified confidence that "scientific men are under definite obligation to experiment upon animals" (LW 2:98; cf. LW 13:333). The reader may reasonably wonder whether Dewey sees the new questions raised, and the potential for reforms highlighted, by his own altered metaphysical map.

One would naturally assume that the evolutionary continuity model elaborated by Dewey would sparkle on the subject of human–animal continuity, as it indeed does in the first chapter of *Art as Experience*. But Dewey is obliged both by his original audience and his own intellectual habits to worry that the principal objection to his philosophy will focus on the degradation of ideals, "betrayal of their nature and denial of their value" (AE, LW 10:26). *Experience and Nature* and *Art as Experience* can be read as Dewey's extended argument that evolutionary continuity implies no such betrayal. Many among today's more progressive, post-Earth Day readers will understandably share the opposite concern, namely that we risk betrayal of the more-than-human world when we fail to celebrate continuity.

On Dewey's map of generic traits of existence, humans live alone on a third plateau (EN, LW 1:208), a field of interaction that includes all mental life and all creative and individuating factors. He distinguished the human plane, the animal plane, and the vegetative plane. All three "planes" or "plateaus" involve the "interaction of a living being with an environment" (AE, LW 10:276). Operations of the "higher" include the "lower," but not vice versa. Here, as with Peirce's doctrine of *synechism* (his version of the postulate of continuity), there are no ontological barriers to continuity between human and other forms of life, though of course developmental constraints in the other direction exist.

The three plateaus are descriptive categories for "fields of interaction," so unlike Aristotle's parallel categories (thinking, appetitive, nutritive), they do *not* support a fixed anthropocentric teleology. Dewey says of the plateaus: "They stick to empirical facts noting and denoting characteristic qualities and consequences peculiar to various levels of interaction" (EN, LW 1:208). As with any mapping, Dewey thus conceived his categorization as fallible and provisional, to be revised in light of ongoing inquiry. Looking back from the vantage point of contemporary research on animal behavior, cognition, emotion, and culture, Dewey overstated the extent to which the behavior of other animals is determined by instinct that is pushed by unthinking appetite. Dewey echoed the prejudice of his contemporaries that all non-human animals act out of blind habit. Today even classical conditioning (a.k.a. the "reflex arc," from which Dewey liberated humans but not other animals) is recognized in any introductory psychology text as involving some cognitive processing.

On Dewey's metaphysical map, the primary relationship of the human field of interaction is means–consequence (such as tool-making and inventions), not cause–effect. The means–consequence relationship is deliberative and entails "responding to things in their meanings," whereas the cause–effect relationship is impulsive and involves "a mere end, a last and closing term of arrest" (EN, LW 1:278). Perception of the past and anticipation of the future, guided by our sociocultural environments, is a prerequisite for skillfully framing and evaluating adaptive means and purposes in the present (UPMP:236–327). Without such perception there could be no control of means, no intelligence, no culminating achievements, nor could we consciously desire something different in the first place. So our behavior would be inflexibly habitual, a reactive discharge of immediately satisfied instinct—driven by chance, not choice. These, Dewey asserted, are traits of the animal plane.

As discussed, culture for Dewey is the way we inhabit nature, but he restricts such inhabitation to humans, and perhaps as a direct result nature at times appears to recede far into the background in his discussions of culture (e.g., FC, LW 13:79).[60] Cultural existence, according to Dewey, is marked by learning ("growth" in Dewey's idiom), which stems from sociocultural interdependence and the fact that meanings enter "that are derived from prior experiences" (AE, LW 10:276). Growth is a sociocultural, not simply physical, gift (DE, MW 9:48). As cultural beings who have internalized linguistic communication by conversing with others (EN, LW 1:135), humans are capable of imaginative forethought and experimental probing. Consequently our experiences do not merely end; they are potentially consummated and fulfilled, perhaps superficially and hastily, but better artistically and perceptively.

There is much that is redemptive in Dewey's theory of the three plateaus. Unless we are subsisting on the animal plane (e.g., attacking someone as a reflex response), human goods are deliberate even if obtuse. Our impulses are at least potentially directed though educated foresight of consequences. Dewey urged us to establish social and material conditions that liberate human energies from enslavement to mechanized habits, toward a life of critical inquiry, social responsiveness, emotional engagement, and artistic consummations. He perpetuated a 1920s picture of animals as unintelligent and unemotional brutes, but at the same time he attempted to throw into relief our human potential as adaptive imaginative animals.

Summary

Dewey rejected metaphysics that pretends to study something beyond experience. On his naturalistic reinterpretation, metaphysics aims to project a provisional "map" to be used as a navigational tool for inquiring into the general characteristics of "experience," by which he meant our natural existence as cultural beings. In his conception of experimental inquiry as mapping, he affirmed the inescapability of selectivity, developed a functional–operational sense of truth that requires action, and asserted the provisional nature of symbolic constructions. He called experimental method the "denotative method," a methodological loop that moves from immediate to mediated and back to immediate experience. Due to the traditional map, troublesome intellectual habits ring true for us, such as dualisms between subject and object, mind and body, theory and practice, spirit and matter, culture and nature, or freedom and necessity. Dewey sought substitutes for preecological, nonrelational, and individualistic maps that were filled with dualistic, "hypostatized" assumptions. His own constructive metaphysical map instead highlighted, for example, temporal quality, precariousness, stability, potentiality, qualitative immediacy, qualitative individuality, relations, and novelty. As with any map, Dewey's was provisional and biased, as illustrated by his depiction of other animals. If metaphysical inquiry is to be experimental it must retravel, inspect, and resurvey the ever-changing experiential terrain and revise past symbolic formulations accordingly.

Notes

1 Irwin Edman, in Experience and Nature (LW 1:405).
2 However, Dewey did not regard metaphysics as inherently more significant than other modes of cultural criticism.
3 On Heidegger and Derrida in comparison with Dewey on metaphysics, see Jim Garrison, "John Dewey, Jacques Derrida, and the Metaphysics of Presence," Transactions of the Charles S. Peirce Society 35, no. 2 (1999): 346–72.
4 Charles S. Peirce, "Letters to Lady Welby," in Charles S. Peirce: Selected Writings, ed. Philip P. Wiener (Mineola, NY: Dover, 1958), 386.
5 For an anthology of expert essays exploring Dewey in the context of ancient Greek philosophy, see Christopher C. Kirby, ed., Dewey and the Ancients (London: Bloomsbury, 2014).
6 In Philip Wheelwright, The Presocratics, Parmenides, F 7B (Upper Saddle River, NJ: Pearson, 1966), 98.
7 In Wheelwright, The Presocratics, Anaxagoras, F 18, 162–63.
8 In Wheelwright, The Presocratics, Anaxagoras, F 15, 162.
9 Aristotle's notion in the Physics that chance is a secondary feature of nature rather than a fundamental one was eventually replaced in the first half of the twentieth century with the idea of chance genetic variation in evolutionary

biology, the "modern synthesis." On chance and spontaneity, see Aristotle, *Physics*, books 4–8.

10 Others before Dewey—such as Herbert Spencer, who coined the phrase "survival of the fittest"—might be mistaken for Darwinian revolutionaries in philosophy. Spencer was more directly influenced by the person and texts of Darwin, and Dewey was heavily influenced by Spencer's general evolutionary outlook. But, as Dewey observed on many occasions, Spencer was himself tangled in the quest for fixity and maintained a Lamarckian view of the biological inheritance of acquired moral intuitions. Spencer misconceived evolution as having a fixed goal that we are automatically moving toward, and on a standard interpretation he attempted to give the approval of biological law to a political view of society that would forever justify the social inequalities of laissez-faire capitalism (see Chapter Five). On the influence of Spencer on Dewey's "Darwinism," see Trevor Pearce, "The Dialectical Biologist, circa 1890: John Dewey and the Oxford Hegelians," *Journal of the History of Philosophy* 52, no. 4 (2014), forthcoming. In a book in preparation, *Pragmatism's Evolution: Organism and Environment in Early American Philosophy*, Pearce argues for the deep influence of Spencer's general framework of organism–environment interaction on Dewey and other classical pragmatists.

11 For new material on Dewey's evolutionary biology and scientific subject matter, see Peter Godfrey-Smith, "Dewey and the Subject-Matter of Science," in *Dewey's Enduring Impact*, ed. John R. Shook and Paul Kurtz (Amherst, NY: Prometheus Books, 2011).

12 See Thomas M. Alexander's Introduction to Dewey's *A Common Faith* (New Haven, CT: Yale University Press, 2013).

13 On the map image, see Jim Garrison, "Dewey on Metaphysics, Meaning Making, and Maps," *Transactions of the Charles S. Peirce Society* 41, no. 4 (2004): 818–44.

14 René Descartes, "Reply to Objections V," in *The Philosophical Works of Descartes*, trans. Elizabeth S. Haldane and G. R. T. Ross, 2 vols. (Cambridge, UK: Cambridge University Press, 1911), vol. 2: 212. Volume from Dewey's personal and professional library, Special Collections, Morris Library, Southern Illinois University at Carbondale. Underlining is in Dewey's hand.

15 See Shannon Sullivan's exploration of Dewey's ecological insights in *Living across and through Skins: Transactional Bodies, Pragmatism, and Feminism* (Bloomington, IN: Indiana University Press, 2001).

16 The far-reaching implications of this insight are underappreciated in current introductory psychology textbooks, which simply gloss Dewey as one of the founders of functional psychology.

17 In Corliss Lamont, ed., *Dialogue on John Dewey* (New York: Horizon Press, 1959), 95.

18 Thomas M. Alexander, personal communication.

19 For an analysis of the metaphorical structuring of ecological imagination that uses Dewey as a platform, see my "Ecological Imagination," *Environmental Ethics* 32 (Summer 2010): 183–203. I develop the notion from an East–West comparative perspective in "Ecological Imagination and Aims of Moral Education through the Kyoto School and American Pragmatism," in *Education and the Kyoto*

School of Philosophy: Pedagogy for Human Tranformation, ed. Paul Standish and Naoko Saito (Dordrecht: Springer, 2012).

20 The *situation* for Dewey is akin to what phenomenologist Merleau-Ponty later called the *chiasma*. See LW 16:281–82 for insights into Dewey's terms situation, problematic situation, and inquiry.

21 See William James, *The Principles of Psychology*, vol. 1 (Mineola, NY: Dover, 1950 [1890]), 246. My reference to the "spread" of an event is derived from Stephen Pepper.

22 Michael Pollan, "Some of My Best Friends Are Germs," *The New York Times Magazine*, May 15, 2013.

23 See Mark Johnson, *The Meaning of the Body* (Chicago: University of Chicago Press, 2007), 267.

24 See Thomas M. Alexander, "Dewey's Denotative-Empirical Method: A Thread through the Labyrinth," ch. 2 of *The Human Eros: Eco-ontology and the Aesthetics of Existence* (New York: Fordham University Press, 2013), 54–71.

25 Raymond D. Boisvert, "Dewey's Metaphysics: Ground-Map of the Prototypically Real," in *Reading Dewey: Interpretations for a Postmodern Generation*, ed. Larry A. Hickman (Bloomington, IN: Indiana University Press, 1998), 150.

26 See Boisvert, "Dewey's Metaphysics," 150.

27 See Josiah Royce, "Supplementary Essay," in *The World and Individual*, vol. 1 (New York: Macmillan, 1899), 502ff.

28 For a technical discussion of careful distinctions regarding logical form in Dewey's "inquiry into inquiry," the 1938 *Logic*, see Douglas Browning, "Designation, Characterization, and Theory in Dewey's *Logic*," in *Dewey's Logical Theory*, ed. F. Thomas Burke, D. Micah Hester, and Robert B. Talisse (Nashville, TN: Vanderbilt University Press, 2002), 160–79.

29 Hickman further clarifies Dewey's usage: "Continuing this analogy, we could say that a judgment is what is made by the batter as a result of (rapid) deliberation about whether he or she will swing the bat at the ball. The pitched ball is thus the proposition and the swing of the bat is the judgment. In this case, as others, deliberation takes into account observed conditions as well as established rules, such as those established to determine strike zones" (Larry A. Hickman, *Pragmatism as Post-Postmodernism: Lessons from John Dewey* [New York: Fordham University Press, 2007], 221).

30 1915.05.04 (03521): Dewey to Scudder Klyce.

31 Dewey developed a participatory theory of imaginative communication that informs his value theory, his theory of democracy, his theory of education, and much of the rest of his philosophy. His most complete analysis, which is beyond the scope of an introductory volume, is chapter 5 of *Experience and Nature*.

32 Cf. Garrison, "Dewey on Metaphysics, Meaning Making, and Maps," 822.

33 Thomas Burke writes: "A major target here will be to explain Dewey's distinction between propositions and judgments. One cannot understand his logical theory as a whole without understanding this distinction. And one must understand his conceptions of inquiry, situations, and other basic notions in

order to understand this distinction." Burke, *Dewey's New Logic: A Reply to Russell* (Chicago: University of Chicago Press, 1998), ix–x.

34 See "Judgment" in the Glossary for Dewey's technical use of the terms judgment and proposition. I am here passing over Dewey's very careful yet technically demanding distinction in his logic between generic and universal propositions (e.g., LTI, LW 12:254ff.). The following selection from *Logic: The Theory of Inquiry* sums up Dewey's technical distinction between affirmations and assertions: "The terms *affirmation* and *assertion* are employed in current speech interchangeably. But there is a difference, which should have linguistic recognition, between the logical status of intermediate subject-matters that are taken for use in connection with what they may lead to as means, and subject-matter which has been prepared to be final. I shall use *assertion* to designate the latter logical status and *affirmation* to name the former. Even from the standpoint of ordinary speech, *assertion* has a quality of insistence that is lacking in the connotation of the word 'affirmation'" (LTI, LW 12:123).

35 Cf. Garrison, "Dewey on Metaphysics, Meaning Making, and Maps," 823.

36 See Garrison, "Dewey on Metaphysics, Meaning Making, and Maps," 820, 829.

37 Richard W. Pogge, "Real-World Relativity: The GPS Navigation System," *Astronomy*, Ohio State Unversity, www.astronomy.ohio-state.edu/~pogge/Ast162/Unit5/gps.html; accessed June 8, 2014.

38 Alexander, *The Human Eros*, 1. Dewey's agrarian heritage was a likely line of influence in his appreciation of culture as part of nature. Thompson and Hilde write: "Agrarian naturalism—the belief that culture and conduct are conditioned by nature because they are of a piece with nature—becomes pragmatic naturalism." Paul B. Thompson and Thomas C. Hilde, eds., *The Agrarian Roots of Pragmatism* (Nashville, TN: Vanderbilt University Press, 2000), 20.

39 From Irwin Edman's draft preface to the third edition of Dewey's *Experience and Nature*, included in *The Correspondence of John Dewey*. See 1954.01.26 (17266): Allan B. Ecker to Roberta Lowitz Grant Dewey.

40 Thomas M. Alexander, "John Dewey's Uncommon Faith: Understanding 'Religious Experience,'" *American Catholic Philosophical Quarterly* 87, no. 2 (2013): 347–62, at 350–51.

41 Alexander, *The Human Eros*, 17.

42 Cf. Raymond D. Boisvert, *John Dewey: Rethinking Our Time* (Albany, NY: SUNY Press, 1998), 124.

43 Boisvert, *John Dewey: Rethinking Our Time*, 124.

44 He paused in a chapter on mind in *Experience and Nature* to caution: "The foregoing discussion is both too technical and not elaborately technical enough for adequate comprehension. It may be conceived as an attempt to contribute to what has come to be called an 'emergent' theory of mind. But every word that we can use, organism, feeling, psycho-physical, sensation and sense, 'emergence' itself, is infected by the associations of old theories, whose import is opposite to that here stated" (EN, LW 1:207).

45 William James, "The Sentiment of Rationality," in *The Works of William James*, ed. Frederick H. Burkhardt, Fredson Bowers, and Ignas K. Skrupskelis (Cambridge, MA: Harvard University Press, 1975–).

46 Dewey's postulate does not exclude experienced discontinuities; indeed, such discontinuities set many problems for inquiry. Hence his postulate is not in opposition to a central thesis of James's radical empiricism, namely that we directly experience both continuities and discontinuities, that these are equally real, and that we must be equally open to both. For a contemporary study of Dewey's principle of continuity as "a guiding assumption for a naturalistic semantics," see Johnson, *The Meaning of the Body*, 10.

47 For the reader interested in more historical connections: In Dewey's view the empiricist George Berkeley had something fundamentally right despite his "immaterialist" theory of the origin of ideas in God. The typical empiricist shaves off Berkeley's theology but keeps his psychology (EN, LW 1:149), with the result that ideas are taken to be subjective. Berkeley, in contrast, perceived that ideas are real and objective. Dewey replaced Berkeley's antinaturalistic theory of ideas with a theory of ideas as "modes of natural interaction" (EN, LW 1:149).

48 In contemporary scholarship on Plato's later works, a sophisticated theory of deep mathematical and logical structures is emerging, a theory that may not violate Dewey's principle of continuity. As Dewey well appreciated, going back to Plato always exceeds the doctrinal accretions of later "Platonism."

49 Paul Thompson, *The Agrarian Vision* (Lexington, KY: University Press of Kentucky, 2010), 132–33.

50 In George Herbert Mead, "The Philosophies of Royce, James, and Dewey in Their American Setting," in *John Dewey: The Man and His Philosophy*, Addresses Delivered in New York in Celebration of His Seventieth Birthday (Cambridge, MA: Harvard University Press, 1930), 103.

51 See Gregory Pappas, *John Dewey's Ethics: Democracy as Experience* (Bloomington, IN: Indiana University Press, 2008) for various interpretations of the philosophical fallacy.

52 Cf. Thomas M. Alexander, *John Dewey's Theory of Art, Experience, and Nature: The Horizons of Feeling* (Albany, NY: SUNY Press, 1987), 109.

53 On East Asian thought in relation to Dewey, see Roger T. Ames, "'The Way Is Made in the Walking': Responsibility as Relational Virtuousity," in *Responsibility*, ch. 3, ed. Barbara Darling-Smith (Lanham, MD: Lexington Books, 2007), 55ff.

54 Mind, as Johnson explains Dewey's position, "is a functional aspect of experience that emerges when it becomes possible for us to share meanings, to inquire into the meaning of a situation, and to initiate action that transforms, or remakes, that situation." Johnson, *The Meaning of the Body*, 76–77.

55 William James, *Essays in Radical Empiricism* (New York: Henry Holt, 1912), xii. Cf. James, *Pragmatism and Other Writings* (New York: Penguin, 2000), 42.

56 See Alexander, "John Dewey's Uncommon Faith: Understanding 'Religious Experience.'"

57 Anthropocentrism has many meanings: it is the view that only humans have moral worth, or that humans are atop a hierarchy of moral worth, or at least that humans are the only sources of value. In popular culture it often includes a belief that the

Earth was created principally for human use. Unlike Dewey, most anthropocentrists regard humans as ontologically separate (i.e., we are distinguished by our discontinuity from nature) and axiologically intrinsically worthy (i.e., we are the only creatures to be valued for ourselves rather than solely as means to others' ends). Some anthropocentrists, however, simply argue that our *primary* commitment should be to help humans live better lives. This last sense, along with the assertion that humans are the only sources of value, applies unambiguously to Dewey. But he did not fully examine the more controversial notion that humans stand atop a hierarchy of value, which he projected in part into his metaphysical map.

58 For a systematic analysis, see my "Dewey and Animal Ethics," in *Animal Pragmatism*, ed. Erin McKenna and Andrew Light (Bloomington, IN: Indiana University Press, 2004), 43–62. Descartes wrote: "[I]t is nature which acts in them [animals] according to the disposition of their organs, as one sees that a clock, which is made up of only wheels and springs, can count the hours and measure time more exactly than we can with all our art" (René Descartes, *Discourse on the Method*, pt. 6, trans. Robert Stoothoff, in *The Philosophical Writings of Descartes* [Cambridge, UK: Cambridge University Press, 1985], vol. 1: 141).

59 Thus, for instance, in Dewey's view there is nothing on the animal plane analogous to love. Nonhumans pursue the "physiologically normal end" of sex without any sort of redirection of impulses—such as in humans results in poetry—into other channels (AE, LW 10:83).

60 In *Freedom and Culture*, Dewey identified six chief factors of culture: (1) law and politics, (2) industry and commerce, (3) science and technology, (4) the arts of expression and communication, (5) "morals, or the values men prize and the ways in which they evaluate them," and (6) social philosophy, "the system of general ideas used by men to justify and to criticize the fundamental conditions under which they live" (FC, LW 13:79).

Further reading

Thomas M. Alexander, *The Human Eros: Eco-ontology and the Aesthetics of Existence* (New York: Fordham University Press, 2013).

Thomas M. Alexander, "Potentiality and Naturalism: Dewey's Metaphysical Metamorphosis," in *Dewey and the Ancients*, ed. Christopher C. Kirby (London: Bloomsbury, 2014), 19–45.

Raymond D. Boisvert, *Dewey's Metaphysics* (New York: Fordham University Press, 1988).

Douglas Browning, "Dewey and Ortega on the Starting Point," *Transactions of the Charles S. Peirce Society* 34, no. 1 (1998): 69–92.

Jim Garrison, "Dewey on Metaphysics, Meaning making, and Maps," *Transactions of the Charles S. Peirce Society* 41, no. 4 (2004): 818–44.

William T. Myers, "Metaphysics: A Defense," *Transactions of the Charles S. Peirce Society* 40, no. 1 (2004): 679–700.

Herbert Schneider, "Radical Empiricism," in *A History of American Philosophy*, ch. 8 (New York: Columbia University Press, 1946), 511–72.

Three

Epistemology reconstructed

Any belief as such is tentative, hypothetical. ... When it is apprehended as a tool and only a tool, an instrumentality of direction, the same scrupulous attention will go to its formation as now goes into the making of instruments of precision in technical fields.

(QC, LW 4:221–22)

Dewey's purpose in *The Quest for Certainty* was, in his own words, to crumble into dust "the chief fortress of the classic philosophical tradition" (QC, LW 4:64). At book's end, a contemporaneous reviewer quipped, Dewey stands sword in hand, high above a bloody field strewn with vanquished philosophers. The book is that destructive. Yet his ultimate aim was constructive: to hypothesize a future "in which experience will itself provide the values, meanings and standards now sought in some transcendent world" (QC, LW 4:63).

Our cultural need, Dewey urged, is to shift away from extraempirical creeds, and this can be furthered by revealing the inherently operative and interactive method of inquiry that the natural sciences use to attain "the most authentic and dependable knowledge" (QC, LW 4:64). This led Dewey to speak not so much of an essence of science but of the morale of science and the generic logic of experimental method. In particular, he admired this method's tendency, at its best, to cut against the grain of our aversion to uncertainty. He admired its "willingness to hold belief in suspense, ability to doubt until evidence is obtained; willingness to go where evidence points instead of putting first a personally preferred conclusion; ability to hold ideas in solution and use them as hypotheses to be tested instead of as dogmas to be asserted; and (possibly the most distinctive of all) enjoyment of new fields for inquiry and of new problems" (FC, LW 13:166–67). These animating traits are not the special possessions of scientists. Through education they can become available to all.

We get our best examples of knowledge—including good maps—through functional–operational procedures that require overt action and hence bear no resemblance to the old split between knowing and doing. Knowing requires acting. So it is time, in Dewey's view, to fire philosophies that perpetuate the outworn wedge between subjective knowers and known objects, including endless reincarnations of the doctrine of truth as pre-existing correspondences between symbols and states of affairs. A rejuvenated empirical philosophy, he argued, would contribute to the refined intellectual instruments we need in order to deal with the most perplexing and significant problems we share in a moving world (see RP, MW 12:152).

Emerson said that "To be great is to be misunderstood" (and not vice versa).[1] Dewey has had his share of such greatness over the past century. The most common interpretive mistakes arise from reactive pigeonholing due to ordinary associations of his key terms, such as experience, pragmatism, empiricism, naturalism, progressive education, instrumentalism, liberalism, and democracy. One prominent Dewey scholar begins academic presentations with a good-humored mantra: "By experience Dewey doesn't mean experience," "By nature Dewey doesn't mean nature," "By mind Dewey doesn't mean mind," and so on.[2]

Take the terms pragmatist and empiricist. Dewey was not a pragmatist in the narrow sense of valorizing expediency, glorifying action for its own sake, or conflating truth with whatever it takes to turn a profit (see LW 2:5). His writings ring with criticisms of shallow American practicality and acquisitiveness, what he called "capricious pragmatism" (EN, LW 1:186). Moreover, although Dewey dubbed his philosophy naturalistic empiricism in *Experience and Nature*, he was a sharp critic of *empiricists* caught up in the old, preexperimental Lockean picture of a veil of ideas obscuring an objective world that is nonetheless taken to be responsible for human knowledge.

Dismantling the epistemology industry

Dewey argued in his newly recovered book *Unmodern Philosophy and Modern Philosophy* that philosophy's failure to contribute much to humanizing techno-industrial civilization has largely been due to persistent "entanglement in alien doctrines that reflect the slow and halting course of institutional change" (UPMP:169; cf. ION, LW 5:108). The vital heart of modern philosophies since the seventeenth century, Dewey argued, has been the progressive course away from outworn creeds haunted by the "hidden and occult" (UPMP:169). Despite doctrinal entanglement, modern philosophies have energetically striven "to get things out into the open, into the public air and light of day where they are open to inspection on equal terms by any and all who are properly equipped" (UPMP:169).

In *Unmodern Philosophy and Modern Philosophy*, Dewey lamented that what goes by the name of modern in philosophy has often been anything but. What is genuinely modern, he argued, is the priority of public over private, open over closed, inspectable over hidden. These priorities are more significant for meriting the name modern than any particular set of conclusions that a philosophy might espouse (UPMP:169). In that modernizing spirit, Dewey wrote in his 1948 preface to the reprinting of *Reconstruction in Philosophy* that *Reconstruction of Philosophy* would have been a "more suitable title" if philosophy is to become more pertinent to the emerging problems of our place and time (MW 12:256).

In order to introduce some of the subtleties of Dewey's reconstruction of as-yet-unmodern epistemology, it may help to set some of his positions in contrast with one of his more recent admirers. In the 1970s through 1990s Richard Rorty (1931–2007) became the most prominent American spokesperson for "anti-foundationalism." That is, he opposed the notion that there can be an immovable bedrock for securing knowledge claims. Rorty's intellectual heroes were Dewey, Heidegger, Wittgenstein, and Donald Davidson, each of whom rejected the self-image of detached, reason-besotted philosophers occupying a purely objective Archimedean standpoint.[3] Rorty was a brilliant philosophical tactician and an engaging writer, so his heroic characterization of Dewey in books like *Philosophy and the Mirror of Nature* (1979) and *Consequences of Pragmatism* (1982) held considerable sway. This was especially true for philosophers who, like me, were introduced to Dewey in the 1980s. Rorty's Dewey delighted in pulling the foundations from beneath the philosophical establishment. Reading Rorty was like taking a hot-air balloon ride, the familiar ground strangely falling away beneath you while you seem to hover motionless. Or, Boisvert suggests, picture the cartoon character Wile E. Coyote suspended wide-eyed above a canyon with the ground suddenly absent.[4]

Rorty's postmodern "ironism," in which we cherish and act upon positions that we nevertheless know cannot be rationally substantiated, became popularly identified with his hero Dewey.[5] The chief target of Rortyans was, and remains, "the correspondence aspect of knowledge identified by philosophical realists."[6] That is, Rorty rejected the prevailing "realist" view that knowledge is an abstract correspondence between mind and world. In Rorty's words: "Now, to put my cards on the table, I think that the realistic true believer's notion of the world is an obsession rather than an intuition." For Rorty a radical constructivism—in which truths are purely linguistic artifacts that are wholly made, not found—was the only route. "About two hundred years ago," he argued with a nod to Kant, "the idea that truth was made rather than found began to take hold of the imagination in Europe. ... The world does not speak. Only we do."[7]

One reaction to Rorty's neopragmatism in the 1980s and 1990s among scholars of classical pragmatism was to defend Dewey from his most visible if careless admirer.[8] Scholars of Wittgenstein and Heidegger mounted parallel defenses. Critiques of Rorty were part of a general movement to distinguish Dewey from purportedly "postmodern" philosophies that were merely chiseled in negative relief by the very assumptions they sought to dislocate. Distinguishing Dewey from Rorty's Dewey helped to clarify and develop key concepts, though at times it outpaced critical reexamination among those in the best position to renew the promise of Dewey's philosophy.

As discussed, Dewey's philosophical coming of age reflected the dominance of Hegelian Absolute idealism in philosophy in the US during the latter nineteenth century. The majority of professional philosophers in the US at that time were Absolute idealists who favored what William James criticized as a static, monistic "block universe," or at least they accepted the ancient Greek identification of knowledge with immutability and endorsed methods at odds with generation, change, process, and open-endedness. Meanwhile, a growing minority of philosophers, largely outside the academy, were empiricists who favored the "phenomenalist" view that any discussion about physical reality is actually about patterns presented to our sensory organs.

In the 1890s Dewey's sympathies joined James in rejecting both the standard idealistic and standard empiricist outlooks. Empiricism is traditionally defined as the view that all knowledge comes from experience, but it is pragmatically defined as habituation toward exposing ideas to experience as test. As discussed in Chapter Two, Dewey's empiricism is characterized by an experimental feedback loop between secondary experience and primary experience. Classical empiricists rejected absolutism and embraced change, but they hid the world's organizational features behind a veil that forever sealed off ideas from access to anything but the flow of sensations. The old empiricists "rested their case finally," Dewey recalled, "upon some weakness in human intelligence or some opaqueness in human experience" which, they held, "prevented access to the absolute and fixed truths and realities which somehow undeniably existed beneath the things of relativity and mere experience" (LW 15:4). These empiricists were predecessors, minus technical sophistication in symbolic logic, of the logical positivists and logical empiricists who gained professional dominance in the US during the 1930s through 1950s.

"The Postulate of Immediate Empiricism" (MW 3:158–67) was Dewey's first full-blown attempt to develop a modern empiricist epistemology free of these pitfalls that characterize what he called the "industry of epistemology" (MW 7:49). Traditional epistemology asked "How does the knowing mind align itself to correspond with known objects?" This guiding question of epistemology is in some circles still synonymous with "doing epistemology." Because many philosophers are narrow intellectualists who have long presumed knowing to be more essential than feeling or doing, they have taken answering this question to be the most important thing a philosopher could be doing.

But recall from Chapter Two that experiencing for Dewey is not limited to knowing, and nature (which encompasses cultural existence) is not limited only to what is knowable. Dewey condemned as "the great vice of philosophy" the outworn view that all experiencing is "a mode of knowing" (EN, LW 1:28), and he called this vice the "intellectualist's fallacy" (QC, LW 4:232). Knowledge is not the only measure of nature (QC, LW 4:233). Examining A, C, G, and T bases of DNA in a molecular biology lab is not inherently more revelatory of nature's potential than dancing. Art celebrates nature's emergent potential, so the "real" includes more than scientific objects narrowly construed.[9] Broadly construed, art is not a science, but scientific inquiry is a precise and operative art. "Scientific thought is, in its turn, a specialized form of art, with its own qualitative control" (LW 5:255).

Traditional epistemology defends knowledge as a unique relationship between subjective knowers and objects known, aloof perceivers and things perceived. This central feature of epistemology was framed long "before the rise of experimental inquiry" (QC, LW 4:134), and Dewey straightforwardly aimed to eliminate its influence (UPMP:182).

For Aristotle there was no problem of mind-world skepticism. The forms instantiated in material things were identical to the forms perceived by the mind, so there was an essential identity between the world as humans perceived it and the world in itself. Aristotle wrote: "A sense faculty is that which has the power to receive into itself the sensible form of things without the matter, in the way in which a piece of wax takes on the impress of the signet ring without the iron or gold" (On the Soul 424a17–24). For almost two millennia after Aristotle's hypostatization of logic (LTI, LW 12:63), most philosophers assumed that one taps into the rational order of the cosmos whenever one thinks logically. But this confidence collapsed along with the medieval cosmos. It was replaced in the seventeenth century with an internal-external dualism that left a burning doubt about the match-up between subjective ideas and objective things-in-themselves.

Twentieth-century philosophy remained mired in this seventeenth-century mindset, so Dewey beckoned in *The Quest for Certainty* that there is "need of thoroughgoing revision of ideas of mind and thought and their connection with natural things." This "is the critical task imposed on contemporary thought" (QC, LW 4:134–35). This task cannot simply be left to scientists. It is possible to accumulate a great deal of experience as a scientist without reflecting much about the nature of knowledge. We need to ask how knowing works when knowing has itself been made a subject of careful investigation (i.e., when we are willing to be empirical about knowing).

As discussed in Chapter Two, Dewey's naturalism extends beyond epistemology to characterize the way we inhabit nature as cultural beings, so it should be distinguished from the narrower meaning of naturalism in contemporary Anglophone philosophy of science. But his naturalism shares with this newer movement a rejection of foundationalism, which in the terminology of philosophy of science refers to any theory that tries to provide epistemology with a "pure" starting point free of any assumptions about the validity of prior scientific work.

What we discover when we are empirical about knowing, Dewey asserted, is that the knower is an active participant in what is known, not an outside spectator of it or passive receptacle. The latter view is a hangover from the metaphysical doctrine of selfhood as an indissoluble soul. "Many who think themselves scientifically emancipated and who freely advertise the soul for a superstition, perpetuate a false notion of what knows, that is, of a separate knower" (HNC, MW 14:123). As with maps and other symbolic representations of the world, knowing is not an affair in which detached spectators observe given objects that are "out there." To know things we journey with propositional representations, selectively engage the existential terrain they hypothesize (often mediated through technologies), seek out other experiences to "interpret and test the evidential value of what is observed" (particularly important when objects are remote in space and time), and revise symbolic formulations accordingly (see LW 14:19).

So Dewey reframed the primary question of epistemology as: How are things experienced "when they are experienced as known things?" (MW 3:159–60). This reframing positioned Dewey to develop his theory of experimental inquiry, to which he later devoted many of his chief works, including The Quest for Certainty (1929), Logic: The Theory of Inquiry (1938), and Knowing and the Known (1949).

The "Oh" of problems, the "Hmm" of inquiries, and the "Good" of judgments

In a nutshell, this is the picture of inquiry and knowing that Dewey eventually developed: A biological organism's life is marked by "the rhythm of loss of integration with environment and recovery of union" (AE, LW 10:20–21). With the human organism, so long as its habits are in equilibrium with its environment, there is no impetus to inquiry (HNC, MW 14:125). When nothing perplexing appears, human experience is characterized not by reflective thought but by the general stream of consciousness, random chains of so-called thought, and prejudicial beliefs. We are on cruise control, whether for better or worse. We act comfortably and credulously on the inertia of our beliefs whenever an occasion is presented.

Reflective thought is provoked by a hitch in the works, when an unsettled world stops being congenial to our expectations. We falter. When factors appear that are incompatible with secured habits, the situation becomes precipitous. It is "disturbed, troubled, ambiguous, confused, full of conflicting tendencies, obscure, etc." (LTI, LW 12:109). "Problematic situations" check our composure.

To say a situation is problematic is to say there is something questionable in it. The term problematic encompasses "features that are designated by such adjectives as confusing, perplexing, disturbed, unsettled, indecisive; and by such nouns as jars, hitches, breaks, blocks." The difficulty is "spread throughout the entire situation, infecting it as a whole" (HWT, LW 8:201). Problematic features interrupt forward motion and deflect it into inquiry (LW 16:282). Problematic situations destabilize, engage, intensify, and stimulate deliberate readjustment to meet the surprises of a moving world. (Recall here that the word situation, for Dewey, includes "diverse elements existing across wide areas of space and long periods of time, but which, nevertheless, have their own unity" [LW 16:281].)

In using the word problem to characterize the impetus to inquiry, Dewey did not intend a set task. Problems solvable by simple means–end engineering were of little interest to Dewey, who recoiled from any outlook that would reduce inquiry to the cognitive and emotional level of changing a flat tire. Dewey's pragmatism was the opposite of a master plan for preselected problems and cut-and-dried solutions.

Nor did he intend something made-up and artificial like Descartes pretending to solve the so-called "problem" of the external world. He wanted to take such blinders off inquiry by facilitating observation and reflection on the emerging situation as it presents itself (see LTI, LW 12:112). Newcomers to philosophical debate suppose that philosophers are arguing for different conclusions to the same agreed-upon problems. But philosophers, no less than any other group, tend to disagree about the nature of the difficulties themselves. Dewey wisely noted that "our disagreements as to conclusions are trivial compared with our disagreement as to problems. To see the problem another sees, in the same perspective and at the same angle—that amounts to something. ... To experience the same problem another feels—that perhaps is agreement" (MW 3:99). Philosophers earn their keep by putting questions well, and "as the saying truly goes, a question well put is half answered" (HWT, LW 8:201).[10]

To deal with a perplexing situation, alternative avenues for restoring stability suggest themselves, and we imaginatively test these in thought as we envision acting upon them. As will be discussed further in Chapters Four and Six, this imaginative "dramatic rehearsal" of alternative scenarios "goes on till some suggested solution meets all the conditions of the case and does not run counter to any discoverable feature of it" (HWT, LW 8:197).[11]

As the aim of deliberation, we select some particular suggested alternative and reject others because this way forward is perceptively felt to round out or harmonize the situation by dealing practically with the conflicting elements or desires that had set us on the path of inquiry (see AE, LW 10:247–48; cf. HNC, MW 14:136). This is what it means for a solution to "make sense." This felt sense of an apt way forward is not merely a subjective mental state; rather, it is an interactive tonal quality that permeates the developing situation and carries deliberation forward. To paraphrase Dewey's essay "Qualitative Thought," to be explored in greater detail in Chapter Six, the pervasive felt quality begins with the "Oh" of a disturbance or ambiguity, and it resolves with the "Good" of reestablished stability. "Oh" and "Good" characterize subject matters, Dewey emphasized; they are not mere personal feelings (LW 5:250).[12]

Active reflection—inquiry, in Dewey's lingo—thus occupies "an intermediate and reconstructive position" between an unstable situation and a temporarily controlled one (EEL, MW 10:331). As revealed in the analysis of maps in Chapter Two, judgments or assertions that mark the satisfactory terminus of inquiry are always provisional. If we follow the denotative (experimental) method, these culminating assertions are subject to ongoing rectification and extension through interactive engagement with an existential terrain that is forever only partially mapped.

In this way Dewey reconstructed rationality, henceforth "intelligence," as an experimental instrument for dealing with perplexing situations.[13] As will be developed in the next four chapters, the aim of intelligent inquiry is to make our fulfillments more secure and more widely shared. Dewey dismantled the old notion of a universal Reason that transcends culture, historical context, social relations, embodiment, and emotion. His own examples highlighted combined individual efforts, as with the joint development of maps and other navigational technologies, "in which one individual uses the results provided for him by a countless number of other individuals, and uses them so as to add to the common and public store" (LSA, LW 11:49). Such social intelligence is always historically situated, so the trying problems we grapple with are sometimes dissolved rather than finally solved.

By intelligence Dewey did not mean the common and objectionable sense well criticized by Stephen Jay Gould in *The Mismeasure of Man*: a capacity that can be accurately quantified as a single number (such as IQ) for each individual in a way that allows all individuals to be scientifically measured and ranked on a high-to-low scale of unchangeable mental limits that will likely be passed down to that individual's children.[14] Here is yet another iteration of the quest for fixity and its twin brother the fallacy of hypostatization. What is the practical difference between an inert, free-floating capacity disconnected from the need to mediate specific situational contexts, and no valuable capacity at all? Intelligence "is a charlatan," Dewey wrote, if taken in this hypostatized way as something behind the presence of "the living, behaving, knowing organism." Intelligence evolved through the same process of differential survival and reproduction that gave other animals fangs or shells or talons. Treating intelligence, IQ, or mind as a real entity "is double-talk; and double-talk doubles no facts" (KK, LW 16:124).[15]

Logic, meanwhile, Dewey recast as the theory of inquiry into problematic situations, yielding judgments that are inseparable from the uneasy contexts that originally gave rise to the inquiries.[16] Given the popular sense of the words knowledge and truth as infallible ideas to which we commit ourselves irreversibly, Dewey came to prefer the term "warranted assertion" to designate the provisional terminus of inquiry. He explained in *Logic: The Theory of Inquiry*: "The term 'warranted assertion' is preferred to the terms *belief* and *knowledge*. It is free from the ambiguity of these latter terms, and it involves reference to inquiry as that which warrants assertion" (LTI, LW 12:16). Contrary to epistemic relativism it is engaged inquiry, not individual point of view, that warrants assertions, but in accord with Peirce's "fallibilism" Dewey held that doubt can never be completely purged from our assertions.

Dewey held that dismissal of the idea of reason, logic, and knowledge as aloof, transcendent, and noncontextual happily spells an end to the pseudo-problems manufactured by much traditional metaphysics, epistemology, ethics, and aesthetics. It concurrently promotes a recovery of philosophical engagement with practical human problems of experience, knowing, moral life, and art.

Deerstalker hats and construction hard hats

In *Novum Organum* Francis Bacon rejected the idea that the mind is readily able to perceive, freeze, and reflect on natural phenomena without any distortions. Yet he thought we could train the mind to catch distorting influences in the act before they have a chance to muddy our mental snapshots of reality. For Dewey, in contrast, the mind is not even in principle a flawless mirror of nature.[17] The nature of mind–world "representation" has received voluminous attention in recent decades, and it is now a rare philosopher who claims that internal conceptions mirror external realities in themselves. But it is not necessary to understand the nuances of contemporary theories of representation to see that Dewey is playing an altogether different ball game. Dewey's philosophical pivot is "the picture of an organism as a force" rather than as a blank slate, mirror, camera, or transparent eyeball.[18] In philosophy of science the debate has nowadays shifted to one between constructivists and realists, so it will help to situate Dewey in this context. The poet Muriel Rukeyser famously said "The universe is made of stories, not of atoms." Are human narratives on one side of a dividing line and physical reality on the other, or is Rukeyser right to imply that humanizing narratives play a role in constituting reality? The question is not an idle one to be pursued only by those with spare time on their hands. Outside the academy, at least, it is common to suppose that some of our ideas mirror "the way things are" in nature, and to act on these conceptions in a self-fulfilling prophecy that often makes a mess of things. So what is responsible for human knowledge: us, or reality?[19] Dewey argued that this is a false dilemma, and he reconstructed old-fashioned empiricism in light of his rejection of both horns of the dilemma.

Dewey agreed with classical empiricists that immediate contact with a more-than-human world sets experimental conditions, but as has been shown he rejected their veil of ideas along with their static notion of knowledge as the passive replication of sensations. His philosophy also resonates with a theme of "scientific realists," despite their usual dualistic mind–world starting point: the sciences quite reasonably aim to represent a portion of the world. Meanwhile, in accord with the postmodern truism that we are limited by our culture's conceptual repertoire, Dewey urged that warranted assertions are no less actively constructed than maps or blueprints. But he rejected extreme forms of purely linguistic constructivism such as Rorty's which see scientists as spiders who spin beautiful and intricate linguistic webs wholly from their own innards, to invoke Francis Bacon's image of scholasticism's "cobwebs of learning."

To see what is at issue here, take the construction of clade trees in biology, which are used to determine the historical branching order of species. Cladistics is a taxonomic method that today usually relies on DNA analysis to construct cladograms in order to classify the evolutionary lineage of species. If Dewey's view of scientific knowledge is on target, a cladogram is a way of mapping biological terrain that is characterized in part by our bodies, neural anatomy, languages, values, and purposes. Cladistics is a trusty tool biologists have constructed to model historic divergences. Conceiving cladograms in this way does not make them any less reliable as a method for modeling species lineage, but it runs counter to the notion that clade trees correctly mirror the biological relationships that are discovered in the external world. Taxonomic classification based on cladistics may be the right tool for the job at hand, but not "right" once and for all, or as a perfect snapshot of the world's biological relationships.[20]

Dewey would reject as dualistic those versions of scientific realism—already fading among philosophers in Dewey's day—which hold that our technological sophistication allows us to reasonably aim to look and see ready-made objects and their relations as they are (and as they were), naked of cultural garb. In the more recent terminology of Jacques Derrida's deconstructionism, Dewey rejects the "transcendental signified." But again, at the same time he would part from extreme constructivist detractors who think we are merely dressing objects up in linguistic robes. Instead we are always immediately in the mix with objects as active, engaged, and creative participants in what is known. The strict or purely linguistic constructivist mistakenly replaces the realist's deerstalker detective hat (picture Sherlock Holmes) with a construction hard hat. In Dewey's more moderate constructivist view, which emphasizes shared practices and operative intelligence, we wear both hats. An interactive and communal empirical method detects and constructs.[21] In The Necessity of Pragmatism, Ralph Sleeper aptly calls this Dewey's "transactional realism."[22]

The seventeenth-century Cartesian philosopher Nicolas Malebranche argued that minds match the world through Divine intervention. Unless one wishes to resurrect such a view, Dewey urged us to settle for the more humble view of Locke and Kant, that we cannot directly perceive a world-in-itself. But Locke and Kant unfortunately took refuge in a hermetically sealed subjectivity that (a) drew its content from an external source about which we "know not what" and (b) made sense of that content by means of conceptual forms that appeared miraculously. On that view, thinking is somehow structured independent of embodied transactions in what phenomenologists helpfully call the Lebenswelt, or lifeworld.

In "Does Reality Possess Practical Character?" (1908), Dewey argued for what was at the time a groundbreaking thesis:

"knowledge makes a difference in and to things" (MW 4:127). He criticized "irresponsively sullen" philosophies that, despite professed adherence to Darwinism, retain an epistemology that is incompatible with "the lessons of physics and biology concerning moving energy and evolution" (MW 4:127). Such philosophies treat knowing as emanating from nowhere rather than as itself a natural, generative mode of situated experience. What, Dewey asked, would it look like to philosophize *sub specie generationis*, from the standpoint of a moving world, instead of *sub specie aeternitatis* (MW 4:141)? It is an often-observed fact about purportedly eternal truths in religion, morality, politics, and economics that they precisely resemble dominant assumptions of a particular historical context. The eternal standpoint consoles us in troubled times, but the "philosophy which tries to escape the form of generation by taking refuge under the form of eternity will only come under the form of a bygone generation" (MW 4:142). Through insensitivity to the generative world about them, some philosophers maintain "monastic impeccability" and immunity from contemporary relevancy (MW 4:142). At its most brazen, the cost is "intellectual lockjaw" and a sort of scholastic pedantry in which the academic philosopher sits in an ivory tower while "burly sinners run the world" (RP, MW 12:192).

The mirror of nature

It has become commonplace in theoretical physics that investigators get at the world only through observation, which in turn alters what is observed. From the standpoint of the old Newtonian clockwork universe, the forces acting on objects are precisely measurable by observers who are in no way factors in experiments. It is assumed that such observations do not require interaction. That is, the observer is assumed to be wholly detached from the inner-workings of what is observed. Give me a precise measurement of forces at work on any object, and, as observed in Chapter Two, on the Newtonian view I can precisely predict its future behavior.

Peirce had argued that chance is a fundamental feature of existence that makes it impossible to determine precisely and infallibly what will happen next in response to a force, and by the late 1920s physics had dissolved this classical Newtonian assumption altogether. To observe any system, the observational system must exchange energy with the system being observed. During this exchange, the two systems function together so that both are changed. Technological refinements can minimize this "observer effect," but in quantum mechanics there is a fundamental "graininess" of matter and energy that affects observation and measurement in a way that better instrumentation cannot overcome.

In *The Quest for Certainty* and "Time and Individuality," Dewey drew from Werner Heisenberg's 1927 "uncertainty principle" to illustrate and empirically bolster his assertion that we cannot simply "look and see" focal objects and their relational fields (see QC, LW 4:156–77 and LW 14:106).[23] Heisenberg revealed a complementary relation between measuring velocity and location.[24] If we want to measure something's simultaneous location and velocity, we must observe it, and we cannot observe without interaction. The uncertainty arises because observing something requires us to exchange energy with it. Take an electron. To watch the electron requires an observational medium such as light. Light energy consists of photons. To pinpoint the electron's location we must use a high-frequency wave that concentrates the photon, but high frequency means high energy, so we have to pay a price for our precise measurement of position: we slap the electron in an indeterminate direction and speed. Or we can pinpoint the electron's velocity by watching with a gentle, low-frequency wave. But the wave is too smeared out to know precisely where the photon is, so the electron's location is now indeterminate. To paraphrase Heisenberg, the more precise our measurement of location, the more imprecise our measurement of velocity.[25] Interaction is unavoidable, and this must render uncertain either the electron's location or its velocity.

Dewey greeted Heisenberg's principle with predictable enthusiasm, arguing that its implications are not limited solely to the tiny quantum level of indeterminate positions and velocities. The principle of uncertainty illustrates that human perception and inquiry are inescapably reagents that contribute new qualities and arrangements to whatever is observed (see HNC, MW 14:26). Knowing is not a spectator sport. If a sport, it is a participatory and team one. Dewey approached knowing as "one kind of interaction which goes on within the world," so he was alert to empirical work bolstering his thesis that knowing is "a participant in what is finally known." Heisenberg's insight, far from suggesting that knowing "gets in its own way, frustrating its own intent," reinforced for Dewey that knowing must return from the ether of a disembodied mind back to the push and pull of interactions—he would later prefer the prefix *transactions* to signify an undifferentiated event—between organisms and environments (QC, LW 4:163–64).

Greater precision by researchers at CERN on the "uncertainty limit" may require a more nuanced reading of Heisenberg. But the illustration clarifies and gives some empirical warrant to Dewey's contention that knowing is a relational *event* from which knower and known, subject and object, are abstracted and then all too often hypostatized. Naked objects and bare relations just do not exist as static things in a relational world (see UPMP:215).[26]

Knowing is not, as a matter of fact, a transcendental affair. Whether it *ought* to be transcendental is irrelevant. The experience of knowing is inseparable from embodied and cultural creatures getting the knowledge. Many epistemologists in Dewey's day, including the logical positivists, blithely assumed they could separate an adequate theory of knowledge from any need to understand the organism that goes about getting the knowledge. Psychologists are welcome to examine the interior organ of knowing, they demurred, but we epistemologists have set our sights higher, on the nature of knowledge itself (see MW 7:49). Rejecting such unempirical nonsense, Dewey scrapped any theory of knowledge that was not at root a theory of inquiry, and he scrapped any theory of truth (or of meaning, the more encompassing concept) that was not at root a theory of human understanding and meaning-making. In Dewey's view *all philosophical problems belong in the context of inquiry*, not in the context of traditional epistemology (LW 16:283–84).

Dewey's reconstruction of epistemology contained both descriptive and normative dimensions, and he did not always go out of his way to distinguish these. That is, he was interested both in how we do in fact come to know *and* how we ought to inquire if we want to do so more effectively. If he sometimes conflated these, it was not due to a lack of analytic rigor, but because he was so intent on highlighting that these two projects are intimately related.

A thoroughgoing naturalist, Dewey analyzed existence, value, and knowledge as coordinated interactions of biological organisms with environing conditions. But he was not an "epistemological naturalist" if this means, on the standard interpretation of W. V. O. Quine's 1969 essay "Epistemology Naturalized," to treat all epistemological questions as ultimately psychological ones.[27] Quine was an anti-foundationalist who helpfully refocused philosophical attention on psychology by approaching what it means to "know" from the standpoint of investigations into the organ of knowledge. Yet the old separation of thoughts from things echoed in the background. As discussed in Chapter Two, the helpful distinction between knower and known, psyche and matter, internal and external, was hypostatized so that epistemologists took dysfunctional dualisms as their starting point. Again, in Dewey's view, to understand the activity of knowing we must start with transactions between knower and known (i.e., with perplexities that engender inquiry), not with a separation of the organ of knowledge from the subject matter of knowledge.

As discussed, for Dewey our investigation into the nature of knowing should be no less empirical than any other inquiry. So our representations of "the way things are"—say, our approach to biological classification—must be interpreted as outgrowths of our peculiar sort of imaginative hominid interacting with social and physical environments. Classifications such as clade trees are not purified representations of ready-made entities, properties, relations, and states of affairs that inhere just as we conceive them in the world independent of human interpretation. Scientific categories are mediated, like all knowing, as outgrowths of our cultural existence in nature. Because they grow interactively from the soil of experienced situations, they are neither purely constructed nor purely discovered. Dewey's conception of interactive mediation draws the arrow in both directions: it neither subjectivizes objects, in the way of strict constructivism, nor objectifies subjects, in the way of spectator theories of knowledge.

In Dewey's view there is not even in principle a single correct symbolic formulation, no God's-eye view, that will finally mirror external nature. For example, Newton perceived that the physical law that explains the falling apple is the same as that which explains the orbiting moon, and he formulated this as the law of universal gravitation. So, did Newton construct the inverse-square law, or discover it? Although some of Newton's contemporaries perceptively noted his inability to explain *why* gravity operated as it did, most believed he had discovered an absolute law of nature. Prior to Einstein, most assumed that Newtonian mechanics worked so well because Newton had described the fixed design of the cosmos and laid bare its fundamental laws. But according to Einstein objects behave as they do because of the geometric structure of their local environments, not because of a distant Newtonian force.[28] Did Einstein get it finally right? Or in the twenty-first century will string theory unseat him with a final unified theory?

We should not expect a *final* symbolic formulation of reality to appear around the next scientific corner any more than we should expect the single correct map of our planet. Rather, *it is our increasingly subtle and sophisticated predictive power itself—our more reliable maps—that gives warrant to our physical assertions.* As will be discussed in more detail below, it is fine from Dewey's standpoint to say that current models are truer, as long as one means by this that, when used as directive hypotheses, these models make us more sensitive navigators of worldly features that had hitherto escaped our notice. As with maps, so with any symbolic representation of the world: the (changing) terrain answers back. Wayward formulations require revision, further active experimentation, and ongoing adjustment.

In sum, Dewey's experimentalism is compatible with the best insights of scientific realism and constructivism while dissolving the artificial dilemma that drives much of their debate. In what was perhaps the most telling introduction to his philosophical *modus operandi*, Dewey wrote in "The Influence of Darwinism on Philosophy": "The conviction persists—though history shows it to be a hallucination—that all the questions that the human mind has asked are questions that can be answered in terms of the alternatives that the questions themselves present. But in fact intellectual progress usually occurs through sheer abandonment of questions together with both of the alternatives they assume—an abandonment that results from their decreasing vitality and a change of urgent interest.

We do not solve them: we get over them" (MW 4:14). Old empiricism held that ideas are inscribed on our minds by objects in the known world, while many constructivists treat our assertions about the world as nothing but language kicking us around. When the subject–object distinction is made in functional rather than dysfunctional terms, we see beyond the false dilemma and recognize that an empirical method is a controlled feedback loop or spiral of detection and construction.

Dewey offered some handholds from ordinary language to help his reader grasp what he meant by a subject–object distinction that is functional or operative.[29] An object, he said, is that which "objects" in the sense that it resists and pushes back (EN, LW 1:184; cf. MW 14:133 and LW 14:27). This is the dual sense in which the object of your affection may object to your offhanded remark. Objects are also the objectives of inquiry, as when I ask "What is your object in reading this book?" In this latter sense objects are the "eventual consummation, an integrated secure independent state of affairs" (EN, LW 1:184). The active subject, meanwhile, selectively "subjects" environing conditions to investigation and adaptation, as when a chemist subjects a sample to analysis. The subject also undergoes; it is subjected to conditions. It is that which "is subjected and which endures resistance and frustration" (EN, LW 1:184).

As factors in regulated inquiries—say, in the context of making a clade tree—we can of course intelligibly distinguish subjects from objects and the subjective from the objective. However, Dewey added, subjectivism—the notion that knowledge is merely a matter of private mental activity—is pure hypostatization. "Subjectivism as an 'ism' converts this historic, relative and instrumental status and function into something absolute and fixed" (EN, LW 1:184). "I should venture to assert," Dewey said in his plainest statement of the fallacy of hypostatization, "that the most pervasive fallacy of philosophic thinking goes back to neglect of context" (LW 6:4–5).

Some truths about the truth I: pragmatism and experimental method

Plato's *Meno* poses one of the perennial questions of epistemology. Suppose you believe that you have found what you were seeking.

How do you know that is what you were looking for?[30] When you and I are equally confident of logically incompatible assertions, how do I know when I have it right? In the *Meno*, Socrates argued that the locus of knowledge is in things beyond experience and that knowing is recalling our prior connection to this realm of idealized things. Two millennia later, Descartes argued that the locus of knowledge is in thought, specifically in the way the human Will reins in error when it is ruled by Reason. For Descartes, when the disciplined mind assents only to clear and distinct ideas, an intuitive bell goes off in the inner space of mind to tell us we found the truth.

Dewey rejected this choice between idealized things (Plato and Aristotle) and internal thoughts (Descartes to Kant) as the locus of truth. He also distanced himself from subjectivistic tendencies in James's writings, as when James says that we know that we know by means of "certain psychological marks." Truth for Dewey is operative. If you find the car keys, then you know because they will start the car. If you find that DNA has a double-helix structure that provides a copying mechanism for genetic material, then you provisionally know because the experimental medium answers the questions you put to it.

In *Consequences of Pragmatism*, Rorty wrote that truth is not the sort of thing one should expect to have an interesting theory about, and he implied that Dewey would agree.[31] Yet Dewey did not jettison truth understood as a function of inquiry. Instead, he rejected the *word* truth due to its cultural baggage: the word inclines us to picture a cocksure knower standing outside of what is known. Dewey aimed to incorporate the *function* of truth within the concept of warranted assertibility. To say an assertion is warranted affirms that it can be trusted, relied upon. For the time being, when we act on the assertion things go as anticipated.

Alas, most of us tend to overrate the warrant of our assertions, and we are properly wary, in George Eliot's words, of "those who are too certain of their own interpretation to be enlightened by anything we may say."[32] Many of our social problems arise from the opposite extreme of Heisenberg's uncertainty principle. Indeed, at the very time Heisenberg was formulating his principle in Germany, the Nazi Party was solidifying what Jacob Bronowski called "a counter-conception: a principle of monstrous certainty."[33]

Western philosophy is rooted in part in Socrates' wise awareness of his own ignorance. Socrates' view of wisdom, *sophia*, implied an existential judgment: humans are sophomoric. As the etymology of the word sophomore implies, we are "wise fools" who think we know things we do not in fact know. What we think we know exceeds what we *actually* know. This causes a great deal of trouble, indeed most of our trouble. American philosopher and US congressional representative Thomas Vernor Smith (1890–1964), influenced by the classical pragmatists, observed that "much of the misery that men inflict upon one another is in the name of and because of their feeling so certain that they know things and that the other fellow does not."[34]

If only that sought-after intuitive bell would go off in our heads whenever we hit upon a true belief, we could individually and collectively escape the perils of ignorance. But due to what the nineteenth-century Scottish psychologist Alexander Bain called a sort of "primitive credulity," we go right on believing whatever we happen to believe until something brings that belief up short. Bain's observation became part of the working psychology of classical American pragmatism, which approached philosophy principally as the critical attempt to replace naïve received beliefs with inquiry.[35]

Unfortunately, as Peirce explained in his watershed 1877 essay "The Fixation of Belief," there is no *psychological* difference between believing a truth and believing a falsehood. Following Bain, he held that whatever we believe, we believe is true until we have some reason to doubt it. The philosophical difficulty, Peirce noted, is that there are competing methods for dealing with perplexities, and these give rise to conflicting views about which assertions hold water. Peirce described ways in which people's beliefs become "fixed," just as plaster becomes fixed or set, and he held that some ways of believing are more reliable than others. One pervasive approach is the method of tenacity, better known as the ostrich mentality. People sidestep their rational capacities and stubbornly avoid situations that might provoke doubt. In Peirce's words: "When an ostrich buries its head in the sand as danger approaches, it very likely takes the happiest course. It hides the danger, and then calmly says there is no danger."[36]

A second approach, the "method of authority," is to hold beliefs because institutionalized authority declares them to be true, as with those who reject evolutionary biology in favor of a fundamentalist interpretation of religious authority. It is very well that we have living traditions to guide and enrich experience, so long as our response to ancestral voices is deliberately investigated, critiqued, and where helpful reconstructed. Peirce evaluated the method of authority with biting sarcasm: "If it is their highest impulse to be intellectual slaves, then slaves they ought to remain."[37]

Rationalist philosophers from Descartes to Kant replaced the method of authority with an *a priori* armchair reasoning approach. The *a priori* method excelled at mixing up intellectual concoctions which appeared—at least to rationalistic philosophers—to determine precisely the position at which they had already arrived. To Peirce, and later Dewey, this was like doing philosophy in a seminary (see LW 6:276). So they turned to experimental, community-engaged, and error-correcting thinking as the most reliable method for arriving at and testing beliefs. No method can divorce inquiry from human interests and social forces, but the experimental-scientific attitude differs from others in the *way* it exposes inquiry to social experience (via science as an organized community of inquirers) and physical interactions (via rigorously controlled tests).[38]

Russell wrote in 1903 that science reveals us alone in a hostile and purposeless universe, our loves and beliefs the meaningless outcome of "accidental collocations of atoms."[39] Dewey, in contrast, emphasized that science is not just about *conclusions*; it showcases a way of living and thinking that embraces intellectual suspense and constant questioning. Suspense is endured gladly in movies and magic, but it is not always welcomed, much less enjoyed for its own sake, in matters touching our most tightly held beliefs. At its best, science marks a way beyond the dogmatism and fanaticism that cling to the idea that beliefs can be declared true without worldly testing. At their worst, scientists may infer authoritative explanations that dress up prejudices, while assuming that their inferences have been singularly determined by the evidence at hand. Yet insofar as a belief is *held* scientifically, it is as provisional, hypothetical, and revisable as a map. Through active testing, we ask the world to answer back, and the answer we hear—filtered through our selective emphases and soaked for better or worse in our intellectual habits—is open to ongoing questioning.

For the classical pragmatists, an empiricist habit of exposing beliefs to experience as test for their viability was regarded as the only possible corrective for overactive bells that toll with subjective certainty. Dewey agreed with Peirce that the tried-and-true method for arriving at seaworthy assertions is that followed by a community of rigorous albeit fallible inquirers putting beliefs to the test in the world. Philosophy or science cut loose from answering to anyone or anything is anemic and irrelevant. Such intellectual insularity is a luxury of nonempirical philosophies.

It is now common to ask whether "scientific knowledge" should be seen as having greater authority than traditional indigenous knowledge not rooted in European thought, and whether "spiritual knowledge" is an oxymoron. Dewey would simply ask what methods most reliably lead to warranted assertions that help us to negotiate the world, regardless of who is doing the knowing. The answer, he argued, is experimental method—broadly construed, but not so broadly as to rely on the clout of tradition or claims to private, inherently inaccessible intuitions. Knowing for Dewey is a process of sustained, organized inquiry, not an immediate insight. As Richard Bernstein insightfully writes of the historical quest for unmediated, noncontingent knowledge, whatever its cultural origin: "a good slogan for Dewey would be: Qualitative immediacy—yes! Immediate knowledge—no!"[40] Knowledge (warranted assertibility) denotes a loop or spiral of tentative results and ongoing investigations, not a timeless intuition or final description.

Dewey treated the natural sciences as exemplars of an exacting experimental method, but he was certainly not "scientistic" in the sense of limiting experimental method to the sciences narrowly construed or reducing knowledge solely to what is garnered by means of the natural sciences. To the contrary, many of his principal works are dedicated to a programmatic, if not always thoroughly fleshed out, extension of "the method of operative intelligence to direction of life in other fields" (QC, LW 4:134–35).[41]

But why should we put such trust in experience and experimentation? Why not read the history of scientific experimentation in the value-laden way we read the history of metaphysics? The history of metaphysics, Dewey observed, is wisely read for the light it throws on values and social context, not for what it finally discloses about "reality" (MW 11:45). If we read Plato's theory of Forms as an eternal revelation of recorded truth we may fail to appreciate Plato's attempt to change his culture, or his enduring participatory role in our cultural history (LW 3:7). Is science not equally value laden? Yes, we should read science in the light of our values and social contexts, in Dewey's view, but empirical methods can guide our redirection of unreliable conceptions of knowledge and self-defeating scientific practices. This confidence in intelligent reconstruction is the clearest wedge between Dewey's progressivism and a postmodern suspicion that treats all philosophic construction work as interest-driven propaganda.

Some truths about the truth II: Dewey's instrumentalism

Dewey's philosophy has long been the object of hyperbolic criticisms. For example, Bertrand Russell, who Sidney Hook recalled as one of Dewey's least favorite people, influentially depicted pragmatism as an American "businessman's philosophy," poisoning the well by associating what Dewey called his "instrumentalist" theory of inquiry with unchecked materialistic consumption, profit maximization, and entrepreneurial practicality. Russell wrote of Dewey in 1922: "The love of truth is obscured in America by commercialism of which pragmatism is the philosophical expression."[42] As Westbrook observes, such criticisms contributed to an absurd view of American pragmatism as "the epistemological fruit of American capitalism, an expedient confusion of truth with whatever it takes to make a buck."[43] Dewey later said of Russell: "I think I can hold, with a minimum of prejudice, that he never has made a serious attempt to understand any view that is different from his own" but instead "trusted to his natural brilliancy to improvise."[44]

Assertions that mature through socially organized, interactively engaged experimental methods are truer, in the Old English sense of truth as treowth, fidelity or trustworthiness.[45] This link between truth and trust is of more than passing etymological interest. We seek judgments that, when acted upon, can be relied on not to go wide of the mark, as in the old directive sense in which an arrow is true to its target. Taking an experimental turn, I cease asking "To what creed should I commit myself irrevocably?" and begin asking "Which belief-habits are trustworthy instrumentalities?"

Dewey gave the name *instrumentalism* to the dimension of his theory of experience that emphasized cognitive experiences of knowing and thinking.[46] He clarified this terminology in a letter to Corliss Lamont in 1940: "Of course I have always limited my use of 'instrumentalism' to my theory of thinking and knowledge."[47] By the 1930s Dewey used instrumentalism more as a historical name for this vital aspect of his philosophy.

Recall that in a radically empirical philosophy cognitive experiences do not stand atop a totem pole as humanity's defining and most essential experiences. This is no slight to intelligence and knowledge. As discussed in Chapter Two, the cognitive originates in and is naturally continuous with the noncognitive (EN, LW 1:28–30). Dewey's instrumentalism focused on the cognitive aspect of experience, what in *Experience and Nature* he called secondary experience, while never losing sight of its natural continuity with noncognitive or primary experience as equally essential terrain for a naturalistic and empirical philosophy.

Unsurprisingly, by instrumentalism Dewey did not mean instrumentalism. The word instrumentalism is overloaded with meanings in contemporary Anglophone philosophy. If instrumentalists reduce all reflection to simple means-end engineering, or value biotic systems only for the sake of control, then Dewey was not an instrumentalist. "Any name [for a philosophy] can only be onesided, and so it seems a pity to have any," Dewey wrote in a 1905 letter. "Meanwhile I think there is nothing to do but to peg away at the analyses of particular problems."[48]

Nor was he an instrumentalist in the idiom of contemporary philosophy of science, which marks off instrumentalism from scientific realism with this question: Is a theory true because it works (i.e., regardless of the way things actually hang together, the theory makes accurate predictions), or does it work because it's true (i.e., it makes accurate predictions because it correctly corresponds to mind-independent reality)? Dewey rejected this either–or framing. The seemingly pragmatic idea that an experimental result is "true because it works" independent of natural structures treats science as an instrument independent of the reality it discloses, hence such instrumentalism is dualistic.

For example, by the late 1500s many astronomers used Copernicus's 1543 heliocentric model for its predictive power while continuing to assert Ptolemy's geocentric model as the realistic description of the cosmos. In contemporary philosophy-of-science jargon, late sixteenth-century astronomers were heliocentric instrumentalists but geocentric realists.[49] But instrumentalism in this sense shuts the experimenter off permanently from immediate contact with real subject matter. Recall that, in Dewey's denotative method, our primary contact with raw, unanalyzed experience is the origin of our secondary symbolic-conceptual frameworks (EN, LW 1:16). As with any propositional mapping, these invisible symbolic frameworks cannot operate as intelligent guides unless we journey back with them to the primary originating context which they nourish (EN, LW 1:39). Consequently, to assert that scientific theories can "work" while standing apart from existential traits is like asserting that a map can work independent of journeying through the territory mapped!

Theories of truth are typically tossed into three categories: correspondence (e.g., Russell), coherence (e.g., Quine), and pragmatic. Dewey was the chief twentieth-century exponent of the pragmatic theory that truths are those transactive understandings we can trustingly act upon. We call an assertion or theory true at least in large measure because it leads to reliable predictions and for the time being resolves problematic situations, not because it is an aloof description of mind-independent reality (correspondence theory) or solely because the assertion coheres with a specified set of other propositions (coherence theory).

The correspondence theorist holds, with D. M. Armstrong, that "The truth of propositions, and so the truth of what is believed, is determined by the correspondence of actual or possible belief-states, thoughts or assertions to reality."[50] For Dewey this is not so much wrong as it is an empty abstraction that does nothing to bolster a spectator theory of truth as objective correspondence. Of *course* existential conditions beyond the subject set the scene for all inquiry and answer our interrogations. Dewey is a realist in the sense that he acknowledges "that certain brute existences, detected or laid bare by thinking but in no way constituted out of thought or any mental process, set every problem for reflection and hence serve to test its otherwise merely speculative results" (EEL, MW 10:341).[51] Consequently, for Dewey the fact that inquiry deals with existences independent of minds is a philosophically uninteresting truism.[52]

Dewey wrote in a 1915 letter: "Philosophical errors come from taking propositional knowledge as referring to the world or 'corresponding' to it or 'representing' or 'presenting' it in some other way than as being direction for the performance of acts to get the world in a specified emphasis."[53] Classic epistemological theories of correspondence and representation are holdovers of the notion that our ideas are sealed up in a substantial soul. In *The Quest for Certainty*, Dewey opposed the dogmatism that springs from the outworn idea that assertions can be true "independent of what they lead to when used as directive principles" (QC, LW 4:221). He later pointed out, tongue-in-cheek, that in an operational and behavioral sense of correspondence the pragmatist *alone* is a correspondence theorist if correspondence means *answering*, as when we answer a letter, or

> as a key answers to conditions imposed by a lock, or as two correspondents "answer" to each other; or, in general, as a reply is an adequate answer to a question or a criticism—as, in short, a solution answers the requirements of a problem. On this view, both partners in "correspondence" are open and above board, instead of one of them being forever out of experience and the other in it by way of a "percept" or whatever.
>
> (LW 14:179)

As noted above in the discussion of Heisenberg's principle, the correspondence theorist could agree with Dewey that the "method of operative intelligence" (QC, LW 4:135) describes how we get knowledge. But here the correspondence theorist and Dewey part ways. The leisure of professional philosophers, Dewey wrote, keeps them spatially distant "from the scene of directly urgent action," and this "makes them peculiarly liable to a hallucination" that "objects of consciousness" are enclosed in a world that is independent of and superior to "the world of outer perceived objects."[54]

And so the correspondence theorist assumes that the way we go about knowing "has nothing to do with knowledge itself" (EEL, MW 10:339). Knowing is of interest to psychologists and educators, but not to epistemologists with their "Special Powers in their Special Armchairs," in Kitcher's words.[55] If we accept this sharp traditional dualism between the process (knowing) and the product (language-world correspondence), we are led to the dubious conclusion that knowing is a mental affair that has "nothing to do with the known object: that it makes a change in the knower, not in what is to be known" (EEL, MW 10:339).

The ends-means continuum: why warranted assertibility is not truthiness

As discussed, Dewey preferred the term warranted assertibility over the words truth and knowledge. To the extent that he discussed truth at all, his notion was that truth is what James had called workability. To many this sounds like politically expedient cognitive relativism, what comedian Stephen Colbert dubs "truthiness." There seems no end to the expedient "warranted assertions" we could concoct if the notion of truth is "cut loose from epistemic accountability to the real world," as E. M. Adams wrote in a criticism of pragmatism.[56] This popular criticism springs from a cultural distrust, discussed in Chapter Two, that has soaked experience and human intelligence in a sense of unreality—as apart from "the real world"—and thereby stymied even the most basic reflection on means and ends. As a criticism of Dewey, its superficiality comes quickly into focus when ends and means are examined. Enter a cornerstone of Dewey's philosophy, to which I will return throughout the rest of this book: the ends–means continuum.

One of the many folk beliefs I grew up with was that clouds do not affect the sunburning power of the sun. Evidence suggests that, to the contrary, UV-A and UV-B radiation is on average reduced with heavy cloud cover. But this awareness may lead people to risk prolonged exposure, which is troublesome given that cloud cover under some conditions can actually increase UV radiation. So the benign folk theory on which I was weaned may "work" to discourage risky behavior. Ubiquitous examples of workability of this sort have led to a popular argument against pragmatism which follows this simplistic train of logic: Assertion A works to attain goal B, but stated as a scientific proposition A is false, therefore truth is essentially unrelated to workability.

How did Dewey respond? To begin, our common-sense beliefs often do not work under experimental conditions when we test them as directive hypotheses. Through cooperative inquiry we resurvey the existential terrain these beliefs propose to map, discover biases, debate mistakes, and construct new maps.

Customary beliefs that tug for our assent generally become customary because they operate as a means to something we desire. So far, so good. Dewey's instrumentalism does indeed hold that consequences "provide the warrant for means employed" (TV, LW 13:229). But *what about all further consequences produced by this means?* Shall we fixate on an isolated piece of overall consequences, "a fragment arbitrarily selected because the heart has been set upon it," and authorize "the use of means to obtain it" (TV, LW 13:229)? This is the mad maxim by which we often live, but it has always been a catastrophic recipe for moral, political, educational, and ecological myopia.

In the solar radiation example, collateral consequences are largely limited to perpetuating unscientific intellectual habits. To see more vividly how the means–end relationship bears on warranted assertibility, take an example in which we pay a higher price to get what we desire. In *Theory of Valuation*, Dewey turned to Charles Lamb's "Dissertation on Roast Pig" for a silly yet memorable illustration:

> The story ... is that roast pork was first enjoyed when a house in which pigs were confined was accidentally burned down. While searching in the ruins, the owners touched the pigs that had been roasted in the fire and scorched their fingers. Impulsively bringing their fingers to their mouths to cool them, they experienced a new taste. Enjoying the taste, they henceforth set themselves to building houses, inclosing pigs in them, and then burning the houses down.
>
> (TV, LW 13:227)

If our ends get their value in isolation from careful appraisal of means, then there is nothing absurd in this behavior. We may attain the end of enjoying roast pork by means of shoving pigs in houses and burning them down, but the value of this enjoyment is obviously related to the extraordinary means by which we bring the consequence about. The first finger-licking enjoyment in Lamb's story was not a result of forethought and effort. But subsequent house-burnings were pursued, in Dewey's lingo, as "ends-in-view." The absurdity of this laborious barbecuing method is clear only when we assess the end in light of the sacrificial means used—building houses and burning them down instead of envisioning other means to bring about the enjoyed result (TV, LW 13:227).

It is essential to critical reflection "to be able to see the end in the beginning" (CC, MW 2:279). When we identify, evaluate, and revise our ends in light of means and consequences, we avoid "the absurdity of any 'end' which is set up apart from the means by which it is to be attained and apart from its own further function as means" (TV, LW 13:227). We make Dewey's point today whenever we assert that justice is not won through terror and retributive violence. Whenever we spotlight a single desired outcome or end-in-view, we must evaluate it with a systemic eye to its consequences for attaining other valuable goals.

In Lamb's story, roast pork is so greatly valued that it is taken to warrant the costly means of building and destroying houses. The means by which individuals, groups, and nations exact justice, defend honor, or safeguard economic liberty are often no saner. The sole alternative to selecting and privileging some fragmentary desired consequence as "the" end is to evaluate desires, ends, and consequences as themselves "means of further consequences" (TV, LW 13:229).

The maxim "the end justifies the means" is an absurdity stemming from the related idea that ends are to be valued irrespective of means. The maxim presupposes either that some miracle will intervene "to prevent the means employed from having their other usual effects," or that the end is so prized that consequences rippling through the entire network "may be completely ignored and brushed aside no matter how intrinsically obnoxious they are" (TV, LW 13:228).

Conditions demand that we extend perception deeper into the sociocultural, natural, interpersonal, and global contexts in which we are embedded. As discussed in Chapter Two, "The visible is set in

the invisible" (EN, LW 1:44). Dewey explained the upshot of this
insight for ends and means in *Theory of Valuation*. It is par for the course
in the physical sciences that "nothing happens which is final in the
sense that it is not part of an ongoing stream of events" (TV, LW
13:229). We can rarely if ever do a single thing. Many decades before
Garrett Hardin formulated this as the first principle of ecology, Dewey
recognized that choices are pregnant with connections. Due to relational continuities, wise deliberations must forecast relevant, over-
lapping ripple effects that spread from alternative avenues for acting.
Whatever end we bring about will engender other existential connections, so it must be evaluated as a potential help or hindrance. The
notion that some objectives are ends-in-themselves is consequently
incoherent and dangerously obsolete. If it were abandoned "not
merely in words but in all practical implications, human beings would
for the first time in history be in a position to frame ends-in-view
and form desires on the basis of empirically grounded propositions of
the temporal relations of events to one another" (TV, LW 13:229).

Dewey on meaning in the context of analytic philosophy

Appraised in the context of twentieth-century Anglo-American
philosophy of language and philosophy of science, Dewey was well
ahead of the curve in arguing against fundamental assumptions of
the logical positivist movement of the 1920s–1950s. Whereas logical positivism limited philosophical analysis of science to abstract
descriptions of its logical structure, Dewey's theorizing about science probed the psychology of human inquiry and the history of
scientific investigation. In this he anticipated post-Kuhnian philosophy of science, which includes rejection of a standpoint of pure
thought and of the encyclopedic view that science develops by progressively accumulating static knowledge brick by brick.[57]

To the extent that Dewey had a theory of the meaning of meaning, he articulated it in *Experience and Nature*. Consider in light of his
theory of maps and mapping:

> A thing is more significantly what it makes possible than what it
> immediately is. The very conception of cognitive meaning,

intellectual significance, is that things in their immediacy are subordinated to what they portend and give evidence of. An intellectual sign denotes that a thing is not taken immediately but is referred to something that may come in consequence of it.

(EN, LW 1:105)

This ball, that ball game, or the proposition "The Red Sox are playing the Cardinals" becomes meaningful through the connections each calls up. Some meanings are limited to conditions under which an assertion may be judged warranted or unwarranted, but meaning is wider than truth. In Dewey's words: "The realm of meanings is wider than that of true-and-false meanings; it is more urgent and more fertile. ... Poetic meanings, moral meanings, a large part of the goods of life are matters of richness and freedom of meanings, rather than of truth." Indeed, "a large part of our life is carried on in a realm of meanings to which truth and falsity as such are irrelevant" (EN, LW 1:307).[58] When analyzing the subset of meanings that we might judge true or false, the assertions of scientists can be misleading. For example, it is common for scientists to say things like "Imagination gets in the way of understanding."[59] This assumes that our abstract concepts are disembodied. But abstract concepts are defined by intellectual habits, many of which are imaginative, so we err when we reify concepts as pure or disembodied. Imagination is not optional in cognitive experience.

Dewey argued long before W. V. O. Quine that statements cannot map states of affairs in isolation but rather depend for their meaning on the context in which they stand in relation to other statements (e.g., see "Context and Thought," LW 6:3–21).[60] Indeed, Dewey was also among the first to argue that meaning is contextual rather than strictly propositional. That is, meaning is not a product of freestanding propositions that correspond one-to-one to sensory impressions of entities, properties, and relations (see LW 6:4–5). Dewey's instrumentalist theory of warranted assertibility should be carefully distinguished, however, from Quine's meaning holism in which the whole web of beliefs is the unit of cognitive significance and truth is an affair of how well parts of the web cohere.

Also like Quine, and decades before Carl Hempel, Dewey repeatedly critiqued verificationism—the idea that a statement's meaning equals its truth condition.[61] Half a century before Wittgenstein's *Philosophical Investigations*, Dewey followed James in rejecting objective reference along with the "essentialist" idea that definitions must be analytic sets of necessary and sufficient conditions. If one insists upon identifying a basic unit of meaning, Dewey argued alongside his friend Mead that actions are better candidates than words or sentences, and he thereby anticipated speech act theory despite lacking its linguistic sophistication.

Dewey's philosophy remains a vital resource for those grappling with the central question of late twentieth- and early twenty-first-century philosophy of language: How is meaning grounded if it has no foundation?[62] Rorty answered that it is simply not grounded in any interesting way, but Dewey took meaning more seriously. He undermined the foundations for absolutistic views of truth, meaning, and value; however, he rejected skepticism (except as a tool of inquiry), radical subjectivism, and philosophies of suspicion in favor of an overall constructive project. Dewey's work is congenial to much contemporary work on cognition and emotion in philosophy and cognitive science, in part because he prioritized the fullness of embodied experience over narrowly conceptual experience. He had "gotten over" still-prevalent assumptions that knowing is the quintessential activity of the human being and that meaning is restricted to truth conditions.

Scientists are not, generally speaking, the best philosophers of science. But in the wake of Kuhn, feminist critiques, and sociological studies, today's scientists do tend to be more aware than were the scientists of Dewey's day that assumptions drive inquiries and that they are constructing abstract models of the world rather than simply seeing the world "as it is." Dewey's tendency to write as though scientists in his own day were more or less rigorously following the denotative method may have been naïve, but his naturalism and sophisticated critique of subject–object dualism are gaining renewed attention by prominent twenty-first-century philosophers of science such as Philip Kitcher and Peter Godfrey-Smith.[63]

Summary

In his instrumentalist theory of inquiry, Dewey replanted knowledge and thought in the soil of organism–environment interactions, conceiving even natural and mathematical laws as tools which evolve over time. If there is a single lesson of the sciences, for Dewey it is that beliefs that mature through interactive engagement with the world are truer to the mark. Experimental method marks a way beyond the dogmatism and fanaticism that cling to the idea that beliefs can be declared true without worldly testing. His experimentalism is compatible with the best insights of scientific realism and constructivism while dissolving the artificial dilemma that drives much of their debate.

Notes

1 Ralph Waldo Emerson, "Self-Reliance," in *Emerson: Political Writings*, ed. Kenneth Sacks (Cambridge, UK: Cambridge University Press, 2008), 59.

2 Thomas M. Alexander (Southern Illinois University at Carbondale).

3 See Raymond D. Boisvert, "Philosophy: Postmodern or Polytemporal?," *International Philosophical Quarterly* 40 (2000): 313–36, at 315ff.

4 Cf. Boisvert, "Philosophy: Postmodern or Polytemporal?," 315ff.

5 Certainly we do, at times, knowingly hold and act on positions with a confidence that outstrips what we judge to be warranted.

6 Boisvert, "Philosophy: Postmodern or Polytemporal?," 315.

7 Rorty, in Boisvert, "Philosophy: Postmodern or Polytemporal?," 315.

8 For a brief discussion of critiques of Rorty, see Michael Eldridge, *Transforming Experience: John Dewey's Cultural Instrumentalism* (Nashville, TN: Vanderbilt University Press, 1998), 205–6. For the general epistemological outlook of one of Rorty's most vehement and astute pragmatist critics, see Susan Haack, *Defending Science— Within Reason: Between Scientism and Cynicism* (Amherst, NY: Prometheus Books, 2003).

9 On Dewey's argument in "The Postulate of Immediate Empiricism" (MW 3:158–67) that what is real cannot be equated with known objects, see Thomas M. Alexander, *The Human Eros: Eco-ontology and the Aesthetics of Existence* (New York: Fordham University Press, 2013), 27–53.

10 Because the problematic situation becomes determinate only through inquiry, "The place for an accurate definition of a subject," Dewey proposed, "is at the end of an inquiry rather than at the beginning" (1932 E, LW 7:9).

11 On dramatic rehearsal, see Steven Fesmire, *John Dewey and Moral Imagination: Pragmatism in Ethics* (Bloomington, IN: Indiana University Press, 2003), ch. 5, "Dramatic Rehearsal," 69–91.

12 Cf. Mark Johnson, *The Meaning of the Body* (Chicago: University of Chicago Press, 2007), 78.

13 For a recent appreciative critique of Dewey's (and James's) theory of thinking and an argument for broadening it to meet educational aims, see Philip W. Jackson, "How We Think We Think," *Teachers' College Record*, 2012, http://www. tcrecord.org/Content.asp?ContentId=16243; accessed June 11, 2014.

14 Stephen Jay Gould, *The Mismeasure of Man*, 2nd ed. (New York: W. W. Norton, 1996).

15 On Dewey and intellectual ability, see Heather E. Keith and Kenneth D. Keith, *Intellectual Disability: Ethics, Dehumanization, and a New Moral Community* (Chichester: Wiley-Blackwell, 2013), 48, 156.

16 See Larry A. Hickman, "Dewey's Theory of Inquiry," in *Reading Dewey: Interpretations for a Postmodern Generation*, ed. Larry A. Hickman (Bloomington, IN: Indiana University Press, 1998), 150.

17 On Dewey in the context of the mirror metaphor, see Richard Rorty, *Philosophy and the Mirror of Nature* (Princeton, NJ: Princeton University Press, 1979).

18 Robert Innis, quoted in Johnson, *The Meaning of the Body*, 77. Johnson adds: "With a Deweyan perspective we are neither mirror, nor carbon paper, nor Kodak fixation. We are systems of mediations of immediacy, fusions of actions, feeling, and meaning." Johnson, *The Meaning of the Body*, 77. Cf. AE, LW 10:22.

19 For an accessible exploration of this question, see Peter Godfrey-Smith's excellent introduction to the philosophy of science, *Theory and Reality* (Chicago: University of Chicago Press, 2003).

20 For insights on realism vs. constructivism in the context of the debate in the 1980s between vying taxonomic methods, see George Lakoff, *Women, Fire, and Dangerous Things* (Chicago: University of Chicago Press, 1987).

21 Dewey's use of the word "construction" differs from current usage. For him construction denotes "the creative mind, the mind that is genuinely productive in its operations" (LW 5:127).

22 Ralph Sleeper, *The Necessity of Pragmatism* (New Haven, CT: Yale University Press, 1986), 3 and throughout.

23 Cf. Aruthur O. Lovejoy, *The Revolt against Dualism* (La Salle, IL: Open Court, 1929). Regarding Dewey's use of Heisenberg's uncertainty principle, Lovejoy wrote that "no metaphysical consequences … can be deduced from the physical principle of indeterminacy except with the aid of purely metaphysical assumptions" (356). There is no reason to assume Dewey would disagree. The uncertainty principle is an illustration of Dewey's point, and it provides some empirical warrant for his metaphysical map.

24 Heisenberg formulates the principle to illustrate a relationship between measuring momentum (mass times velocity) and measuring position. I am simplifying this as velocity and location. Heisenberg explains that the uncertainty of the momentum measurement multiplied by the uncertainty of the position measurement is greater than or equal to Planck's constant divided by two.

25 See Werner Heisenberg, *The Physical Principles of the Quantum Theory* (Mineola, NY: Dover Publications, 1949).

26 More controversially, Dewey held that his view accords with an interpretation of the quantum-mechanical view: that scientific objects are ultimately statistical.

27 W. V O. Quine, *Ontological Relativity and Other Essays* (New York: Columbia University Press, 1969).

28 Einstein drew from the nineteenth-century concept of a "field" of force (created in all points in space around an object), which proposed that objects behave as they do because of their local environment. (Michael Faraday and

James Clerk Maxwell are among the "big" names in nineteenth-century field theories.) Prior to Einstein this nineteenth-century work was still under the sway of Newton's view of gravity.

29 Students of Ludwig Wittgenstein will recognize an affinity with Dewey's operative theory of ideas or concepts. In Stephen Toulmin's explanation of Wittgenstein: "an 'idea' or a 'thought' which is not associated with such sets of operations serves no more purpose (and so has no more *meaning*) than an 'idle wheel' added to a clock mechanism, which drives nothing and so has no intelligible effect" (in QC, LW 4:xviii).

30 Cf. John J. McDermott, *The Drama of Possibility: Experience as Philosophy of Culture* (New York: Fordham University Press, 2007), 450.

31 Richard Rorty, *Consequences of Pragmatism* (Minneapolis, MN: University of Minnesota Press, 1982), xiii.

32 George Eliot, *Daniel Deronda* (New York: Random House, 2002 [1876]), 600.

33 Jacob Bronowski, from "Knowledge or Certainty," 1973 BBC television series, *The Ascent of Man*, http://www.indiana.edu/~jkkteach/P553/bronowski.html; accessed June 11, 2014.

34 Thomas Vernor Smith, *Creative Sceptics: In Defense of the Liberal Temper* (New York: Willett, Clark & Co., 1934), 7.

35 See Max Fisch, "Alexander Bain and the Genealogy of Pragmatism," in *Peirce, Semeiotic, and Pragmatism*, ed. Kenneth Laine Ketner and Christian J. W. Kloesel (Bloomington, IN: Indiana University Press, 1986).

36 Charles Sanders Peirce, "The Fixation of Belief," in *Philosophical Writings of Charles Sanders Peirce*, ed. Justus Buchler (Mineola, NY: Dover, 1955), 12.

37 Peirce, "The Fixation of Belief," 14.

38 In "Wayward Naturalism: Saving Dewey From Himself," in *Pragmatism and Inquiry* (Oxford: Oxford University Press, 2012), Isaac Levi has cogently argued that Dewey needs to be rescued from a failure to take seriously the need to avoid error in inquiry. Although the *Correspondence* reveals Dewey personally at pains to avoid error (e.g., 1927.03.24 [04684]: Dewey to Scudder Klyce), Levi is at least correct that the purposeful avoidance of error is no more central to Dewey's theory of inquiry than it was for James. Dewey anticipated the critique, which he regarded as arising from the intellectualist's fallacy and the related assumption of an already-completed world of static, mind-independent scientific objects to be known. Dewey rejoined that a philosophy that embraces a world of real novelty "will indeed recognize that there is in things a grain against which we cannot successfully go, but it will also insist that we cannot even discover what that grain is except as we make this new experiment and that fresh effort, and that consequently the mistake, the effort which is frustrated in direct execution, is as true a constituent of the world as is the act which most carefully observes law. For it is the grain which is rubbed the wrong way which more clearly stands out. It will recognize that in a world where discovery is genuine, error is an inevitable ingredient of reality, and that man's business is not to avoid it—or to cultivate the illusion that it is mere appearance—but to turn it to account, to make it fruitful" (MW 11:50).

39 Bertrand Russell, "A Free Man's Worship," in *Why I Am Not A Christian* (Sidney: George Allen & Unwin, 1957), 107.

40 Richard J. Bernstein, *John Dewey* (New York: Washington Square Press, 1966), 92.

41 In his Introduction to the critical edition of *The Quest for Certainty*, Stephen Toulmin critiques Dewey's book as more programmatic than substantive (LW 4:xviii).

42 Dewey cited this quote and responded to Russell in "Pragmatic America" (MW 13:306). He again responded to such accusations in his classic 1925 essay "The Development of American Pragmatism" (LW 2:3–21).

43 Robert B. Westbrook, *John Dewey and American Democracy* (Ithaca, NY: Cornell University Press, 1991), 114.

44 In Jay Martin, *The Education of John Dewey: A Biography* (New York: Columbia University Press, 2002), 325. In 1940 Russell wrote a book critiquing Dewey's epistemology, *An Inquiry into Meaning and Truth*. Dewey responded in 1941 with "Propositions, Warranted Assertibility, and Truth," in the *Journal of Philosophy* (LW 14:168–88). Thomas Burke renders a verdict on the debate: "Dewey's views are very much more timely these days than ever before, whereas Russell's way of thinking about logic is now passé." Burke, *Dewey's New Logic: A Reply to Russell* (Chicago: University of Chicago Press, 1998), xi.

45 The social organization of science is a crucial part of knower–known interaction in the sciences. Dewey's views on social organization in the sciences were skeletal in comparison to some contemporary philosophers of science zooming in on this vitally important yet underdeveloped area.

46 More precisely, Dewey wrote late in his life that he had used the term instrumentalism for "that aspect of my theory of knowledge" that hypothesized that "scientific subject-matter grows out of and returns into the subject-matter of the everyday kind" (LW 16:291).

47 1940.09.06 (13667): Dewey to Corliss Lamont. Cf. Thomas M. Alexander, "John Dewey's Uncommon Faith: Understanding 'Religious Experience,'" *American Catholic Philosophical Quarterly* 87, no. 2 (2013): 347–62, at 351.

48 1905.01.02 (01827): Dewey to A. W. Moore.

49 Richard Dewitt, *Worldviews: An Introduction to the History and Philosophy of Science*, 2nd ed. (Oxford: Wiley-Blackwell, 2010).

50 D. M. Armstrong, *Belief, Truth and Knowledge* (Cambridge, UK: Cambridge University Press, 1973), 137.

51 In a 1909 letter Dewey commiserated with James: "I have repeated *ad nauseam* that there are existences prior to and subsequent to cognitive states and purposes, and that the whole meaning of the latter is the way they intervene in the control and revaluation of the independent existences." Quoted in Herbert W. Schneider, *A History of American Philosophy* (New York: Columbia University Press, 1946), 553. See 1909.03.21 (04583): John Dewey to William James.

52 Among the dissenters to this as a truism would be idealists who "start with a power, an entity or substance or activity which is ready-made thought or reason and which as such constitutes the world" (EEL, MW 10:338).

53 1915.05.04 (03521): Dewey to Scudder Klyce.

54 1915.05.07,08,09 (03525): Dewey to Scudder Klyce.

55 Philip Kitcher, *Preludes to Pragmatism: Toward a Reconstruction of Philosophy* (Oxford: Oxford University Press, 2012), xviii–xix.

56 E. M. Adams, *The Metaphysics of Self and World: Toward a Humanistic Metaphysics* (Philadelphia, PA: Temple University Press, 1991), 30.

57 Dewey's method of operative intelligence, unlike Thomas Kuhn's notion of radical incommensurability in *The Structure of Scientific Revolutions*, points a way to explaining how comparative judgments across scientific models can be warranted, just as we can make judgments about different maps in light of the journeys we are taking. Things we missed on one map are fronted on another map, and this objectively alters our negotiation of the territory. See, for example, Dewey's discussion of the 1921 deflection-of-light experiment (testing a prediction of Einstein's general theory of relativity), where he showed a penetration that the logical positivists lacked (see EN, LW 1:16).

58 Cf. Johnson, *The Meaning of the Body*, 265–69.

59 Ecologist Kerry Woods, public presentation at Green Mountain College, Poultney, Vermont, April 12, 2011.

60 "Habits of speech, including syntax and vocabulary, and modes of interpretation have been formed in the face of inclusive and defining situations of context … We are not explicitly aware of the role of context just because our every utterance is so saturated with it that it forms the significance of what we say and hear" (LW 6:4–5).

61 On Dewey, verificationism, and related subjects, see R. W. Sleeper's excellent introduction to LW 14:ix–xxiv.

62 For example, see Mark Johnson's *The Meaning of the Body*.

63 See Peter Godfrey-Smith, *Theory and Reality* (Chicago: University of Chicago Press, 2003), chs. 10 and 15; Kitcher, *Preludes to Pragmatism*; and Godfrey-Smith, "Dewey and the Subject-Matter of Science," in *Dewey's Enduring Impact*, ed. John R. Shook and Paul Kurtz (Amherst, NY: Prometheus Books, 2011). For perspectives on Dewey's notion of construction and reconstruction as it relates to scientific knowledge, see Peter Godfrey-Smith, "Dewey and the Question of Realism," *Noûs* (forthcoming 2014) and Philip Kitcher, "Deweyan Naturalism," in *Pragmatism, Naturalism, and Religion*, ed. Matthew Bagger (New York: Columbia University Press, forthcoming).

Further reading

Michael Eldridge, *Transforming Experience: John Dewey's Cultural Instrumentalism* (Nashville, TN: Vanderbilt University Press, 1998).

Larry A. Hickman, *Pragmatism as Post-Postmodernism: Lessons from John Dewey* (New York: Fordham University Press, 2007).

David L. Hildebrand, *Beyond Realism and Antirealism: John Dewey and the Neopragmatists* (Nashville, TN: Vanderbilt University Press, 2003).

Philip Kitcher, *Preludes to Pragmatism: Toward a Reconstruction of Philosophy* (Oxford: Oxford University Press, 2012).

Four
Ethics reconstructed

A moral philosophy which should frankly recognize the impossibility of reducing all the elements in moral situations to a single commensurable principle, which should recognize that each human being has to make the best adjustment he can among forces which are genuinely disparate, would throw light upon actual predicaments of conduct and ... would lead men to attend more fully to the concrete elements entering into the situations in which they have to act.

(LW 5:288)

The problem with wallpapering an old house is that the lines vary from room to room, so wallpaper neatly squared by the eye in one room appears crooked from the next. The effect is a bit jarring. The well-tested solution is to square the first strip of wallpaper to the world, not to the room, by following the vertical line of a weighted string called a plumb line. Descartes ran with this image as a metaphor for the leveling effect of pure reason in the *Discourse on Method*: "As far as all the opinions I had accepted hitherto were concerned, I could not do better than undertake once and for all to be rid of them in order to replace them afterwards either by better ones, or even by the same, once I had adjusted them by the plumb-line of reason."[1]

It is a common presumption that one's own moral formulation has been adjusted by the singular plumb line of reason, direct intuition, or divine authority. As such one's peculiar brand of moral rectitude occupies an exclusive logical space. In Descartes' seventeenth-century understanding, the "plumb-line of reason" squares our individual judgments with the fixed geometry of God's creation.

But in Dewey's view no plumb line of pure thought or transcendental reason is required as a leveling reference to orient our scientific, moral, or aesthetic inquiries. Nor has such a universal plumb line ever been available.

The problem is not that Descartes selected a tool for his metaphor. His image is ironically a pragmatic one, highlighting that we use improvable intellectual instruments to enlighten judgment. Tools such as plumb lines are forged in response to situational needs, evaluated and refined by how well they meet these needs. In Dewey's view we need all the help we can get to square our judgments with our best ideals and to square our scientific inquiries with our highest standards of open scrutiny. We need to make judgments less specious, exclusive, "arbitrary, capricious, unreasoned" (EN, LW 1:320).

But consider Descartes' metaphor a bit further. On the Cartesian coordinate plane—the one we all graphed pairs of integers with when we were in high school geometry—a plumb line can be described as a segment of fixed length that is part of a straight line extending across space. The Cartesian line has no curves, and any segment of it has only one possible correct measurement. For Einstein, in contrast, a plumb line would be understood to follow the Earth's local gravitational lines through curved spacetime, and observers in relative motion would correctly disagree about a segment's length. In this way physics was transformed into a relational dance in the twentieth century. Meanwhile, absolutistic moral philosophies kept one foot in the seventeenth century. Dewey's is a relational moral philosophy of the twentieth century, a new philosophy for dealing with new facts.

Multidimensional moral experience

The central dogma that unites ethical theories, whatever the differences that divide them, is that they must identify the fundamentally right way to organize moral reflection. On this view we can set aside our emotional lives and our hodgepodge of customary beliefs in favor of rationally ordered rules, priorities, or laws derived from a foundational principle or supreme unifying concept that correctly distills and resolves moral problems.

Moral skeptics agree that this is indeed an essential assumption for doing ethics, and they reject it. Moral skeptics say it has been an exercise in futility to try to discover or erect a closed system of ready-made principles to live by. But they too often blithely accept the central dogma that ethics is a quest (albeit a hopeless one) for such principles. The practical result is that the moral skeptic may fail to shine any light between extremes of haphazard drifting, on the side of relativism, and fixed doctrines, on the side of absolutism.

Dewey constructed an ethical pluralism that rejected the central dogma. In 1930 he presented an essay titled "Three Independent Factors in Morals" (LW 5:279–88) to the French Philosophical Society in Paris. The essay was published in French and did not appear in English translation until resurrected in 1966 by Jo Ann Boydston, editor of the critical edition of Dewey's works. Dewey scholarship of the last twenty-five years has benefited greatly from this interpretive key. From a more practical standpoint, the essay provides a very general map of ethical theorizing for the student of ethics who encounters a smorgasbord of conflicting yet illuminating theories with little way of organizing them to do practical work. "Three Independent Factors in Morals" offers an organizational scheme or house of theory for the many value orientations encountered when studying ethics, especially when read alongside Dewey's 1932 revision of the *Ethics*.

To illustrate this smorgasbord of value orientations, consider some stances in contemporary environmental ethics. Here are some highly simplified snapshots of ethical debates regarding hunting, stripped of the nuance and analytical sophistication that actual philosophers bring to their ethical theorizing. The utilitarian inquires: Should relevantly similar interests of all currently existing sentient beings be accorded equal consideration when we are deciding how to act? If so, if we permit a nonbasic preference for hunting to trump an animal's basic interest in going on living, does this produce the greatest overall good for all morally considerable beings? The deontological rights theorist objects that the utilitarian is blind to the fundamental question: Do some nonhuman animals possess characteristics that make them bearers of rights that we are duty-bound to uphold? If so, actions treating such an animal as a mere instrument for others' ends fail to conform to the dictates of right action, no matter how much purported good or fulfilled desire comes of it. The virtue ethicist in turn wonders: What traits of character are cultivated by hunting, and do these contribute to a thriving shared life?

Adding to the questions, the biocentrist asks: Is sport hunting compatible with respecting an animal as a fellow center of life pursuing its own evolved good? The ecocentrist steps in to urge that all of the above miss the forest for the trees by unwisely limiting moral considerability to individuals and relegating species and systems to a secondary and supporting role. Instead, says the ecocentrist, we should take our cue from natural processes and ask: Is culling of some animals ecologically obligatory for the good of the system, regardless of whether anyone prefers to pull the trigger? Moreover, given the sad conditions of industrial animal agriculture, might hunting offer many people a sustainable source of locally harvested, free range animal protein while reconnecting them with natural cycles?

Recall that I am greatly simplifying highly articulated and subtle positions, but these moral philosophies do tend toward a single focus. Dewey's pluralism embraced the fact that when we ask different questions, we see different connections and possibilities, and this is an aid to both moral deliberation and the democratic development of policies. There is a siren lure to the hyperrationalist's search for grand unifying concepts and for metaethical organizing principles that aim to swallow all that is best in competing orientations. In Homer's *Odyssey*, Odysseus and his crew pass the island of the sirens, whose song promises to tell their futures. His men heed Circe's council: They stop their ears with wax and tie Odysseus securely to the ship's mast. The siren song of classical ethical systems promises something even more alluring: a universal plumb line to square our moral reasonings with the social world. Ethics students should not stop their ears, but they should perhaps tie themselves to the mast. No matter how carefully elaborated their moral principle, it will rarely focus their attention on all the relevant situational factors that they ought to note and deal with. Dewey shared the spirit of William James's pluralism: "The word 'and' trails after every sentence. Something always escapes. 'Ever not quite' has to be said of the best attempts made anywhere in the universe at attaining all-inclusiveness."[2]

In opposition to the monistic search for a single principle or unifying concept to explain and direct moral life, Dewey asserted that "there are at least three independent variables in moral action" (LW 5:280). He described the following three general characteristics of moral experience, which are often at odds with each other: demands of communal life (the root of deontological theories of justice and duty, such as Immanuel Kant's), individual ends (the root of consequentialist theories, such as John Stuart Mill's utilitarianism), and social approbation (the root of virtue theories, such as Aristotle's). The identification of three primary factors conveniently encompassed the three chief Euro-American ethical theories, and Dewey knowingly exaggerated differences among the three (LW 5:503). Pinning down a precise number of primary factors in moral life is far less significant than Dewey's argument that moral philosophers have generally abstracted one or another factor of moral experience as central and uppermost, hypostatized it (as discussed in Chapter Two), then treated this factor as the self-sufficient starting point for moral inquiry and the foundational bedrock for all moral justification.

In sum, the concepts of duty, virtue, and the good highlight irreducible factors that operate in any moral situation; that is, the three cannot be boiled down to one. Classic moral philosophies that privilege only one of these concepts did not drop from the heavens. They were forged in part as tools to understand and deal concretely with everyday social situations, consequently they do have practical value for streamlining moral deliberation. This practical value can be liberated by putting these tools to work attending to the complex textures and hues of conflict-ridden moral situations (see 1932 E, LW 7:6). Rigorous reflection on goodness, virtues, and obligations is a means to "the continuous reconstruction of experience" (RP, MW 12:185) that is more inclusive, meaningful, and value-rich. Unfortunately, competing monistic bedrock concepts vie as bottom lines in traditional ethical theory, and so they too often sacrifice nuanced perception and engaged problem-solving in favor of armchair theoretic clarity that may actually render moral problems more opaque.

Morally uncertain situations, Dewey urged, require us to intelligently reconcile inherent conflicts between conflicting factors. Should I have an abortion? Should a soldier shoot upon command?

Should a security analyst blow the whistle on government intrusions into privacy? To see these questions through the lens of only one factor—as at bottom a matter of rights not consequences, of duty not virtue, of what is right not what is good, of what I should do and not who I should become—risks bringing deliberation to a premature close.

Chuang-tzu's fable "The Frog of the Well" gave rise to a Chinese idiom for tunnel vision: "like looking at the sky from the bottom of a well." If indeed traditional moralists see the sky from the bottom of a well, this does not imply that they perceive their patch of sky less clearly than they should. They are presumably expert in that part. The problem arises when they ignore the rest of the sky on the assumption that their patch is all that warrants moral consideration. It is fair to add that we are all frogs in the well, inescapably limited by our standpoints and contexts. Dewey's pragmatic pluralism in ethics built on his more general theory of operative intelligence to chart a course making the best of our contingency and provincialism.

In Dewey's ethics, there is more than just surface tension between independent moral factors, so conflicts between them are not merely specious. *No single principle, standard, law, concept, or ideal rooted in just one factor can operate as a moral bottom line that accommodates whatever is of moral worth in the rest.* That is, no single factor of moral life—the right, the good, or the virtuous—is the central and basic source of moral justification to which all morality is reducible. Instead, when we begin our moral deliberations with the troubled situation, we discover that diverse factors are *already* in tension with each other. Our foremost practical need is for fine-tuned habits of character that enable us to continuously coordinate and integrate these tensions. When a theorist errs in the direction of abridging moral life and editing out the plurality of situational tensions that tug at us, we should not be surprised that a relative few find much use for that theory when facing real, unsettled circumstances.

Especially outside the academy, many of those who are drawn to the cropped moral images prevalent in classic theories savor a sense of moral certitude that can accompany them. Consider the influence on activists of utilitarian philosopher Peter Singer, author of the classic *Animal Liberation* (1975).[3] Those who take seriously his rigorous arguments on behalf of animals cannot fail to be moved in some way by them. His own acceptance (in a moderated form) of the central dogma of ethics is no doubt a factor in his ability to radicalize advocates, but it is also his greatest liability. In his engaging and aptly titled Ethics into Action, the "preference utilitarian" rationally discerns the ethical thing to do to satisfy the greatest number of already-existing individual preferences, then urges activists to turn up the emotional rhetoric to get it done.[4] But such certitude can exact a fee: absent ongoing sensitivity and reflection to elicit differences and give them an appreciative hearing, the activist—if he or she is dogmatic—may bluntly ignore what does not fit his or her preestablished trajectory. He or she may not consciously wish to freeze out other people with a stake in the process, or presume them to be dull or irrelevant, but this is too often the actual result. When this occurs, there is a failure to coordinate workable solutions in a way that inclusively develops individual capacities and durably modifies problematic conditions (see RP, MW 12:192–93).

We get a great deal of subjective reinforcement in the moment when our moral deliberations culminate in a resolute plan of action, and this lends a psychological motive to the quest for a theory or belief that will banish our doubts. The aim of ethics is of course to mediate objective difficulties, and no practical ethicist knowingly aims merely to "banish doubt" by resolving an ethical conundrum in the psyche. The aim of ethics is to thoughtfully guide action. Ethicists best achieve this goal when they help us to paddle, with revisable moral convictions, against the swift psychological current that propels people toward subjective moral certainty.

Philosophical ethics at its best can proffer hypotheses that enlarge perceptions and "render men's minds more sensitive to life about them" (RP, MW 12:91–92). In Dewey's view it is valuable only insofar as it renders this service. Traditional ethical theories are helps on the moral journey: even a one-dimensional map of a multi-dimensional landscape can help us to be more perceptive of and responsive to the terrain. The search for finality and completeness itself has nevertheless largely been a distraction except as it has, almost by happy coincidence, enlarged perceptions and made us more sensitive to the world about us. Where they have succeeded in doing good work despite the central dogma of ethics, their good work too often becomes the enemy of better work. Abandoning the quest, as well as the tone, of finality in favor of artistically and experimentally developing projects with distinctive emphases and angles would help rather than hinder the future growth of these traditions.[5]

Dewey's ethical writings

Dewey's writings on ethics of course offer no explicit guidance for many contemporary problems. He is perhaps best understood by a twenty-first-century reader as drafting designs for a house of theory within which we might "do ethics" in a way that is more sensitive to situational facts. The layout of his "house" of theory may appear odd to a reader coming to this chapter in isolation from prior chapters, particularly for a reader who has some background in mainstream Anglo-American ethics. Dewey may appear to be ducking questions that he thinks he has dissolved, and his house may appear wrongly organized. Some (though certainly not all) of the high-traffic areas of analytic ethics (i.e., problems taken to be central, such as the "is/ought" problem) are tucked away in a back closet. Meanwhile, the outbuildings of analytic ethics (i.e., issues taken to be of marginal or supplemental importance, such as the role of imagination in moral deliberation) are found in Dewey's family room.[6]

He approached ethics as the practical art of helping people to live richer, more responsible, and more emotionally engaged lives. He rejected as self-defining and circular the classic hunt for a univocal principle that purports to correctly conceive and resolve ethical quandaries about right and wrong, or to finally solve conflicts over values in advance of the situations in which these conflicts arise. He equally rejected the reactive notion that, absent governance by an overarching rational criterion, we are set adrift with only customary conditioning as rudder or sail. Instead, he refashioned the competing blanket principles of ethical theory so that they could be better used as deliberative tools to help us deal reflectively with distinctive factors of situations. He also advanced a theory of character as inherently social and historical, developed a theory of moral deliberation as fundamentally imaginative, and prescribed a democratic moral ideal informed by aesthetic values. (The last will be developed in Chapter Six.)

Dewey's principal ethical writings included his 1908 and 1932 *Ethics* textbooks (coauthored with James H. Tufts) as well as *Human Nature and Conduct* and *Theory of Valuation*. These writings together engage all approaches typical of philosophical ethics today: descriptive ethics (neutral descriptions of moral thinking and behavior, which includes moral psychology), metaethics (bird's-eye analysis and critique of the central concepts and projects of ethics), normative ethics (formulation and justification of basic moral values), and applied ethics (application of all-the-above to specific areas of activity). In this jargon, Dewey's most distinctive work in ethical theory consisted of metaethical analyses that relied on a redescription of moral experience.

In his 1932 *Ethics*, Dewey argued that deliberate ethical reflection is born of the need to act with patience and courage amid the inevitable ambiguity and doubt that daily arises when we are "confronted with situations in which different desires promise opposed goods and in which incompatible courses of action seem to be morally justified" (1932 E, LW 7:164). Ethical reflection is needed when the way forward is not well lit or when multiple paths beckon. Ethical theory is simply a more systematic working through of the reflection generated by such moral conflicts.

There is a popular but misguided notion of ethics as the study of good versus evil, or of how to get people to do the right thing when they are tempted otherwise. Take a bank employee tempted to steal or embezzle money. The sort of moral struggle involved here quickens the pulse of the individual involved, but Dewey observed that it does not occasion much ethical reflection unless the temptation involves sincere perplexity about right and wrong. If the employee has already determined to embezzle, the only "reflection" involved may be of the tail-wagging-the-dog sort that will allow the unmediated desire to govern conduct (1932 E, LW 7:164).

The absolute prohibitions, commandments, and catechisms of customary morality cry that their own exclusive fixed mooring is humanity's lone moral hope amid storms of lawlessness, disorder, and chaos. Customary catechisms tend to be long on rules but short on tools to intelligently deal with novel challenges and opportunities. Take a citizen who is habituated to be loyal to country, yet her country is engaged in a war that her religious convictions set her against. She is not struggling between a clear good, on the one hand, and the temptation to do wrong, on the other hand. There is a conflict, Dewey observed, between two incompatible duties, and she must choose "between competing moral loyalties and convictions" which "get in each other's way" (1932 E, LW 7:165). Reflection is forced by the situation. Although our everyday moral quandaries are usually less momentous, we are daily torn between incompatible options. Each option may intuitively tug at a desire to uphold this or that conviction about rights, duties, ends, goods, and responsibilities. *Incompatible goods and colliding duties are the rule in moral experience, not the exception.* Theories of reflective morality, of ethics, are generalized extensions of this ordinary sort of thinking (1932 E, LW 7:165).

Dewey argued in *Reconstruction in Philosophy* that moral philosophers have fled the insecurity of troubled situations in their quest for a certainty even greater than the fervent opinions held by those conventional parrots of reactive mores whom philosophers rightly distrust. Having unseated the moral monarch of custom, they still contest which monarch of *reason* shall rule from the old throne. Moral philosophers seeking a single ethical ruler to govern deliberation, or taking the absence of such a ruler to spell the end of ethical theory, missed the democratic revolution.

Most Western ethicists still want three things from a theory: "the right way to reason about moral questions" based on principle-driven moral agency, a clear procedure for resolving moral quandaries, and a single right thing to do.[7] In the main ethical theorists have answered the call to negotiate moral conflicts with their own sorting devices for determining the right way to deal with them. As mentioned, they have tended to regard conflicting ends, goods, and duties as merely apparent (i.e., resolvable through rational analysis) rather than as intractable. This would be fine if moral problems could be solved by hitting upon a unified, coherent, and compelling arrangement of symbols in the inner space of consciousness. But the locus of moral problems is situational and interactive. Existential situations do not reliably fit our tidy rational classifications.

When we approach the principles and rules of monarchical ethical theories as substitutes for personal decision-making and democratic dialogue, we don blinders. We tend to oversimplify and overlook the situational features and alternatives that most require our attention. There is always, Dewey observed, some portion of the relational network of any moral situation that legitimately presses for consideration yet is not spotlighted by our inherited moral frameworks. So our certificates of virtuousness, dutifulness, or goodness invariably lack luster upon closer inspection.

Moreover, as discussed in prior chapters, a lesson of physics and ecology is that what we see is always situated within what we do not see. One "moral" of this is that it is a rare instance when our choices can exhaustively respond to all that warrants our attention. As a consequence moral experience is unavoidably tragic, in the classical Greek sense: In any moral situation there are more things to which we ought to respond than we can. There is no escaping this existential thicket, only the pretense of escape into our own intellectual caves. Dewey's ethics points a way beyond the usual cultural attitudes of resignation, guilt, and shame that we learn to cope with the weighty burden of seemingly inexhaustible "oughts." We select and ignore, as we must (see Chapters Two and Three). Moralistic sermonizing begins when we forget that we have done so. Thus James's pragmatic pluralism, as Dewey endorsed it, "accepts unity where it finds it, but it does not attempt to force the vast diversity of events and things into a single rational mold" (LW 2:9).

Facts and values

In Dewey's view there is no essentially separate realm that marks off "moral" issues from those that are practical or factual. To say "the act ought to be done" differs only verbally from saying "this act will meet the situation" (EW 3:108–9). "You ought not to steal" is not *essentially* different than "You ought not to plant beans outdoors in the New England winter." In contrast, G. E. Moore famously asserted in *Principia Ethica* (1903) that any candidate for a "moral fact" would have to involve some "non-natural property." This bequeathed to the twentieth century the odd notion that statements about natural facts ("is" statements) must be sharply enclosed as inherently distinct from statements about values ("ought" statements).

As Hilary Putnam helpfully explains, what Dewey did instead "was develop a naturalistic picture of the way in which intelligence can be applied to ethical problems, and especially to social problems. For Dewey, ... ethical problems are simply a subset of our practical problems, in the ancient sense of 'practical'—problems of how to live—and it can be a *fact* that a certain course of action or a certain form of life solves, or better resolves, what Dewey called a problematic situation."[8] If I "ought" to do something, it is because of what the situation "is." Whatever I do to meet the situation changes it. Ideally my response will be as sensitive and perceptive as possible to the existing relationships, but any response to the situation will be what Dewey in an early essay playfully called "the 'is' of action" (EW 3:105).

Dewey regarded it as a truism that we cannot simply deduce how we ought to behave as an implication of factual descriptions. But this does not mean that the connection between situational facts and our normative judgments is no better than a wild guess. It is a practical inference of an inductive sort. We daily test such inferences as hypotheses that are drawn from the evidence at our disposal, and (if we are thinking well) we judge such inferences to be warranted and well-grounded, or unwarranted and groundless, by the consequences of acting on them (LTI, LW 12:424). Not only can one intelligently infer an "ought" from an "is," but one cannot responsibly avoid doing so.

In *Theory of Valuation*, Dewey pointed out that people impulsively or habitually prize many things that, upon reflection, cannot be justified as praiseworthy. The prized and praiseworthy, valued and valuable, desired and desirable: Although common speech does not always reflect the logical distinction, the former word in each pair highlights in Dewey's ethics a habituated felt motive, while the latter is a term of reflective judgment. The distinction parallels that already referenced in Dewey's 1938 *Logic* between affirmations and assertions.[9]

Reflective value judgments are like maps that we have journeyed with and assessed. They have "existential import" (LTI, LW 12:123), which simply means that we act on these judgments and, for better or worse, we thereby reshape the moral situation. Our considered judgments are most reliable when they develop through the guidance and direction of colloquy with others, and through the use of moral principles and ideals, instead of in detachment and isolation. There are limitations of even the most refined moral understanding, so criticism is always necessary, with no standpoint immune from ongoing revision. When we plant a crop or take a journey, we know the test is in the reliability of our methods, not in whether we started with the right intellectual abstractions. The same holds for moral life.

Moral imagination

In his redescription of moral inquiry, Dewey laid bare under-appreciated deliberative capacities, chief among which is imagination. In a memorable passage from *Anne of Green Gables*, Diana says to Anne: "'It's easy for you because you have an imagination, ... but what would you do if *you* had been born without one?'"[10] Diana places Anne's imaginative powers on a pedestal to be admired as something most people lack, something godlike that cannot be nurtured by education. Both children share a romantic view of imagination as a "power that enters into the world on the wings of intuition, free of the taint of contingency and history."[11] Imagination in Dewey's view, in contrast, is a concrete cognitive capacity as ordinary and integral as flexing our muscles (DE, MW 9:245). It is not the special province of poets or daydreamers. It is as ordinary and practical for humans as singing and nest-building is for birds, or gnawing and dam-building for beavers.

His ethical theory can be foreshortened from the standpoint of his theory of imaginative forethought in deliberation. Following the lead of Plato's low appraisal of imagination in the *Republic* and *Ion*, philosophers of the eighteenth-century Enlightenment were suspicious of any central role for imagination in ethics. "Nothing is more dangerous to reason," Hume wrote in the *Treatise*, "than the flights of the imagination."[12] Hume was the greatest Enlightenment champion of the role of sympathetic emotions in moral life, but he nonetheless presented imagination as a wayward mental faculty that may oppose intellect and so must be subordinated. On the still-prevalent Enlightenment view, rationality is dispassionate and calculative while our flickering imaginations are the teenagers of the mind. Imagination's cool and collected parent, reason, has assigned its self-indulgent offspring a limited task—to reproduce mental images—which it might at any moment shirk in a flight of fantasy.

But imagination is not limited to fantastical inventions. Dewey highlighted imagination as it functioned concretely in the life of the artist, the moral decision-maker, the scientist, the student. He approached imagination not as a flighty faculty with a subsidiary role in cognitive life, nor as a gaseous inspirational power descending from on high, but as an essential function of human interaction: our capacity of "realizing what is not present" to the senses (LW 17:242).

Perhaps the term imagination should be jettisoned as hopelessly entangled in Enlightenment mistakes, ironically including the hypostatized misconception that there is such a thing as a discrete "faculty" of imagination. Contemporary cognitive scientists studying the same function define it helpfully as a form of "mental simulation" shaped by our embodied interactions with the social and physical world.[13] This meshes well with Dewey's view, but he chose to retain and reconstruct the word to accord with a functional psychology. Imagination encompasses our capacity to form and reproduce visual, auditory, motor, and tactile images (e.g., LW 17:242), but most importantly imagination plays an active and constitutive role in reflection.

Imagination emerges, Dewey asserted, through early childhood play. Very young children begin to understand the world metaphorically by carrying over "one experience into another" (LW 17:262). The toddler who sees a stack of blocks as a tower is no longer limited to the world as immediately presented to his or her senses. "The Omaha house is closed," our five-year-old informed his visiting grandparents as they were departing back to their Nebraska home. He saw the disappointing situation before him in light of a familiar possibility: One cannot go to a store, restaurant, or school when it is closed, so there is little point in going to a closed house. Eventually, though perhaps less charmingly, through more complex imaginative simulations children come to see the actual conditions and challenges they face in light of what is possible, what is before them in light of what could be.[14] Dewey said in his 1902 lectures on education at Brigham Young University: "Imagination really is the transferring of one experience over into another" (LW 17:264). In this way children, and adults, develop the natural force Dewey called intelligence.

Reason-giving is the gold standard for moral deliberation in university ethics courses. It is an important and ill-developed skill, one that requires imagination. Nonetheless, a focus on reason-giving as the essence of wise deliberation has marginalized the importance of imaginative simulation. Ethicists betray a lingering suspicion of imagination. Imagination, it is thought, "leaps and swerves" while rational intellect at its best advances "by rule-guided steps."[15] Even some philosophers who highlight its import prescribe that we "clip the wings of imagination" to keep "imaginings on track."[16] This is in part due to cultural identification of the *imaginative* simply with what is imaginary, unreal, or fanciful. The imaginative experiences of special interest to Dewey were those that are interactively engaged and rooted in problematic circumstances, not subjective. A subjective fantasy may follow the same neural channels, but imagination in Dewey's sense is the medium in which we extend perception deep into the place and time in which we live.

Intentional acts are possible only through imagination. For example, planting a seed is an imaginative act, indeed a prophetic one. The gardener sees and values the seed and soil in light of what they promise for a distant harvest. The focus of intentional acts like planting a seed is concretely on the present, yet attention is expanded beyond what is under our nose so that past lessons and future prospects "come home to us and have power to stir us" (ACF, LW 9:30). Imagination "supplements and deepens observation," Dewey observes, by affording "clear insight into the remote, the absent, the obscure" (HWT, LW 8:251). Through imagination things before us are significant of things absent, as with the natural historian who sees fossils as records of prior events that constituted them (HWT, LW 8:126).

There could be no scientific, aesthetic, or moral thinking without the intervention of imagination. "Only imaginative vision," Dewey urged, "elicits the possibilities that are interwoven within the texture of the actual" (AE, LW 10:348). Imagination needs promising channels, not clipped wings.

More precisely, there are two aspects of imagination in Dewey's ethics, which operate simultaneously:

1. *Empathetic projection*. As Mead described it, empathy is taking the attitude of another. Empathy stirs us beyond numbness so we

pause to sort through others' aspirations, interests, and worries as our own. Empathy is distinct from the Golden Rule, which asks you to put *yourself* in the position of another and discern what you would have done "unto you." Dewey defined empathy as "entering by imagination into the situations of others" (1908 E, MW 5:150; cf. 1932 E, LW 7:268–72). (Dewey and Mead followed the lead of Scottish and English writers in calling such direct valuing *sympathy*, but their usage fits the term empathy in contemporary ethics.) In sharp opposition to Kant's disparagement of empathy as *morally* (though not prudentially) unnecessary, even subversive, for Dewey it is through such sensitivity that we avoid cold-blooded callousness and indifference. For Dewey, as for contemporary feminist care ethicists, empathy is a necessary condition for moral deliberation. Without it there would be no "inducement to deliberate or material with which to deliberate" (1932 E, LW 7:269). A multifaceted sympathy is a virtue, at least up to the point that empathetic care threatens to block any action.

2. *Creatively tapping a situation's possibilities.* Empathy provides the primary felt context of moral reflection, without which we would not bother with the other aspect of imagination: seeing what is before us in light of a wide survey of what is possible in a situation. Surveying and forecasting is the most important phase of moral deliberation (indeed all deliberation), in which we *dramatically rehearse* alternatives prior to acting on them irrevocably. In novelist Wallace Stegner's words, imagination is our means for shaping definite contours, lines, and forms "out of the fog of consequences" that we call our past and future.[17]

As discussed in Chapter Three, for Dewey inquiry is born of troubled situations. We are propelled to act despite being brought up short by perplexing circumstances. Disrupted action evokes deliberation, which Dewey described as an indirect and vicarious mode of action that substitutes for direct action by placing before us "objects which are not directly or sensibly present, so that we may then react directly to these objects, ... precisely as we would to the same objects if they were physically present" (HNC, MW 14:139). Deliberation, Dewey said, is "a kind of dramatic rehearsal" in magination. If only one alternative for dealing with a problematic situation were to present itself, we would act on it without hesitation. But when alternatives contend with one another as we forecast the consequences of acting on them, the ensuing suspense sustains deliberation (HWT, LW 8:200).[18]

There is an obvious evolutionary benefit of a neural adaptation that enables experimental simulation: "An act overtly tried out is irrevocable, its consequences cannot be blotted out," Dewey observed. "An act tried out in imagination is not final or fatal. It is retrievable" (HNC, MW 14:132–33). From plotting your next chess move to struggling over a reproductive choice, *dramatic rehearsal is a capacity for crystallizing possibilities for thinking and acting and transforming them into directive hypotheses.* Whatever else may or should be involved in moral deliberation, in Dewey's view it must at least be compatible with these psychological operations, which are fundamentally imaginative.

An incisive critic of narrowly utilitarian calculation (e.g., HNC, MW 14:147–50), Dewey urged that what is most at stake in moral life is engaged imaginatively rather than via calculative rationality, if the latter is understood on the standard view as cold accounting. What is most at stake is "what kind of person one is to become" and what kind of world one wishes to participate in making (HNC, MW 14:150). Next to basic questions of physical nourishment, health, and security, these are the most fundamental human questions. We bet our lives on a conviction that the better answer is found in one direction rather than another. Our choices express who we are and who we will become. "Every choice sustains a double relation to the self. It reveals the existing self and it forms the future self" (1932 E, LW 7:286–87).

Calculative rationality and a value hierarchy may suffice for making a provisional choice in a situation in which there is no fundamental tension between goods, ends, responsibilities, rights, or duties. But dramatic rehearsal is the way we negotiate less tidy moral territory, and moral life is memorably untidy. Understanding the psychology of imaginative deliberation may help us to more effectively map that terrain.

To the extent that utilitarian theories limit our dramatic rehearsals to consequences that are immediate and localized, Dewey opposed them. By the time he wrote his great social and political works in the wake of the 1929 Wall Street collapse, it was apparent that such narrowness was alarmingly out of step with complex social conditions. He was also keenly aware that it is easier to think atomistically and individualistically about the roots of problems that are in fact systemic and institutional. We are lately realizing what Dewey counseled decades ago, that contemporary moral perception needs supplementation and expansion beyond the speck of self-interest and pleasure-seeking around which many daily consumer concerns orbit. Scientific literacy has become vital to this. But even the most thorough scientific knowledge will overwhelm rather than enhance moral reflection if that knowledge is not framed by imagination in a way that relates one's individual biography to one's encompassing environment and history.

Imagination is essential to the emergence of meaning, a necessary condition for which is to note relationships between things. "To grasp the meaning of a thing, an event, or a situation," Dewey asserted, "is to see it in its relations to other things" (HWT, LW 8:225).[19] Take an everyday ecological irony. Many migratory songbirds I enjoy in summer while drinking a morning cup of coffee are declining in numbers, in part because trees in their winter nesting grounds in Central America have been bulldozed to plant coffee plantations. Awareness of these relationships amplifies the meaning of my cup of coffee as new connections are identified, discriminated, and employed "as means in a further course of inclusive interaction" (EN, LW 1:198). In imagination we hold these connections before attention as we reflect, and this confers relational significance upon otherwise mechanical and superficial experiences. Such imagination permeates a situation "deeply and widely" (ACF, LW 9:13), and it opens the way for critical assessment and redirection of individual and institutional behaviors. Should I drink shade-grown coffee? Donate to wildlife conservation groups? Support habitat protection in trade agreements? Put the concern on the back burner? Ideally, this amplification of meaning operates as a means to intelligent and inclusive foresight of the consequences of alternative choices and policies. No option will be perfect, each will proliferate new questions, and each must be considered in relation to other problems and goals.

As with the coffee example, many remediable moral failures stem from maldevelopment of our capacity to oscillate in our imaginative rehearsals between things and relevant relations. Economists and ecologists have long emphasized that it is essential to forecast and facilitate outcomes so we can better navigate systems. It is through imagination that relational perceptiveness enters into practical, aesthetic, and scientific deliberations so that we are able to understand focal objects through a fuller scope of connections distant in space and time.

The starting point and principles

In *Utilitarianism*, Mill echoed the received view that "the morality of an individual action is not a question of direct perception, but of the application of a law to an individual case."[20] For Dewey, in contrast, the term "applied ethics" is potentially misleading: ethics is always practical. What could it mean to apply, to put into action, a theory like Dewey's that asks you to *start* with the situation at hand? Dewey's ethics were Shakespearean in spirit, beginning in *medias res* with the emotion-soaked muck of real circumstances of competing values and diverse goods. That is where we actually find ourselves in our moral lives: the thicket of deliberation about what it is best to do. Dewey rejected as a fantasy the notion of a purified rational perspective from nowhere. There is in his view no universal plumb line, no singular moral compass, no inerrant moral intuition, no God's-eye view. But *neither is ethics arbitrary*.

Philosophical analysis can help to identify the often-unexamined principles, organizational patterns, or customary assumptions underlying behaviors and beliefs. Of course these implicit principles are not commonly held in the detached and abstract way of a professional philosopher. These principles are often latent and hard to articulate, not consciously applied and debated. Many contemporary ethicists understandably identify "doing ethics" with an attempt to benefit human conduct through analysis and critique of such underlying principles. Philosophical analysis teases them out to see what trajectory they commit us to when acted upon. The (re)constructed principle can thereby be evaluated by the work it does when used as a tool. As a tool it is never final or complete; it is subject to ongoing refinement. And as a tool it is never the starting point of ethical deliberation; it is something we reach for in the thick of the problem.

This is the heart of Dewey's ethics: The starting point of deliberation is a problematic situation. We reach for our toolbox of principles and ideals not to deduce the right thing to do, but to help us attend more perceptively and responsively to situational factors.[21]

The constructed tools of ethics are not fixed metrics that have been analyzed and justified by an autonomous, detached, dispassionate individual consciousness. Yet much contemporary "applied ethics," despite sophisticated stabs at a defensible moral epistemology, still tends to approach ethical decision-making *as though* universal metrics are being applied to concrete cases. At its extreme, applied ethical discourse may give the appearance of prefabricated principles in search of problems. When ethicists appear to have the parameters for an answer ready before a question has even arisen, they may not succeed in helping people see their way between absolutism and arbitrariness. Dewey argues that principles can help us to feel and think our way through a conflicted relational web, but the standpoint of being *situated* or placed should be the primary one in moral deliberation rather than standpoints steeped in the quest for a universal plumb line, such as divine commands, universal laws of reason, timeless moral intuitions, natural laws, or universal maxims.

To see how Dewey's reconstruction of ethics can nevertheless be "applied" to contemporary problems absent any fixed metric, consider a problematic context far removed from his own. Debates over animal use and treatment have become standard fare in philosophical ethics since the 1980s, with special ferocity in the areas of biomedicine and agriculture.[22] Perhaps the touchiest area concerns what we choose to eat, with many diets vying for "the best." To illustrate Dewey's moves, take two out-of-the-mainstream diets competing for center stage: an omnivorous diet relying on grass-fed animal husbandry, and a vegan diet seeking to abolish animal agriculture. Each seeks to respond to problems stemming from our industrialized food system, such as chemical runoff, overuse of antibiotics, resource depletion, and animal confinement that suppresses natural behaviors. There is nothing extraordinary about this particular dispute among moral reformers. It is replaceable for purposes of illustration with any other current heated controversy, some more consequential, in which disputants typify the outworn cultural assumptions about ethics that Dewey urged us to get over.

Drawing in part from trailblazing work on "perennial poly-culture" by the agriculturalist Wes Jackson, Virginia farmer Joel Salatin advocates an approach to agriculture and eating that requires less tilling (hence less soil depletion) than exclusively vegetable-based agriculture, is well adapted to colder climates, and does not rely on long-distance transportation of conventionally produced grain. From the standpoint of Dewey's ethics, this or any other promising hypothesis should be evaluated in light of how well it directs behaviors to solve shared problems. But Salatin is no prag-matist in his ethics. He wields the sword of righteousness. For example, he argues that the "right" diet must be based on grass-fed animal husbandry if it is to mimic perennial natural cycles, so it must include meat. From his standpoint vegetarians are hypocrites (if they eat dairy and eggs), and the best that can be said of vegans (those who consume no animal products) is that at least they are not hypocrites. Indeed Salatin, who is a Christian fundamentalist, believes vegans and vegetarians commit a sacrilege against nature (and God) by refusing to enter the cycle of eater and eaten.[23]

Despite faddish proliferation of books and blogs proposing the correct, best, or "natural" diet, Dewey's ethics provides no basis for assuming that such a thing can be determined in advance of the situations that require us to make dietary choices. There are multiple ways to pursue better lives in relation to food, and no diet exhaus-tively deals with all of the often incompatible exigencies inherent in agriculture and eating. Practical ethicists would generally agree that there can be no such thing as the correct diet. But neither, from Dewey's standpoint, is there any single right way to reason about diet-ary choices. Still, dietary choices are not arbitrary. We do not need an absolute dietary compass to perceive that many choices and policies do little to move us toward a more humane, just, healthy, and sus-tainable food system. Nor do we need such a compass to infer and test ways forward—such as the hypotheses of perennial polyculture and veganism—to judge by their consequences the extent to which these hypotheses are well grounded or groundless.

Salatin makes several popular assumptions about moral life, including the central dogma of ethics. There is, he assumes, a right way to reason about moral matters, a single accurate way to conceive the human-nature relationship, and hence a right (omnivorous) diet.

Ironically, vegan abolitionists share the same assumptions when they argue that "meat is murder" and that all animal agriculture is slavery that violates animal rights. For the abolitionist, an animal's sentience or subjectivity grants it rights comparable to the human rights Jefferson celebrated in the Declaration of Independence: life, liberty, and the pursuit of happiness. These rights, abolitionists claim, trump any interest humans may have in killing, penning, or experimenting on animals, and violating these rights simultaneously degrades the environment of all species and worsens human health. The analogy to human slavery highlights for abolitionists the dismal treatment customarily accorded to those we regard as property, emboldening their activism with absolute moral conviction.

Each disputant starts with the same assumption about ethics: a bedrock, a correct worldview, a single right principle. They simply disagree about which. The fundamental agreement is what charges their polarization. Dewey rejected this culturally dominant starting assumption. He proposed a pragmatic approach to vexing ethical issues as a realistic aim of moral education, even if it is not always a realistic aim for already-polarized situations. A practical result over time is that polarized positions may lose their winner-take-all prescriptive force, thereby liberating their respective insights for accommodation in a broader-based, more intelligent inquiry.

In Dewey's view moral education should aim to help youths be patient with the suspense of moral inquiry, distrustful of tunnel vision, aware of the fallibility and incompleteness of any deliberation, and imaginative in pursuing relational leads. At its most successful, such an education helps moral debates to be more honest, open, and productive. It also makes moral inquiry harder work. But there is need for confidence without puritanical fervor, courage in mediating troubled situations without need or expectation of certainty, and bold ameliorative action without fatalistic resignation or paralyzing guilt.

Dewey reconstructed ethics as a way for us to help each other and the next generations to become more perceptive and more responsible. The question dietary warriors, and the rest of us, should ask is which methods and habits trend in this direction, and which do not. Many do not. Some do. We should be grateful that those which do will be approached through different conceptual frameworks with their varying dominant emphases, and the resulting tensions will stimulate ongoing inquiry as we grapple with the transitions ahead. There is ample room, for instance, for diets that rely more or less on animal agriculture, and for advocates of the same, just as there are usually more mutually traversable ways forward in any polarized debate than are seen by mono-focused disputants.

In praise of theory

Those who demand certainty rather than guidance from an ethical theory will be disappointed. But the problem may lie more with their expectations than with the theory. On their own, traditional ethical theories are neither enriching nor obfuscating. But critical examination of their holdover assumptions frees them up to be used as aids to imaginative reflection (EN, LW 1:40). Dewey found the baby in the bathwater of classic systems, but he was especially intent on criticizing those who point to the baby as proof that the system was right all along. That is, he argued that the praiseworthy accompaniments of classical ethical theories have no indissoluble connection to the monistic systems that spawned them (see MW 10:5). Classic theories such as Kantianism and utilitarianism contain fertile ideas despite and not because of their attempts at logical exclusion. Thanks to them "the horizon has been widened; ideas of great fecundity struck out; imagination quickened" (MW 10:5). An organizing principle such as Kant's practical imperative or Mill's utilitarian maxim provides a way of

> looking at and examining a particular question that comes up. It holds before him certain possible aspects of the act; it warns him against taking a short or partial view of the act. It economizes his thinking by supplying him with the main heads by reference to which to consider the bearings of his desires and purposes; it guides him in his thinking by suggesting to him the important considerations for which he should be on the lookout (1932 E, LW 7:280).

It is difficult to imagine a serious reader of Kant or Mill who has never found them helpful for checking a tendency toward selfish gratification. Classical systems can help to make judgment more intelligent, less biased by what Dewey called "the twisting, exaggerating and slighting tendency of passion and habit" (HNC, MW 14:169). But in Dewey's view these aids to reflection can be better sustained and expanded when freed of the straitjackets of classic systems. For example, when we respond to the call of moral duty over and against sell-outs to narrow practical expedience, we need not retreat with Kant to a fantasy realm of pure reason to explain our choice. At our best, in Dewey's view, when we opt out of a convenient and self-serving course we are exercising imaginative moral artistry that takes the longer view of practical consequences, the wider appraisal of pressing communal demands, and the more complete engagement with our best reflective ideals.

Emerson famously wrote that "a foolish consistency is the hobgoblin of little minds." He did not say consistency is foolish, only a consistency that fails to meet situations. Returning to dietary choices, consider the case of a vegetarian couple living abroad, invited to dine at the home of new acquaintances. Sitting down with their hosts to a meticulously prepared dinner, they find steaks on their plates. Suppose they eat gratefully. From a neo-Kantian animal rights standpoint, they are sellouts or people of weak will who have just committed a transgression. At the logical extreme of animal rights, eating the steak is the moral equivalent of eating a person to honor a host. The absolutistic tenor and artificial clarity of this judgment is not a peculiarity of animal rights theories. It stems from the fact that the Kantian deontologist limits deliberation to universalized maxims purified of sensitivity to particular relationships and concrete circumstances. Yet these relations and circumstances constitute the ethical situation. It is not that the couple's usual dietary choices are irrelevant, or that their concerns about animal treatment are negated when they are in the role of guest. The point here is simply that they are in the thicket of ethical life. They cannot simply rest on their usual dietary habits to meet the situation well. Their choice to eat the steaks may indicate fine awareness and rich responsibility for the consequences of their choices, along with an ability to perceptively read and respond to situational particulars. Or perhaps there were other options they missed.

Everyday rules do not have the scope of fundamental principles, laws, or maxims, but they are not essentially different from general principles in the way they function. A rule like "Look both ways before crossing the street" helps children to focus attention and economize reflection, lest they be injured. Such rules are implicit and habitual for most adults, absent conditions that may require greater reliance on externally imposed limits. A Dewey-inspired ethics employs principles, rules, and unifying concepts as directive hypotheses. As discussed, Dewey defended their use as tools even as he decried the idea of a mythic true north for setting moral compasses. Unidimensional tools cannot on their own do multidimensional jobs.

Fundamental moral principles, laws, and maxims are not truths that receive their warrant from some realm of pure thought or spirit beyond history, context, and place. The foundational principles and procedures of modern Western moral philosophies have made many people confident that that they are acting within precise moral limits. Yet we do not mostly suffer from lack of confidence. We do "suffer from lack of ... detached and informed criticism" (LW 17:110). No matter how rigorous the rational demonstrations of our ethical theories may be from the standpoint of the armchair or lectern, confidence does not entail responsibility to the situation at hand.

Rules and protocols are effective when they help rather than hinder responses to particular needs. A friend of mine was recently driving on a busy urban freeway en route to the airport when his car broke down. Worried about missing his flight, he phoned a taxi. "We can't send a taxi without a street address," he was duly informed of the company rule. "I'm on the freeway, so I don't have an address," he replied. After several minutes of this, a manager eventually grabbed the phone, frustrated after overhearing his employee: "Sorry about that; just tell me where you are."

Plato was aware long ago that legalistic morality is maladaptive because something invariable cannot keep up with the pace of circumstances. Law, he wrote in the *Statesman*, "is like a self-willed, ignorant man who lets no one do anything but what he has ordered and forbids all subsequent questioning of his orders."[24] When the traditional moralist snubs situational considerations as an inferior locus for motives and justifications, he or she paves the way to becoming what Mark Twain called good "in the worst sense of the word."

Some principle-based ethicists classify Dewey as a "moral particularist," the view that moral principles are crutches and that the ideal moral agent is sensitive rather than principled. Instead, Dewey rejected both horns (of course) of what is nowadays known in Anglo-American ethics as the generalist-particularist debate.[25] This debate is often illuminating, but it fails to fully appreciate either the profound instrumental value or the myopic limitations of principle-based reasoning. It is true that we may find convenient excuses for self-interested action when, instead of submitting ourselves to the governance of principles, we limit ourselves to surveying the concrete particulars of a situation. But it is equally true that we excuse unresponsive behaviors by reference to universal maxims.

To loosely paraphrase Henry James, it is a foolish consistency that fails to sacrifice a dictum or code when considerations of a finely perceived situation demand it. No codified rule can replace a flexible and discerning imagination. We need the economizing of thought that principles and rules afford. We also need the guarding against partisan bias, the summarizing of prior wisdom, and the intellectual parameters.[26] These needs clarify the pragmatic value of armchair thought experiments for scrutinizing and adjusting precepts, so ubiquitous today as to be synonymous with ethical theorizing. But at the same time, it is increasingly recognized that ignoring imagination contracts perception and leaves deliberation coarse and monochromatic.

Edwin A. Burt suggested that "if he had to pick a single word to typify Dewey's philosophical work, it would be 'responsibility.'"[27] We derive more psychological comfort from being Right than from being responsible. Armchair systematizing that attempts to delineate a latitude and longitude of rectitude, or that approaches ethics as rational justification of an inherited moral system, is useful, but it is not on its own responsible enough. It leaves moral imagination flat and lifeless. It does not skillfully transform troubled situations in light of discovery of integrative paths of mutual growth. A situation at hand may require integrative ways forward that are not currently recognized as alternatives, creative and value-added resolutions that preserve and carry forward the propulsive desires that had previously been in conflict—as with two children being persuaded to play catch with a ball they had been fighting over.[28] Ethicists drop the ball if they offer instead a picture of moral life that is content to leave moral experiences incomplete and underdeveloped, without the depth and breadth required to grasp inherent connections and relationships. Our greatest social need is to awaken dormant imaginative capacities to be more context-responsive. Sadly, imagination neglected is as likely to turn to fleeting self-serving pursuits or to promotion of authoritarian control, regardless of how well-oiled our detached ethical analyses may be.[29]

The social basis of character

Modern European-descended political philosophy and ethics has assumed in the main that humans are defined in isolation rather than in relation. The model of free-willing, autonomous moral agency has dominated Western ethics. It has been considerably eroded among professional ethicists since Dewey's day, but it too often lingers as a habitual assumption. There is, the classical story ran, an unchanging moral realm of free will that does not depend for its structure on physical or social systems. This mental power of free will is best ruled by transcendental rationality or supernatural authority.

As we saw in Chapter Two, Dewey rejected these dubious notions. Mind and will are functions of the way we inhabit nature as imaginative cultural beings. That is, they are complex functions of the doings and undergoings of encultured, embodied, historically situated organisms, continuous with physical systems. We commit the fallacy of hypostatization whenever we abstract an emergent individual away from social relationships and then assert or assume that the individual is self-sustaining.

Dewey concurred with Mead in observing that individuality emerges through a developmental process, and it is not set over-and-against our association with others. The self does not arise in the absence of others. Ecologists study the way individual organisms arise together and act together, and the human organism is no exception (see PP, LW 2:250). The child's selfhood is formed socially. Although desires, intentions, and choices originate in singular beings, there is no soul-like "seat, agent or vehicle" of selfhood that does the perceiving, imagining, and reasoning for us (HNC, MW 14:124). The self is not like a seed awaiting the right external conditions to actualize its pre-existing form. Nor is the self a genetically hardwired wind-up device. But neither is selfhood the product of mechanical and thus precisely controllable stimulus-response events. Dewey associated the latter view with what he called the "extremely narrow and dogmatic" tenets of psychologist John Watson's behaviorism.[30]

In opposition to social contract theorists such as Hobbes, Locke, or Rousseau, Dewey argued: "There is no sense in asking how individuals come to be associated. They exist and operate in association. If there is any mystery about the matter, it is the mystery that the universe is the kind of universe it is" (PP, LW 2:250). We grow into a social milieu shot through with complex, stable, and often conflicting customs. Such heritable cultural and subcultural patterns set the stage for personal habituation, and they are the principal objects and tools of philosophical criticism. From sublime arts to genocide, our preestablished social circuits set the scene.[31] They operate as neural paths of least resistance, and through them potential meanings are revealed and in greater proportion concealed.

Dewey used the everyday word habit to capture the propulsive power of latent recurring tendencies. He included private behavioral patterns, what we call good or bad habits, but he also used the word habit in a deliberately imprecise way to sweep in physical posture, evolving customs, symbol systems, conceptual frameworks, myths, metaphors, beliefs, virtues, and prejudices.[32] He explained this broad usage in *Human Nature and Conduct*:

> We need a word to express that kind of human activity which is influenced by prior activity and in that sense acquired; which contains within itself a certain ordering or systematization of minor elements of action; which is projective, dynamic in quality, ready for overt manifestation; and which is operative in some subdued subordinate form even when not obviously dominating activity (HNC, MW 14:31).

Habits form our characters, which Dewey defined along Aristotle's lines as "the interpenetration of habits" (HNC, MW 14:29). Habits operate as active means, projecting themselves for better or worse into actions. They, and not some mythical free will, are the fundamental instruments of conduct, so much so that when we lack the relevant habits and thus the relevant moral "intuitions" (HNC, MW 14:26), our conduct misses the mark. Without stability in our habitual attitudes, moral experience would be a sequence of disjointed acts and there could be no such thing as developmental potential. George Eliot wrote in this vein about the importance of "good and sufficient ducts of habit without which our nature easily turns to mere ooze and mud, and at any pressure yields nothing but a spurt or a puddle."[33] In that case, Dewey said, conduct could not be morally significant, as no act could be "judged as an expression of character" (1932 E, LW 7:170).

Our sense of who we are, how we understand situations, how we relate to the social and natural world, and what we see as possible courses of mediation all depend significantly on the stable habits that we inherit, share, and live by. Dewey described the moral import of this: "The community ... in which we, together with those not born, are enmeshed ... is the matrix within which our ideal aspirations are born and bred. It is the source of the values that the moral imagination projects as directive criteria and as shaping purposes" (ACF, LW 9:56).

Habits mostly unconsciously shape our dramatic rehearsals, enabling us to coordinate situational tensions and to envision an indefinite future together. An organization of avenues for thinking and acting would be largely unavailable—again, for better or worse—if habits did not mark them out. Indeed, Dewey concurred with Mead that thinking itself is an "inner conversation" carried on in a locus pervaded by the language(s), traditions, and institutions of a particular human environment.[34]

In Dewey's view, the principal social role of philosophy is the interpretation, evaluation, criticism, and redirection of culture. As children we inherit values along with our speech. "It is not an ethical 'ought' that conduct should be social," Dewey urged. "It is social, whether bad or good" (HNC, MW 14:16). Because the customs that possess us precede our choices, many ideas and ideals seem naturally right, beautiful, or true. We did not opt for our presuppositions, and we are mostly unaware of them, so we take them to be inevitable and uncontroversial. This makes it challenging to intelligently evaluate and reconstruct them. Left uneducated, the human tendency is unfortunately to champion customs in blind conformity or to dismiss them in reactionary defiance.

We cannot entirely bypass the customs and recurring attitudes that structure our dramatic rehearsals and thereby inform conduct and policymaking. They do some of our thinking for us and so must be examined, evaluated, and criticized. To the extent that contemporary research opens up greater knowledge of these organizational circuits and their inner workings, we are supplied an inroad to better understanding, appreciating, and gradually altering the inescapable context of our moral imaginations.

Does this emphasis on morality as social make Dewey a cultural relativist? The anthropologist Franz Boas, who developed cultural relativism as a methodological tool, was among Dewey's Columbia University colleagues. Dewey's principal work predates the occasional conflation among moral philosophers of the terms "cultural relativism" and "moral relativism."[35] The former is a methodology in anthropology that aspires to nonethnocentric descriptions of cultural practices, while the latter is a dissenting position in ethics on the issue of whether any set of individual or cultural norms or practices can be substantially justified against any other set of norms. On the issue of moral relativism, as throughout his work, Dewey steered between what he identified as equally untenable extremes. He felt no temptation to justify an ethical theory of ultimately ethnocentric principles that masquerade as universals and so are threatened by anthropological methods.

What anthropological evidence supports, on Dewey's interpretation in "Anthropology and Ethics," is both variability and stability across cultures. There is of course "relativity in the actual content of morals at different times and places." But such relativity "is consistent with a considerable degree of stability and even of uniformity in certain generic ethical relationships and ideals" (LW 3:22). At least two factors account for this stability. First, although popular claims about an unchanging human nature are grossly exaggerated, we share recurrent psychophysical needs such as requirements for food, security, sex, companionship, social recognition, and artistic making. Second, we share basic preconditions for living together, such as some level of peace and internal order (LW 3:22).

As discussed, when habits get out of equilibrium with the flux of environing conditions, moral experience becomes problematic, and this is the source of deliberation. So as a necessary condition for moral growth and achievement, habits must be open to intelligent reconstruction. We are by definition used to them, but inflexible habits are maladaptive because mechanisms for blind routine cannot keep up with a moving world. To be genuinely responsible and self-disciplined is to be empowered and educated to overhaul prevailing habits in order to manage problems of the insistent present. It is thus a perverse irony that so many try to inculcate responsibility in the young by "molding" them in past designs simply because these hardened habits may once upon a time have helped us to cope (HNC, MW 14:48–49). Of course, regardless of how mal-adaptive they are, habits do not magically disappear simply because we tell them to. Habit-change demands support from objective conditions. We should be wary of the habitual biases we cultivate, as the embodied mind has no easy reset button.

Dewey's emphasis on individuality as the locus of desire and choice, along with his championing of democratic inquiry, stands in contrast with collectivistic tendencies in East Asian views. But it is noteworthy that Dewey completed *Human Nature and Conduct* during his second year in China, and there are affinities which were rein-forced during those two years.[36] Bao Zhiming describes the Con-fucian model of selfhood: "Ultimately, man is social, hence relational. ... Man as an individual abstracted away from the social and political relationships he is born into never enters the picture of Confucius' ethical world."[37] Our reasoning, in Dewey's view, does not stand outside of culture. It does not hover above that to which we are accustomed. A dominant assumption in most schools of Western philosophy has been that moral knowledge arises through the exercise of a rationality that transcends customary morality and hence stands on *terra firma*, but what is needed in moral life is not a substitute for customs, but to adopt more "intelligent and significant customs" (HNC, MW 14:58).

Summary

Moral zealots are often fearful of ambiguity and so cling desperately to settled codes as fixed compass points. Philosophical ethics stands in opposition to such zealotry, but it has in the main egged on winner-take-all value disputes, and as a result it has been lost in an ink cloud of logical one-upmanship. For example, Dewey argued in his 1932 *Ethics* and "Three Independent Factors in Morals" that ethical theorists have abstracted one or another factor of moral experience—such as duty, for Kant—as central, forgotten the rich context from which it was abstracted, then treated this factor as the self-sufficient starting point for moral inquiry. On Dewey's view that moral situations cannot be reduced to a single primary factor, the role of moral philosophy and practical ethics shifts. Dewey's ethics aimed not to establish a singular moral bedrock, but to help us become more imaginative and responsible.

Notes

1 René Descartes, *Discourse on Method* (New York: Penguin Books, 1968), 37.

2 William James, *A Pluralistic Universe* (Cambridge, MA: Harvard University Press, 1977), 145.

3 Peter Singer, *Animal Liberation* (New York: Harper Perennial Modern Classics, 2009).

4 Singer, *Ethics into Action* (Lanham, MD: Rowman & Littlefield, 1998). As a caveat, Singer's book was explicitly written for a popular audience as a guide for activists. His philosophical writings are cautious and probing. See, for example, Dale Jamieson, ed., *Singer and His Critics* (Oxford: Blackwell, 1999).

5 For criticisms (and appreciations) of aspects of Dewey's pluralism, see Robert B. Talisse, *A Pragmatist Philosophy of Democracy* (New York: Routledge, 2007).

6 For an excellent introduction to both Dewey's value theory and metaphysics, see James Gouinlock, *John Dewey's Philosophy of Value* (Atlantic Highlands, NJ: Humanities Press, 1972). Gouinlock wrote the book as a response to debates in analytic ethics about the "is"/"ought" distinction in the 1960s and 1970s, but the book remains a timely introduction to Dewey's house of theory despite the demise of the "is"/"ought" debate as "the" purported core problem of ethics.

7 For example, R. M. Hare asserts that his Kantian-utilitarian hybrid ethical theory is "the right way to reason about moral questions." R. M. Hare, "Why I Am Only a Demi-vegetarian," in *Singer and His Critics*, ed. Dale Jamieson (Oxford: Blackwell, 1999), 247–68.

8 Hilary Putnam, "Reflections on Pragmatism," in *Dewey's Enduring Impact: Essays on America's Philosopher*, ed. John R. Shook and Paul Kurtz (Amherst, NY: Prometheus Books, 2011), 52.

9 On affirmations and assertions, see Chapter Two.

10 Lucy Maud Montgomery, *Anne of Green Gables* (New York: Grosset & Dunlap, 1908), 290.

11 Jonathan Levin, *The Poetics of Transition* (Durham, NC: Duke University Press, 1999), 87.

12 David Hume, *Treatise of Human Nature*, bk. 1, pt. 4, §7, 267. On Hume and sympathy, see Annette C. Baier's classic *A Progress of Sentiments: Reflections on Hume's Treatise* (Cambridge, MA: Harvard University Press, 1991).

13 George Lakoff, *The Political Mind* (New York: Viking Press, 2008), 241. Cf. Benjamin K. Bergen, *Louder than Words: The New Science of How the Mind Makes Meaning* (New York: Basic Books, 2012).

14 Cf. Thomas M. Alexander, *The Human Eros: Eco-ontology and the Aesthetics of Existence* (New York: Fordham University Press, 2013), 194.

15 Stuart Hampshire, *Innocence and Experience* (Cambridge, MA: Harvard University Press, 189), 126.

16 Emily Brady, "Imagination and the Aesthetic Appreciation of Nature," in *The Aesthetics of Natural Environments*, ed. Allen Carlson and Arnold Berleant (Peterborough, ON: Broadview Press, 2004), 166.

17 Wallace Stegner, *Angle of Repose* (New York: Penguin, 1971), 444.

18 For a more detailed treatment of Dewey's theory of imagination, see my *John Dewey and Moral Imagination: Pragmatism in Ethics* (Bloomington, IN: Indiana University Press, 2003), including ch. 5, "Dramatic Rehearsal." Dramatic rehearsal is one phase or function of the deliberative process. But this function is so essential for Dewey that it lends its name to the whole process.

19 As Johnson explains Dewey's position: "The meaning of something is its relations, actual or potential, to other qualities, things, events, and experiences." Mark Johnson, *The Meaning of the Body* (Chicago: University of Chicago Press, 2007), 265.

20 John Stuart Mill, *Utilitarianism* (Indianapolis, IN: Hackett Publishing Co., 2002 [1861]), 2.

21 For a thorough analysis of Dewey's ethical starting point, see Gregory Fernando Pappas, *John Dewey's Ethics: Democracy as Experience* (Bloomington, IN: Indiana University Press, 2008), 20ff.

22 For a pragmatist approach to animal ethics, see Erin McKenna and Andrew Light, eds., *Animal Pragmatism* (Bloomington, IN: Indiana University Press, 2004). More recently, see Erin McKenna, *Pets, People, and Pragmatism* (New York: Fordham University Press, 2013).

23 Joel Salatin, presentation at Green Mountain College, Poultney, Vermont, November 2011. Journalist Michael Pollan advanced Salatin's view in his best-selling book, *The Omnivore's Dilemma*, while distancing himself from Salatin's libertarian-agrarian-Christian-conservative idiom. See Michael Pollan, *The Omnivore's Dilemma* (New York: Penguin Press, 2006).

24 294a–c. Plato, *Statesman*, trans. J. B. Skemp (Indianapolis, IN: Hackett, 1992), 66.

25 For a discussion of this debate in the context of Dewey's ethics, see Pappas, *John Dewey's Ethics*, 51ff. See David Bakkhurst's careful distinction of pragmatist from particularist ethics in "Pragmatism and Ethical Particularism," in *New Pragmatists*, ed. Cheryl Misak (Oxford: Oxford University Press, 2009). For a criticism of my own Dewey-inspired situational and instrumental theory of the role of principles in moral inquiry, see Mark Coeckelbergh, *Imagination and Principles: An Essay on the Role of Imagination in Moral Reasoning* (Basingstoke: Palgrave Macmillan, 2007).

26 Cf. Martha C. Nussbaum, *Love's Knowledge* (Oxford: Oxford University Press, 1990), 99.
27 Quoted in Larry A. Hickman, *John Dewey's Pragmatic Technology* (Bloomington, IN: Indiana University Press, 1990), 196.
28 The example is Alexander's in *The Human Eros*, 199.
29 This does not, however, address the extent to which principles are best emphasized in order to operate most effectively as mediating tools, and indeed this is a matter of current debate.
30 1934.01.03 (02088): Dewey to Frank Connor.
31 Cf. Maurice Merleau-Ponty, *The Phenomenology of Perception*, trans. Colin Smith (Atlantic Highlands, NJ: Humanities Press, 1962), 87.
32 Dewey's catch-all term habit appears too vague and sweeping from the standpoint of contemporary psychology and cognitive science. He had no theory of how intellectual habits are blended and systematically linked to form complex cognitive models, but his work on habit accords with the contemporary view that complex conceptual networks are indispensable, irreplaceable, and unavoidable. See Chapter Eight.
33 George Eliot, *Daniel Deronda* (New York: Random House, 2002 [1876]), 139.
34 George Herbert Mead, "The Social Self," in *Selected Writings*, ed. Andrew Reck (Chicago: University of Chicago Press, 1964), 146.
35 For example, see James Rachels's widely anthologized "The Challenge of Cultural Relativism," in his *The Elements of Moral Philosophy*, 3rd ed. (New York: Random House, 1999), 20–36.
36 See 1921.02.23 (07207): Dewey to James H. Tufts. For a book-length investigation, see Jessica Ching-Sze Wang, *John Dewey in China* (Albany, NY: SUNY Press, 2007).
37 Bao Zhiming, "Language and World View in Ancient China," *Philosophy East and West* 40, no. 2 (1990): 195–219, at 207. Quoted in Carl Becker, "Language and Logic in Modern Japan," *Communication & Cognition* 24, no. 2 (1991): 169.

Further reading

Steven Fesmire, *John Dewey and Moral Imagination: Pragmatism in Ethics* (Bloomington, IN: Indiana University Press, 2003).
James Gouinlock, ed., *The Moral Writings of John Dewey*, rev. ed. (Amherst, NY: Prometheus Books, 1994).
Mark Johnson, *Morality for Humans: Ethical Understanding from the Perspective of Cognitive Science* (Chicago: University of Chicago Press, 2014).
Todd Lekan, *Making Morality: Pragmatist Reconstruction in Ethical Theory* (Nashville, TN: Vanderbilt University Press, 2003).
Erin McKenna, *Pets, People, and Pragmatism* (New York: Fordham University Press, 2013).
Gregory Fernando Pappas, *John Dewey's Ethics: Democracy as Experience* (Bloomington, IN: Indiana University Press, 2008).
Jennifer Welchman, *Dewey's Ethical Thought* (Ithaca, NY: Cornell University Press, 1997).

Five

Social-political and educational philosophy reconstructed

Liberalism is committed to an end that is at once enduring and flexible: the liberation of individuals so that realization of their capacities may be the law of their life. It is committed to the use of freed intelligence as the method of directing change.

(LSA, LW 11:41)

The most pressing problem of modernity, in Dewey's view, is to humanize techno-industrial civilization, "making it and its technology a servant of human life" (ION, LW 5:108). The job of intellectuals is to perceive and critically respond to this unrealized opportunity for humane cultural reconstruction. Dewey argued in *Individualism, Old and New* (1930) that as industrial civilization developed, philosophers and other intellectuals were among the many individuals who lost any coherent social function. By facing the shared problems of our civilization and helping to guide inquiry into them, intellectuals could take the first step toward recovering a public function.

Yet due largely to doctrinal entanglements, philosophy has too often defected from public engagement in favor of esoteric problems manufactured by other philosophers. Dewey summed up this spirit of public engagement in "The Need for a Recovery of Philosophy" (1917): "Philosophy recovers itself when it ceases to be a device for dealing with the problems of philosophers and becomes a method, cultivated by philosophers, for dealing with the problems of men" (MW 10:46). As a consequence of their "abdication of responsibility" (ION, LW 5:110), philosophers have failed to contribute as much as they might. This chapter introduces Dewey's own public engagement with cultural problems through his progressive social-political and educational philosophies. To keep the scope manageable, I emphasize Dewey's arguments that bear on twenty-first-century debates.

The democratic ideal

Democracy is widely equated with majority rule, as though it means no more than "one person, one vote," with duties exhausted at the polling booth. Steven Kiernan counters that "a democracy without an engaged populace is like a monarchy without a king."[1] Through his relationship with Addams and Hull House, Dewey in his Chicago years had come to see democracy not just as a way of arranging a political and legal system, but as a way of life that breaks down exclusionary social barriers and opens up diverse points of contact. Democracy is far more than a form of government or system of laws, Dewey asserted in a frequently cited passage in *Democracy and Education*. It is "primarily a mode of associated living, of conjoint communicated experience" (DE, MW 9:93).

The great philosopher of democracy opposed democracy if it is taken in the "neoliberal" sense of barely regulated market capitalism in which a position of economic privilege increases political access. The moral meaning of democracy, Dewey said, "is found in resolving that the supreme test of all political institutions and industrial arrangements shall be the contribution they make to the all-around growth of every member of society" (MW 12:186). Throughout his career he held that the chief obstacle to this all-around growth "is found in our economic régime" (LW 5:274). Indeed he held this to a fault, tending for example to analyze racism as mostly an economic problem.[2]

For Addams and Dewey it was not enough merely to passively believe, with Kant, that all humans should be equally respected for their innate dignity. Anticipating key insights of the "capabilities approach" to international economic development associated today with the important work of Martha Nussbaum and Amartya Sen, Addams and Dewey urged that we must actively establish conditions in which capacities are fulfilled instead of being arrested by denied opportunities.[3] The democratic ideal is a working faith in the possibilities of the person on the street, "in the potentialities of human nature as that nature is exhibited in every human being irrespective of race, color, sex, birth and family, of material or cultural wealth" (LW 14:226). Democracy as a way of life is forever on the lookout for socially imposed limits that stunt individual development, limits that arise from a self-fulfilling belief that constructed barriers—say, a purported need to be mastered—are found inside individuals as changeless psychological conditions (UPMP:345).

Democracy as a way of life also requires disciplined intelligence to interpret and evaluate the way things are, and it requires imagination to see what is before us in light of what could be.[4] Although Dewey, who was tone deaf, would not have used this metaphor, consider the cooperative freedom exemplified in jazz. As with the ordered flexibility and cohesive improvisation of a jazz combo, democratic citizenship may be immediately enjoyed while bringing about something enduringly good that is neither prefabricated nor slapdash. Just as the jazz musician can potentially remake and expand the tradition of the art form, so educated citizens can potentially redirect their communities and culture(s) through refined perceptiveness, discernment, creativity, expressiveness, courage, foresight, and communicativeness. Such artistic–aesthetic traits should be among the aims of education.

Dewey was one of the most influential liberal thinkers of the twentieth century, but he was not a *liberal* if that term is taken in the classical sense (discussed below), or if liberal is taken in the sense of centralized "command and control" by autocratic and elite experts in bureaucratic management who build efficiencies into systems by doing the deciding for us, from school governance to state and federal governance. Problematic situations are not helped much when we set ourselves up as enlightened moral or political czars for whom inclusive deliberation inconveniently gets in the way. A keen ear for other voices is not simply nice; it is the way we make decisions and policies that can best be trusted.

The political heart of Dewey's democratic ideal is inseparable from his theory of active, *cooperative* inquiry discussed in Chapter Three. In Plato's *Republic*, the philosopher–ruler is in the best position to make decisions because he or she sees practical circumstances under the form of universal and unwavering Truths. Very few humans can access Truth, so most must be led by the few. For Plato a monarchical meritocracy is best, and democracy is mob rule degenerating into tyranny. (To be more precise, Plato explored this position in the Republic. Plato provided Dewey's "favorite philosophic reading" precisely because "the dramatic, restless, cooperatively inquiring Plato of the Dialogues" always had a practical and social turn of mind and was never the doctrinal figure later embalmed by unimaginative Platonists [LW 5:155].)

For Dewey, in opposition, a decision-making process gains legitimacy and direction by openness and inclusion. In Dewey's view democracy requires inclusive deliberation, not only in institutional and governmental decision-making, but also as an engaged everyday habit. Democracy gains traction as an ideal when we realize that less inclusive approaches—in which "the decider" makes a call that ignores stakeholders—understandably raise suspicions about aims, interests, and background assumptions.[5] Less inclusive approaches also raise issues of transparency and accountability, and they frequently lead to myopic and hence unworkable policies (see PP, LW 2:235–372). Far from shying away from complex tensions and divergences, a democratic approach to decision-making seeks them out and welcomes them. Democratic decision-making ideally responds to, evaluates, criticizes, and thoughtfully incorporates different voices.

Democracy is still rudimentary in its extant political forms, Dewey observed in The Public and Its Problems (1927), but even these forms to some degree inform a public spirit of consultation to uncover troubles and to organize the expertise to deal with them. He made this point in one of his pithiest lines: "The man who wears the shoe knows best that it pinches and where it pinches, even if the expert shoemaker is the best judge of how the trouble is to be remedied" (PP, LW 2:364).

In A Theory of Justice, the neo-Kantian political theorist John Rawls argues for a procedural impartiality that guards against biases. For Dewey, in contrast with Rawls, justice can only be worked out through the practices of actual communities. Although Rawls's theory of justice is not basically concerned with criminal justice, the standpoint of his "original position" accords well with the depiction of justice in the American legal system as a blindfolded goddess. Procedural impartiality is an important instrument for checking biases, especially valuable in circumstances in which trust has disintegrated. But it would be mistaken, in Dewey's view, to regard the blindfold of justice as the ideal for equality. Blind impartiality is not the only way to compensate for arbitrariness, parochialism, and corruption. It is second best. Social ethicists such as Addams and Dewey urged that the best way to deal with such biases is through communicative, caring engagement in which no one's concerns are rejected out of hand.

Like community (and today sustainability), democracy is an ideal, hope, and standard, not a fact. It is something for which we aim. "There is no short-cut to it, no single predestined road which can be found once for all and which, if human beings continue to walk in it without deviation, will surely conduct them to the goal" (1932 E, LW 7:350). Democracy, in Reinhold Niebuhr's words, finds "proximate solutions for insoluble problems."[6] By opening deliberation to a "greater diversity of stimuli," each participant "has to refer his own action to that of others, and to consider the action of others to give point and direction to his own" (DE, MW 9:93). This is a check, albeit an imperfect one, on exclusivity and partiality. Integrative values may emerge to reconstruct and harmonize, albeit tenuously, conflicting desires and appraisals among different individuals and groups (PP, LW 2:328).

Of course we can democratically make bad decisions. When we have made a decision we too often resort to a series of rearguard measures, shoring up defensive arguments and tidying up the details *ad hoc*. Such artificial clarity and circling of the wagons is especially likely in the face of intense public scrutiny or international criticism. The result is that polarization replaces democratic discourse, and both sides in a dispute act as if they possess universal moral compasses while the other has thrown theirs overboard. Their compasses, of course, point to different norths. Cynically chalking these unlovely facts up to petty human nature does nothing to meet the principal educational need, Dewey argues, which is to *improve* "the methods and conditions of debate, discussion and persuasion. That is the problem of the public" (PP, LW 2:365). Through an educated public, democracy can become self-correcting.

The experimental attitude and the democratic ideal

Dewey argued that it no longer seems a pipe dream to believe that we can democratically secure better lives (LW 5:269). Modern empirical methods and techniques have brought a dramatic shift in our intellectual attitudes and morale (LW 5:269). We have reached "down into nature" (EN, LW 1:13) and gained much greater understanding and control of the means to intelligently direct our lives toward valued ends. Experience now has new possibilities, a new method of revelation. Due to this shift in methods, he argued, we are gradually learning to trust experience and experiment as our guide instead of fleeing for guidance to a mythic transcendent realm.

The old morale distrusted social intelligence as a natural force. Nature was principally a realm of frustration and unfulfilled promises. It was too precarious to "contain the arts by which its own course could be directed" (LW 5:269). The new experimental and naturalistic morale offers "some measure of intelligent direction," albeit no imminent Utopias (LW 5:271).[7] For Dewey there was nothing *inevitable* about progress toward greater and more widely shared human fulfillment, regardless of how rigorously experimental our method may be. His view was that whatever progress *is* possible, its potential is best tapped by means of the operative method of intelligence.[8]

The opposing view of intellect as a remote spectator is, despite honorable intentions, in practice allied with the social and political *status quo*. What Dewey in *Reconstruction in Philosophy* called the "aristocratic" mode of philosophy divorces pure thought and logic from common, practical life. The aristocratic philosopher retreats from practical experience to the wide eternal truths of the spirit and consequently stands aloof from the vast majority of people who are relegated to accomplishing rote goals (MW 10:45).[9] At the close of *Unmodern Philosophy and Modern Philosophy*, Dewey makes what he calls a "cynical" suggestion that the "writing class"—in which he includes philosophers—suffers from an inferiority complex. We place our own cognitive activities atop a hierarchical totem pole while relegating practical activity to second-class status, as compensation for the fact that our wider social surroundings consistently place narrowly practical activity above knowing (UPMP:345).

He occasionally referenced physical engineering as an analogy for how we can democratically secure social arrangements that turn potential human goods into actual ones (MW 10:263). The engineering metaphor stemmed from his adamant rejection of the old dualistic separation of a realm of the cultural from a realm of the physical (see Chapter Two). As a result, he made positive references to "social engineering" (e.g., RP, MW 12:179; LW 9:297; LW 15:260), a choice of words that backfires for readers weaned on Aldous Huxley's dystopian novel Brave New World. Doubtless the work of engineering can be imaginative, creative, and free of servility to predetermined ends, but the usual notion of engineering runs opposite to this, against the grain of Dewey's philosophy. Due to his unfortunate, or at least untimely, choice of words, references to social engineering understandably played into the hands of critics, as well as some admirers, who identified his outlook with precisely the narrow utilitarian expediency he rejected, or held that he endorsed social manipulation with too little regard for subjectivity and difference.

The experimental method of patient, engaged, cooperative inquiry, in contrast with pure Cartesian thought, has wrought monumental achievements, yet it is too often restricted to narrow technical applications and lopsided financial gain. Organized experimental communication is capable of imaginative discoveries that unsettle and revise lazy intellectual habits (see ION, LW 5:116). When this experimental attitude is enlivened by the democratic ideal, Dewey prophesied, it may be organized to become the method and morale by which we establish material and social conditions whereby all individuals could have a more humane life (see LSA, LW 11:48–49 and ION, LW 5:114–16). This is practicable through educational reform.

Emergent individualism

In Reconstruction in Philosophy (1920), Dewey examined the three standard Western alternatives then conceivable for the relationship between individual and society. First, classical liberalism held that "society must exist for the sake of individuals" and that the sphere of the individual must be sharply marked off from the sphere of the political (RP, MW 12:187). Extreme individualists held that society does not define individuals; rather, self-sufficing individuals (complete within themselves) define society. Second, on the top-down communist or statist view, "individuals must have their ends and ways of living set for them by society" (RP, MW 12:187). Extreme socialists held that society defines individuals. Finally, the Hegelian view held that individual and society are correlative manifestations of a single superorganism, and society requires "the service and subordination of individuals" while simultaneously "existing to serve them" (RP, MW 12:187).

Dewey rejected the lost atomist, the coerced statist, and the subsumed organicist as poor metaphysical maps (see Chapter Two) and unworkable models for building democratic communities (see RP, MW 12:190–91). Each offers a highly generalized map of the self-world terrain that has inspired millions to make the journey, but none approaches its own social-political map as provisional and experimental. Consequently, specific and concrete observations by these millions of travelers do not adequately feed back to revise their conceptual maps.

As discussed in prior chapters, in Dewey's philosophy there is no such thing as a self-sufficing individual, nor is society the cumulative product of atomistic individuals associating with each other. The particular social medium on which we depend, with its languages, traditions, and institutions, penetrates our thoughts, beliefs, and desires; channels our impulses; and funds our aims and satisfactions (AE, LW 10:274–75). The evidence of the social sciences would at any rate appear to be on Dewey's side, that individuality is an interactive social *achievement* and a creative emergent process. It is not a preexisting natural gift, metaphysical nugget, or sacrificial object. By seeing humans in relation instead of in detachment, he dissolved the starting question of social contract theories: How do atomistic individuals join together to form a society or nation-state (RP, MW 12:194)?

If I built a business, I did so in the existing infrastructure achieved through associated life, which also helped to create my own individuality. If I am homeless, the same holds. There is nothing in this realization that points to a Hegelian superorganism that sinks the individual. The Hegelian organicist theory had especially attracted Dewey in his youth, but it trivializes conflicts and oppression while presenting subordination to the state-organism as a requirement for people to realize true freedom and individuality (see LSA, LW 11:20). In Hegel's own antidemocratic treatment of the state-organism, individuals are replaceable and interchangeable. Consequently, Hegel wrote in the *Phenomenology of Spirit*, "the individual must all the more forget himself."[10]

For better and for worse, Dewey noted, "Individuals will always be the centre and the consummation of experience, but what an individual actually *is* in his life-experience depends upon the nature and movement of associated life" (LW 5:275). When that life is marred by ignorance and injustice, individual vitality is aesthetically restricted and intellectually distorted for both the haves and the have-nots. This includes the preening displays of those who attempt "to secure happiness through the possession of things, social position, and economic power over others" (LW 5:274). We each have a responsibility to aid in the progress of institutions which will succeed in realizing the potentials of those around us.

Radicalism for grown-ups

Genuine transformation of deeply entrenched habits, systems, and institutions may appear a distant, and receding, hope. Dewey urged us to take stock of the fact that change is always afoot. Our history is filled with the revolutionary *effects* of shared reflection and non-violent action. In 1968 Dr. Martin Luther King Jr. was assassinated three miles from my childhood home in Memphis. I was raised in a climate of racist fear, always on the "right" side of literal tracks that divided (and divides) classes and races throughout the culturally segregated and homophobic American South. At this writing the American president is a bi-racial black man, and same-sex marriage is supported by the majority of Americans. What change needs is direction, a channel for energies. It is due in part to the thoughtful mediation of many who came before us that our civilization is, even from a gloomy point of view, better off than it might otherwise have been.[11]

As Westbrook observes, and Alan Ryan has moderated somewhat, Dewey's was a minority voice, more radical than the frequent depiction of him as the standard-bearer of American liberalism.[12] If perceiving the need for radical changes makes one a radical, Dewey wrote, "then today any liberalism which is not also radicalism is irrelevant and doomed" (LSA, LW 11:45). Democracy's goal is radical "because it requires great change in existing social institutions, economic, legal and cultural" (LW 11:298–99).

The eventual consequences of democratic social action cannot be entirely predicted and predetermined. We see the significance of great movements in hindsight, rarely at their source (see LW 6:99). Standing by the Grand Canyon, we appreciate the importance of that little trickling stream high in the Colorado Rockies. It is sometimes said, mistakenly, that Dewey advocated only incremental rather than revolutionary change. Instead, he advocated durable revolutionary change—at the Grand Canyon scale—through cooperative social action informed by education in operative intelligence. His "renascent liberalism" is a window through which to envision possibilities that could be effected on the other side of that transformation: a way of organizing society "that will make possible effective liberty and opportunity for personal growth in mind and spirit in all individuals" (LSA, LW 11:41). His aims were those of a liberal radical, particularly in his relentless pursuit of economic and social justice.

Dewey's meliorism is at the heart of this radical democratic vision. He followed William James in distinguishing meliorism from optimism and pessimism. On James's approach to clarifying concepts, the meaning of a concept is best clarified by asking how it disposes us to act. The Pollyanna optimist—say, regarding racial equality or greenhouse gas emissions—trusts that everything is going to work out fine, no matter how I live. The pessimist thinks everything is going to go to hell, no matter how I live. On a practical level both agree that things will go well or ill regardless of my actions, so I can disengage and sit on my hands. The meliorist, in contrast, says there is no guarantee that one's actions will nudge matters toward the better, but be assured that such self-fulfilling action has always been the necessary ingredient for bringing about whatever amelioration is possible.[13]

Dewey understood his melioristic social and political outlook to be simultaneously realistic and idealistic. The self-described realist in economics and politics deals with social conditions "as they are" and calls this practical. "Economic reform or international peace would be nice," she says, "but I cannot afford to trade in impracticable ideals that pretend to finally displace and overcome all institutional defects." Her nemesis is the doctrine-thumping ideologue. But from a pragmatic standpoint she and the ideologue are two peas in a pod: each commits the perfectionist fallacy, namely that any version of the good must be realized all at once. Vague visions of a future world are far removed from existing circumstances, so the self-proclaimed realist dismisses remote ideals in favor of what amounts to submission and "putting our trust in drift" (LW 15:254). From his earliest days Dewey rejected both extremes as patently unrealistic nonsense, out of touch with our own dynamic social history and ultimately serving class profit. When ideals like equality or freedom are set up as "some remote goal to be finally accomplished" (LW 17:66), they fail as a working method and resource for deliberately taking the vital step ahead.

Dewey would accuse us of abdicating our intelligence if we accepted what he said as timeless or authoritative. As Peirce observed, nothing blocks the road of experimental inquiry more than the sense that we are infallible. Yet this very spirit of fallibility led many on the political left to reject his reconstruction of liberalism. If I say "let's experiment on this promising idea," perhaps very few will listen, but if I say "follow me, for this is the ultimate and exclusive truth," then perhaps more people will follow.

Along these lines, Dewey's reception among Chinese Marxists in the early 1920s was especially telling. He was out of step with the rising ideology of violent upheaval. In a letter during his second year in China, Dewey remarked: "The whole temper among the younger generation is revolutionary, they are so sick of their old institutions that they assume any change will be for the better—the more extreme and complete the change, the better. And they seem to me to have little idea of the difficulties in the way of any constructive change."[14] In a scathing review of a lecture series Dewey gave in 1921, Chinese Marxist philosopher Fei Juetian summed up the absolutist view that would carry the day: "If I tell the world that we should experiment with socialism and see if it works, people would think that I am crazy and would oppose this experiment. If I proclaim that socialism holds the ultimate truth to solving problems in today's society, that there is no better theory than socialism, people will become interested in its practice and help transform the theory into a reality."[15] The quest for certainty is real, but if the hazard of liberalism is a tendency toward evasion, the hazard of revolutionary zeal is losing a historical perspective and "abandoning in panic things of enduring and priceless value" (LSA, LW 11:6).

Ironically, Fei was making a narrowly pragmatic argument on behalf of absolutism. He wrote that "the experimental method would not work in reality because no one would want to risk their lives and their properties simply for the sake of experiment."[16] Dewey responded, as he would more famously respond to the Soviet exile Leon Trotsky in 1937: "Work" for what end?[17] Absolutist ideology eventually worked to bring about a communist revolution in China, just as it had in Russia. But did it bring about the goods for which the revolution was fought? Did it lead to what Marx called the dictatorship of the proletariat, or to a "dictatorship over the proletariat" (LW 11:331)? Fei's narrow, capricious sort of pragmatism deliberately invented absolutes in order to generate the will to accomplish a prefabricated egalitarian end taken to be valuable in itself. His prophecy was self-fulfilling, but it was not the only or most complete fulfillment afforded by the circumstances. With respect to absolutes, those with low tolerance for ambiguity try to purchase freedom from doubt, but at the cost of shortchanging the democratic spirit. Fear of sane doubt has long been a prelude to atrocity as people cling to the illusion of ironclad certainty.

The notion that liberals bring sugar to actions that require vinegar is common today, particularly in distinctions that pit radical philosophies against liberal ones, such as radical feminism versus liberal feminism. Is liberalism an ineffective, fair-weather, milk-and-water political philosophy that should be rejected by tough-minded progressives who are willing to take a stand? This question was the theme of *Liberalism and Social Action* (1935) which Dewey penned in the middle of the Great Depression and on the eve of the Second World War, as Marxist ideology in the United States was gaining momentum over liberalism. Progressivism in politics has long been opposed to conservatism. "But today," Dewey noted, attacks from conservatives "are mild in comparison with indictments proceeding from those who want drastic social changes effected in a twinkling of an eye, and who believe that violent overthrow of existing institutions is the right method of effecting the required changes" (LSA, LW 11:5).

Dewey's was a radicalism for grown-ups, those with the courage and patience to secure the "democratic means to achieve our democratic ends" (LW 11:332). Or as Addams earlier made the point in her 1922 book *Peace and Bread in Time of War*: "Social advance depends as much upon the process through which it is secured as upon the result itself" (in LW 15:195).

This emphasis on democratic means was the heart of Dewey's response to the Soviet exile Trotsky after chairing the "Dewey Commission" in Mexico City in 1937 (see Chapter One). On the face of it Trotsky agreed with Dewey regarding the interdependence of means and ends, and they agreed on the liberation of humanity as the end-in-view. The two quickly developed intellectual and moral respect for each other. But Trotsky was beholden to Marxist dogma regarding the invariable law of all social development, and his view that the sole means to the liberation of humanity is violent class struggle was *deduced* from this absolute social "law" and *not* from wide survey of the situation and thoughtful forecast of consequences. Consequently, Trotsky *imported* the social means (violent revolution) from a separate source and thereby failed to rigorously examine which means would more likely lead objectively to the desired results (LW 13:351–52).

Liberalism, old and new

Dewey told the story of liberalism by exploring the outdated assumption that one's outlook is derived by inference from "Nature" and hence reflects inherent and unchanging conditions (see UPMP:345). Pronouncements about what is "natural" are among the chief obstacles that each generation confronts as we struggle to change social conditions that are in fact of our own making and so are susceptible to change. Consider tired defenses of extreme inequalities, such as the old Aristotelian defense of slavery as the best arrangement for those born with slavish natures.

In a peculiarly consequential inference from nature, Dewey observed in *Liberalism and Social Action*, the Physiocracy (Nature + rule) movement in pre-Revolutionary France proposed a political philosophy based on imitating nature's ways so that the ideal society's economic system would mirror nature's patterns (see LSA, LW 11:10). The Physiocrats popularized the term laissez-faire as a slogan against excessive regulations. Their interpretation of nature was of course pre-Darwinian and preecological, so they saw nature as unchanging.

The Scottish moral philosopher and economist Adam Smith and others later replaced the Physiocratic focus on *physical* nature's unchanging ways with the notion that it is instead *human* nature that is fixed and unalterable. Smith's view was that humans are essentially atomistic yet sympathetic creatures who strive above all to maximize self-interested satisfactions. He took a partial glimpse of our nature and froze it forever as an essence transcending history and environment.[18] His theory is today identified with "classical liberalism," but it was simply "liberalism" until the late nineteenth century. Today, a controversial and highly selective reading of Smith is identified with economic conservatism and neoliberalism.

Smith argued in *The Wealth of Nations* (1776) that our acquisitive and self-serving tendencies are the universal beating heart of all cultural existence. This beating heart serves the greatest good when it circulates labor and goods through the economic and political circulatory system of capitalism. Or to shift the metaphor, free market capitalism is the economic engine ideally suited to running on the fuel of our acquisitive human nature. Smith was personally deeply sympathetic to the plight of workers, and he supported government regulation where required to ensure free competition. But what he called "do-gooders" who propose seemingly benevolent regulations interfere with patterns permanently established by human nature. They pave the road to hell with their good intentions. Do-gooders, Smith argued, gum up the works of the free market system, which, when the natural liberty of citizens is freed of interference from governmental action, invisibly and automatically ushers our self-interested pursuits toward a happy collective result that maximizes aggregate happiness (see LSA, LW 11:9ff.).

As Dewey observed, Smith provided the rationale for a historic shift of economic power from aristocrats to merchants. By the late eighteenth century, the commercial classes (the industrialists, in

Britain) had latched onto Smith's theory of political economy. The utilitarian Jeremy Bentham, who with James Mill helped to popularize the term "laissez-faire" (which Smith never used) in Britain, would develop a variation of the theory to successfully gain radical legislative reforms. This helped to move Britain away from the outdated aristocracy-based common laws that were holding back—that is, restricting the economic liberty of—the rising commercial class.

It should be no criticism of a philosophy to observe that it is incomplete and cannot be transported in all of its essentials from one culture and period to another. Our philosophies grow out of our dealings with the problems of our own place and time, so they are all compensatory and transitional. There are profound constraints placed on the success of a political philosophy by social structures and our biological inheritance, but we should not look back to past philosophers for final formulations of these constraints. We should look to them for tools, historical perspective, and hopefully inspiration to deal with current perplexities.

Dewey's theoretical tools were well-honed in part because he was deliberately forging them to deal with practical historical problems. Most of these problems persist today. Perhaps most notably, the general contours of conservative and progressive worldviews, especially in the context of economic freedom, are laid bare by Dewey in the 1920s–30s in ways palpable to a contemporary reader. Meanwhile, some of our own most pressing political topics played little part in public discourse during Dewey's life—such as abortion and gay marriage, the two principal indicators of political party affiliation in the United States today.[19]

Had classical liberal economists in the early nineteenth century understood themselves to be making a historical and contextual response to specific conditions in Britain, Dewey argued, this intellectual history lesson might be just that. But laissez-faire liberalism, as it came to be called, was presented as the correct theory of economics—for all times, places, and persons. It was as certain as Newton's laws of motion: the scientifically correct way to reason about economics, founded on the bedrock of the correct description of human nature. Physics today is several revolutions removed from its classical Newtonian roots, but economic ideology retains its classical lines. An economic theory that had been progressive and liberating at its inception became economic gospel. It asked us to trust in Nature, not cooperative planning, so aside from securing free markets it did not charge government or other social institutions with any purpose to optimize consequences toward valued ends (see LW 15:254).

Dewey argued, in opposition to the policy of laissez-faire, that social institutions such as government, business, and religion are bound by a social purpose that can imbue their activities with a meaning that has been obscured and confused by the old liberalism. "That purpose," Dewey forcefully declared in *Reconstruction in Philosophy*, "is to set free and to develop the capacities of human individuals without respect to race, sex, class or economic status. And this is all one with saying that the test of their value is the extent to which they educate every individual into the full stature of his possibility" (RP, MW 12:186). Toward this end, there are values of the outmoded liberalism that should endure as we reorganize social institutions: we should aim to "secure the blessings of liberty" for all to develop fully their individual capacities and to freely inquire (LSA, LW 11:25). To achieve these redefined liberal aims through means better suited to them, we must be willing democratically to use governmental and intergovernmental power to change the way we organize society instead of supposing that local, national, and global markets will on their own take care of realizing these values for us.[20]

A century ago, Dewey saw that the then-rising consumer economy reinforced lives in which our imaginative energies are spent on thin and superficial personal dramas rather than being invested in shared goods that have breadth and depth. Commercial interests have "interwoven our destinies" (MW 10:193), but these interests have been shaped and directed by a philosophical outlook that dangerously narrows our sympathies.

Dewey was particularly interested in the many justifications twentieth-century defenders of laissez-faire liberalism offered for why we should not strive for equality as an ideal. In *Liberalism and Social Action*, he explored the two most common defenses of the economic status quo that developed as it became apparent that "disparity, not equality, was the actual consequence of *laissez-faire* liberalism" (LSA, LW 11:29). The first line of defense used to justify vast economic

disparities was to glorify virtues of personal responsibility and entrepreneurial initiative. Even before the fights for social security and
minimum wage in the 1930s, conservative critics criticized the
dependency of a nanny state that creates a coddled class who cannot
get out there and succeed. In a laissez-faire meritocracy, the story
runs, virtues of "initiative, independence, choice and responsibility"
are duly rewarded (LSA, LW 11:29).

When former President George W. Bush blamed the infamous
collapse of the Enron corporation on a "few bad apples" rather than
on systemic policy failures, he could count on little pushback from
an American electorate habituated to classical liberalism. Prosecut-
ing these rotten apples, Bush assured Americans, would preserve a
sound economic system from spoilage. Increased government
regulation over free trade, on the other hand, would rot a noble
economic system that justly rewards the American entrepreneurial
spirit of self-disciplined individualism and thereby fuels the engine
of global progress.

Dewey argued that this popular fairy tale reinforces a "ragged
individualism" that does little to transition us toward the "rugged
individualism" it claims to value. We do indeed need many more
rugged individuals who are unafraid of the existing social order and
its sacrosanct values, but classical liberalism is not a reliable means
to that end (LSA, LW 11:29). This lack of efficacy is amplified in a
globally interconnected society far from the preindustrial American
frontier (ION, LW 5:45). Even the mythic entrepreneurial individual himself or herself is lost within a socioeconomic system that
makes a farce of the democratic ideal. What is needed is a more
anchored individualism joined to ideas and ideals that engage
"cooperative individualities," but antiegalitarian thinking and a
romanticized rags-to-riches mythology leaves us directionless and
confused (ION, LW 5:75; FC, LW 13:79).

The second line of defense that laissez-faire liberals used to
legitimate great economic disparities was to cite natural inequalities.
According to Herbert Spencer, Andrew Carnegie, and other "social
Darwinians" at the turn of the last century, government aid to
nonelites perpetuates the weak and vulnerable and allows them to
reproduce. During America's progressive age Dewey was the most
influential critic of social Darwinism—which is a social and

political theory, not Darwin's biological one (i.e., not Darwinism).[21] By insisting upon natural inequalities and a minimal role of government, social Darwinians had in effect elevated the "wants and endeavors of private individuals seeking personal [economic] gain to the place of supreme authority in social life" (LSA, LW 11:136).

It is obvious that people have differing capacities, but this has no logical bearing on equality as a moral ideal. What philosophers call "simple equality," the idea that all goods should be distributed equally, is mostly a straw man presented by antiegalitarians. It is a much-parodied view. In his 1961 dystopian short story "Harrison Bergeron," Kurt Vonnegut masterfully imagines a society that equally distributes talent, beauty, and intellect by handicapping all who have more than their fair share. Vonnegut's story pointedly illustrates the absurdity of simple equality, but it is much more importantly a cautionary tale about the popular tendency to value political ends such as justice, equality, and liberty irrespective of the results of the social means we use to attain them (TV, LW 13:229). This was Dewey's point. If his social and political philosophy could be distilled to a slogan, it would be: Steer clear of anyone's ends which are not stated "in terms of the social means he is using."[22]

Simple equality is not the terrain of serious philosophical dispute. What *is* disputed is the meaning of equality of opportunity. For Dewey it meant "establishing the basic conditions through which and because of which every human being might become all that he was capable of becoming" (LW 11:168). One person is morally equal to another when each has like opportunities for developing unlike capacities (see 1932 E, LW 7:346).[23]

Consider access to health care. For the laissez-faire liberal (a.k.a. the conservative), if the laws governing health insurance, prescription drugs, or birth control are the same for everyone, then this implies equal opportunity to purchase it as a commodity. From that angle, equal opportunity and liberty already exist in many industrialized countries, and it is unclear why progressives are fussing about it. For Dewey, in opposition, genuine equality of opportunity is a high notion expressed in our old democratic moral ideals. The modest and often flawed legislation passed under Franklin D. Roosevelt's 1930s "New Deal" was responding to a crisis provoked by classical liberalism: namely, in Dewey's words, that legal or merely formal liberty does not on its own amount to effective or actual liberty. Equality and freedom under the law is only a start, though it is a start, toward equalization and liberty in practice. Such equalization demands a transformation of our false and fragile economic order because an equal opportunity to develop ourselves "is impossible when vast economic inequality is the established rule" (LSA, LW 11:168).[24]

Democracy begins in conversation

A graduate of any high school in the United States once learned in an American history class—and then promptly forgot—about the debates that raged in the 1790s between Hamiltonians and Jeffersonians on the appropriate scale of national government. Alexander Hamilton and the Federalists advocated a powerful, centralized adaptation of familiar monarchical systems, while Thomas Jefferson and the Democratic Republicans envisioned a less centralized form of government organized along lines akin to New England town meetings as units small enough for face-to-face communication and noncoercive problem-solving. Although the Federalists collapsed as a party, their more centralized vision was gradually realized, ironically in part through Jefferson's own presidency.[25] The great federal projects of the nineteenth and twentieth centuries followed, from the Union Pacific railroad to Hoover Dam to the man on the moon. Amid resource scarcity and an increasingly volatile climate, many of today's supporters of local sustainable agriculture and locally generated renewable energy see their advocacies in an early Jeffersonian light.

In *Freedom and Culture*, Dewey explored and affirmed three pillars of Jefferson's democratic outlook, shaved of a Creator, natural rights, self-evident truths, and aristocratic assumptions. First, American democracy is experimental, and judicial "idolatry of the Constitution as it stands" is undemocratic (FC, LW 13:174). "Is it constitutional?" is a less significant question of legislation, jurisprudence, and action than "Is it wise?" Law alone cannot protect civil liberties. Dewey quoted Jefferson: "We might as well require a man to wear the coat which fitted him when a boy, as civilized society to remain ever under the regime of their barbarous ancestors" (in FC, LW 13:174).[26]

Second, John Locke wrote in the late seventeenth century about the necessity for securing natural rights to life, liberty, and property. Dewey agreed with Jefferson's revision: not property, but "the pursuit of happiness." For Jefferson the property held by an individual is not a claim that the government is duty-bound to uphold. It is secured by rights that are constructed through a social pact. The pursuit of happiness, on the other hand, was for Jefferson an inherent, untradeable right that must be secured against the arbitrary will of others, particularly against the impositions of government officials and wealthy plutocrats (FC, LW 13:177).

Third, community for Jefferson was an ideal that incorporated but went beyond associating with each other. Community meant more than what we call "society." It involves, in Dewey's expanded version of Jefferson's ideal, communication in the sense of sharing ideas and emotions, or jointly envisioning projects that foster value-rich individual lives (FC, LW 13:176).[27] Prior to the world wars of the twentieth century there was no lack of associating and certainly no lack of reactive crowd conformity. But there was not a great deal of community and communication, particularly not across ethnic and national boundaries. The First World War proved that interdependent societies formed by industrialization had been unable to form an integrated community to envision a national or international future together. Dewey argued in *The Public and Its Problems* that this disintegration was due in considerable measure to the stagnant individualistic framework of laissez-faire liberalism (PP, LW 2:315).

What Dewey sought, and credited Jefferson with articulating, was a more fulfilling life, a more widely shared liberty, and a more durable happiness. Due to repeated economic dislocation, Jefferson's democratic ideal—and it was always a moral ideal, not just a narrowly utilitarian one—became obscured and confused (FC, LW 13:178). The theologically based individualism that preceded classical liberalism held that everyone counts *one* because we are all equally created in the image of God. As this notion lost its cultural traction, free market individualism co-opted Jefferson's democratic ideal and its moral force waned (FC, LW 13:179). The pursuit of personal flourishing was shunted into consumptive forms of hyperindividualistic association that are ill-fitted to experimental intelligence, an equal economic footing, and a citizenry educated for democratic decision-making.

Dewey said that "democracy must begin at home, and its home is the neighborly community" (UPMP:176; PP, LW 2:367–68). He had in mind face-to-face conversations with family, friends, and neighbors in the local community as a participatory medium for awakening our slumbering democratic imagination—from schools to markets to neighborhood associations and meetings (PP, LW 2:371). "Democracy begins in conversation," he said at his ninetieth birthday party.[28] He was well aware in the 1930s and 1940s, however, that functional communication at a distance was rapidly developing and that this would to a considerable degree come to stand in for physical proximity (UPMP:177). We have vastly more information about the world than our ancestors did, Dewey wrote seventy-five years ago, but many people are overwhelmed by momentarily exciting yet unfathomed information that is prepackaged for consumption. We like prepared ideas as much as we like prepared foods, Dewey noted (FC, LW 13:95–96).

In his academic bestseller *Bowling Alone* (2000) and in subsequent research, sociologist Robert Putnam cites evidence of an increasing decline of trust and community in the United States despite increasing association across distances and time. In our own dispersive age of globalization and connectivity, we should consider with Dewey whether the national and global problems and transitions we face might be better solved with a democratic citizenry that has also learned to deal with vexing problems at a more manageable scale. At a neighborly scale we can imagine more concretely the situations at hand, assess relevant information, and mediate conflicts to converge upon solutions. Parochialism abounds, but in Dewey's view communal ties and interactions can also expand and reinforce our perceptions and judgments by enabling us to draw on a cumulative wealth of experience, which is preparatory for effectively engaging and reforming national and international affairs and institutions.

Of course community is not identical to democracy—it is necessary, but not on its own sufficient. There have been totalitarian societies, and pockets of community, "arousing the emotion of common intolerance and hate" (UPMP:176). These reactive, antidemocratic societies have built internal and external walls between in-groups and out-groups, forbidding free communication and equal participation in the conduct of life (DE, MW 9:105).

What are the originating conditions of such societies? Dewey argued in the 1940s that the ascension of totalitarian states in the twentieth century grew out of a loss of community, or at least a loss of healthy community. Contrary to the common view, atomistic individualism and totalitarianism are not polarities. Each developed from customs and institutions—including religious institutions with their archaic maps of existence—too outdated to deal with changed conditions and needs. These customs and institutions disintegrated and maladjusted individuals, leaving them in Dewey's terms "lost," which is to say alienated. This is to be expected when we journey with an obsolete map of the self-world relationship. "This seemingly sudden outbreak of totalitarian collectivism," Dewey argued with a helpfully italicized image, "was in fact the breaking *through* the surface, into overt manifestation, of underlying phases of the previous individualism" (LW 15:215). Yet we continue to fail to engage in open and shared inquiry to reintegrate lost individuals into democratic communities and institutions (see UPMP:xxxviii).

Democracy as a way of life expresses a social hope that we can expand communities and gain intimacy in relationships while celebrating individual liberties. Dewey emphasized pluralistic participation and relative decentralization (consonant with the use of governmental power to secure effective liberty for all) in opposition to the politics of centralization and total unification. He saw democracy as exemplifying what is best in communal existence, and he identified democratic societies as those capable of securing "flexible readjustment" of social institutions (DE, MW 9:105).

But how do we direct culture toward democracy? Dewey's faith in democracy was, at bottom, faith in the educative capacity of experience. "Faith in democracy," he urged, "is all one with faith in experience and education" (LW 14:229).

Democratic education vs. industrial education

The locus of social reconstruction, Dewey declared in his widely read manifesto "My Pedagogic Creed" (1897), must be education

particular figure, it was psychologist Edward Thorndike (1874–1949). Thorndike, an early behavioral psychologist who was an active proponent of eugenics and changeless hereditary intelligence, sought to develop a quantitative educational science. He held that administrators and teachers could implement the findings of this scientific research through an industrial management system. Administrative progressives sought to establish efficient educational mechanisms and filters such as mass standardized testing to measure and prepare future employees with the knowledge and skills needed to serve industrial sectors. As Ellen Lagemann observes, Thorndike saw education as "a technique for matching individuals to existing social and economic roles."[31]

There were other concurrent movements for educational reform in the first half of the twentieth century, with many permutations—in *The Struggle for the American Curriculum*, Herbert Kliebard distinguishes four movements. I will follow Labaree's and Lagemann's distinction of two principal channels down which these various movements flowed to affect twenty-first-century speech and practices.[32]

When policymakers and administrators speak today of "educating for careers," it is wise to investigate their meaning. While professor of philosophy at the University of Michigan in 1893, Dewey had influentially written:

> If I were asked to name the most needed of all reforms in the spirit of education I should say: "Cease conceiving of education as mere preparation for later life, and make of it the full meaning of the present life." And to add that only in this case does it become truly a preparation for later life is not the paradox it seems. An activity which does not have worth enough to be carried on for its own sake cannot be very effective as a preparation for something else.
>
> (EW 4:50)

Accordingly, Dewey rejected what he called "trade education" and instead championed holistic incorporation of callings and vocations into a rich cultural education. We do not promote cultural education when we cut it off, with no feedback loop, from the motivating curiosity and interest students have in engaging life's ever-evolving practical occupations. That cultural feedback loop and academic lifeline also gives greater significance and direction to practical life. Such an education achieves democratic ends by equipping students with the tools they need to intelligently overhaul current practices and create new vocations, institutions, and systems.

In diametrical opposition to Dewey, administrative progressives ushered in the age of trade education as a "means of securing technical efficiency in specialized future pursuits" (DE, MW 9:326). Dewey sought to establish conditions for personal flourishing (intellectual, aesthetic, and moral), imaginative inquiry, democratic participation, and lifelong learning. The administrative progressives sought a padded yoke for the industrial workforce so that the plow could be pulled more efficiently.

Dewey argued that curriculum and instruction in formal schooling are too often either:

- overintellectualized (in the sense of ignoring practical life and the child's native curiosity and interests), or
- overpractical (in the sense of being training grounds for specialized skills).

Traditional "great books" advocates tended to overintellectualize education. In 1944 the presidents of the University of Chicago and Columbia University attacked Deweyan progressive education as "a most reactionary philosophy" that had, they claimed, led to wayward and undisciplined youths. These traditionalists argued that an "education for freedom" requires us to sharply separate liberal education in the classics from vocational education. Education in our highest cultural peaks, they urged, is dumbed down when we fail to segregate it from an education for practical occupations. Asked during an interview about these remarks, Dewey dismissed them as "childish." He replied that the University of Chicago president "calls for liberal education of a small, elite group and vocational education for the masses. I cannot think of any idea more completely reactionary and more fatal to the whole democratic outlook."[33] Dewey had concisely summed up his view in a 1932 letter: "The cultural and the vocational overlap."[34] Regardless, in the 1940s Deweyism became a blanket label for the ills of a lax educational system with academic standards too low to keep up with the Soviet Union during the coming Cold War.

Administrative progressives were overpractical, perpetuating "the industrial régime that now exists" in a way that turns educators and students into serfs for a "feudal dogma of social predestination" (DE, MW 9:328). His view of childhood learning underlaid this sharp condemnation. Children are alert to affairs beyond our labels and sorting mechanisms, beyond what McDermott memorably calls our grown-up "linguistic condom."[35] Dewey was keenly attentive to what he and James called the "plasticity" of children which, together with an appreciation of the child's native sociality and curiosity, formed the roots of his educational vision. If our primary educational aim is to "mold" the plasticity of children to fit the specifications of our extant economic infrastructure, then we straitjacket the child's potential, and our best hope for cultural growth and transformation is directed down the very channels that are implicated in our problems. This does not cultivate democratic intelligence. Dewey recognized long before our twenty-first-century economic, environmental, and geopolitical struggles that riding the highway of the consumer economy is not just problematic when we hit an obstacle; it can be equally problematic when the traffic is moving as it is supposed to move.

Dewey asked what practical social benefits could genuinely accrue when curriculum developers, policymakers, and school administrators trump the interests of the child with the purported interests of society instead of educating children to participate in the intelligent redirection of society. Does it serve the public good to extinguish the spark of imagination and curiosity in a child? Does it serve the public good to relegate teachers to functionaries under the surveillance of an administrative bureaucracy? Do we educate for democracy when we reduce teachers to technicians who administer lessons and implement the findings of educational researchers? This is perhaps education for plutocracy, aristocracy, or monarchy, but it is not education for democracy.

Who won, Dewey or Thorndike? Lagemann's judgment reflects the consensus among educational historians: "One cannot understand the history of education in the United States during the twentieth century unless one realizes that Edward L. Thorndike won and John Dewey lost."[36] Labaree clarifies that Thorndike won for control of actual school structures and practices, while Dewey won for control of the rhetoric that guides schools of education.[37] A saying popular among university professors of education is: "We talk Dewey, and we do Thorndike."[38]

Despite still-popular hand-waving toward Dewey's child-centered rhetoric, from the standpoint of Dewey's philosophy the tragic flaw of much current educational practice is that it is situated in institutional structures that systematically sacrifice the emotional and aesthetic lives of children. When schooling is too narrowly practical, it does not support emotional "development of the healthy animal, development of affections, relations of the children to each other and to parents" (LW 17:515). When education is approached as the machinery for efficiently producing the industrial workforce, or traditionally as a means of static cultural transmission, it "strikingly exhibits a subordination of the living present to a remote and precarious future. To prepare, to get ready, is its keynote. The actual outcome is lack of adequate preparation, of intelligent adaptation" (HNC, MW 14:185).

But education is not merely preparation. It is growth: my growth, our growth. Growth, and not subsistence alone, is the defining characteristic of biological organisms. Consequently, "education is all one with growing; it has no end beyond itself. The criterion of the value of school education is the extent in which it creates a desire for continued growth and supplies means for making the desire effective in fact" (DE, MW 9:58; cf. AE, LW 10:20).

Despite Dewey's opposition, administrative progressivism was the main channel down which the still-developing notion of education-as-business eventually flowed. Dewey's concerns go well beyond contemporary critiques of "diploma mills" and "degree factories," as though our problem is principally one of academic standards. On an industrial model, educating whole persons for lifelong growth is replaced by education as just another industrial sector, on a par with any other sector. Education's job is to manufacture skilled labor for the market in a way that is maximally efficient.[39] Knowledge on this model is a market commodity, teachers are delivery vehicles for knowledge content, and students are either consumers or manufactured products. Educational institutions on the industrial model are marketplaces for delivering and acquiring content, tuition is the fair price for accessing that content, and the high-to-low grade differential is the means for incentivizing competition. It is not clear where growth, community, and democracy come into the picture.

Drudge work in an educational factory is not, Dewey argued, a means to high culture or high quality of life. A school or industry may gain efficiency and increase productivity by frustrating human fulfillment. "Action restricted to given and fixed ends may attain great technical efficiency," he noted, "but efficiency is the only quality to which it can lay claim" (MW 10:45). The school may train more students with fewer teachers, and an industrial sector may produce more clothes, cars, or animal protein to meet market demands with lower overhead costs. These products can then be used, or put to work to produce more things. *The industrial imagination stops here, with efficient production.* This is useful, but what else has been unintentionally made, to which industrial thinking is oblivious? Have we made narrower lives? Have we embittered and disabled? Have we anesthetized moral and ecological sensitivity? Have we made life more "congested, hurried, confused and extravagant" (EN, LW 1:272)? Efficiency is a means, but it becomes deadening when it is worshiped as an inherently worthwhile end.

When we say an activity is useful, we mean it fulfills a need. The deepest of human needs, Dewey argued, "is for possession and appreciation of the meaning of things" (EN, LW 1:272; cf. LW 5:66–76). But this is precisely what is sidelined and unsatisfied by administrative progressivism and by much of the industrial status quo. In the terms of existentialism and Marxism, human existence is left alienated (see LW 5:66–76).[40] The technologies of mass production and consumption have produced, Dewey believed, "everywhere a hardness, a tightness, a clamping down of the lid, a regimentation and standardization, a devotion to efficiency and prosperity of a mechanical and quantitative sort" (LW 3:134). When social interactions are tight and mechanical, they are also unimaginative. Goods of human life are repressed rather than enjoyed, and difficulties are treated in isolation rather than comprehensively.

Imagination enables us to stretch beyond our conditioning (i.e., the way we have been constructed by our history) and to tap into present possibilities. Its engagement is "the only thing that makes any activity more than mechanical" (DE, MW 9:244). Imagination enables us to be genuinely creative while also tapping the experiences—including "mis-educative experiences" (EE, LW 13:27)—of others. To choke it is culturally suicidal.

Progressive pedagogy in moral education

In *Interest and Effort in Education* (1913), Dewey addressed a fiery debate between conservatives and progressives. Conservatives underscore effort in education, and they accuse progressives of sugarcoating that weakens the self-discipline needed to face unpleasant matters. Progressives underscore interest, and they accuse conservatives of a tough-it-out method that eventuates not in vigorous self-discipline but in dullness or narrowness. Dewey argued that both misconceive the educational object as something external to the self, something "outside the sphere of self" that must either be *made* artificially interesting or mastered through sheer exertion of will (MW 7:156).

As Dewey articulated most forcefully in *Art as Experience*, whenever we have a purpose we desire to realize, we have a durable interest in moving it along. When learning an idea, fact, or skill is called for as part of a student's own growth, teachers do not need to occupy themselves with creating "momentary excitations" that catch attention, nor do they need to appeal to will power.

Interest is "the identification of mind with the material and methods of a developing activity" (MW 7:195, 197). Effort, meanwhile, is a demand for persistence and "continuity in the face of difficulties" (MW 7:174–75). Interest and effort are essential to learning and growing, but they are not aims on their own. When we strive to understand and establish the conditions that elicit interest, both interest and effort develop spontaneously. Dewey wrote: "When we recognize there are certain powers within the child urgent for development … we have a firm basis upon which to build. Effort arises normally in the attempt to give full operation, and thus growth and completion, to these powers. Adequately to act upon these impulses involves seriousness, absorption, definiteness of purpose; it results in formation of steadiness and persistent habit in the service of worthy ends" (MW 7:159–60).

It is beyond my limited scope to discuss curricular content and educational materials, but a case study may offer a holistic glimpse of transformative Deweyan pedagogy. Dewey observed that we all learn in concentric circles of increasing abstraction. Children in his "laboratory school" at the University of Chicago at the turn of the last century learned mathematics and economics through a carefully designed, and challenging, curriculum that included gardening as well as cooking in the school kitchen. For a contemporary parallel, take the Edible Schoolyard project at the Martin Luther King Jr. Middle School in Berkeley, California. Children from the inner city plant, nurture, and harvest food in a schoolyard garden, cook it in the school kitchen, and consume it in the dining hall. These activities are not superadded onto the "real" curricular work at the school; they are thoroughly woven into the curriculum.

Through an ongoing rhythm of doing and reflecting these children learn, for example, about the recycling loop of growth, maturity, decline, death, and decay. The educational materials are communicated socially, but they are not "a special isolated set of facts and ideas" (MW 7:250). Rather, the information is organically assimilated. Because this knowledge is shared with a new generation in an active, personal, and direct way that connects information to observation and experiment in an applied context, it is an achievement that is more readily retained and put to work. Far from "useless pedantry," it is of value in the direction of life (MW 7: 250).

In their daily activities in the Edible Schoolyard, children are continuously developing their capacity for ecological simulation in the garden, in the kitchen, in the dining hall, and in the brick-and-mortar classroom. They explore how food cycles in the garden intersect larger natural systems: the water cycle, the cycle of seasons, and the like.[41] When all goes well, these children are intrinsically motivated to learn through passionate engagement in the activities.

As part of the curriculum, these children also experience first-hand the aesthetic, moral, and intellectual value of noticing and tracing the hidden relationships wound up with everyday food choices. This sets conditions for them to learn that every action has systemic consequences. That ecological factoid is today dispensed in all schools, but secondhand information does not equip children as well to become the kinds of people who habitually take a measure of active responsibility for these rippling consequences. Having a great deal of free-floating information that hitches only to other information does not on its own make one informed in any functional way (MW 7:250–51). But children engaging in the Edible Schoolyard may be a bit wiser in navigating life's terrain. They are "preparing for success," to invoke the overused catchphrase—not success in their ability to out-consume others, but success in their ability to perceive and respond effectively and productively in a moving world.

The Edible Schoolyard is one educational model among many that may enable our civilization over time to better negotiate complex social and natural systems. These are moral aims, and, as shown in Chapter Four, Dewey did not shy away from discussing moral education, so long as we approach it not as a separate area of study but as formal and informal efforts to selectively cultivate behavioral dispositions. He did, however, raise a yellow caution flag to warn against propagandistic Orwellian reeducation. Any reflection on the aims of moral education must compensate for at least three all-too-common mistakes:

1. Moral education is confused with moralistic lessons. This style of instruction is inherently undemocratic, ethically misguided, and pedagogically bankrupt. It does not take personal or cultural transformation seriously, but seeks only to perpetuate established mores.
2. Education is too often conceived narrowly and dualistically as content mastery in a formal classroom while the classroom is conceived as a (mostly) value-free space. Moral education, in that case, is at best an oxymoron, at worst a bad idea.
3. As discussed in Chapter Four, most Westerners conceive moral maturation primarily as progressive sophistication in applying rules and principles. As a result, much of what might pass for "moral education" is too cut-and-dried to imaginatively mediate real muddles.

Perhaps the greatest challenge for moral education in the twenty-first century, as for the twentieth, arises from the fact that we are culturally challenged when it comes to intelligently guiding scientific discoveries and technical developments. One source of our confusion is the dualistic tendency to draw a very bright line separating our sciences and technologies from our moral ideals, the material realm of facts from the ideal realm of values, and the natural from the human. Much of our moral heritage was developed, canned, and preserved on a shelf well before the development of modern science, and long before twentieth- and twenty-first-century technologies. Pickled morals would be fine if they enabled us to deal with the problems we currently face. But they do not, so we experience what Dewey called a "cultural lag." Our moral heritage lags far behind the new and complicated techno-industrial society that it must speak to. Recent scientific discoveries and technical developments are at the tip of a historical iceberg of basic habits and institutions that are too deeply established to be easily inspected, evaluated, and changed (LW 15:199–200; cf. QC, LW 4:203–28).

In "Dualism and the Split Atom: Science and Morals in the Atomic Age" (LW 15:199–203), written in 1945 just after the atomic bombings of Hiroshima and Nagasaki, Dewey reasserted his trust in the possibility for intelligent direction of technological innovations as the only live alternative to a destructive laissez-faire outlook. But only education, he repeated, can bring about the essential cultural transformation. The wedge between our moral heritage, on one side, and our troubled industrial–technological circumstances, on the other side, has been driven deeper by zealous guardians of morality intent on separating received dogmas from the sort of empirical inspection and methods that would destabilize them (LW 15:201). Faith, hope, and love endure, but their meaning and expression are tied up in inflexible doctrines. There is a misfit between these doctrines and problematic factual conditions, and uncritically perpetuating the doctrines does not improve the fit. Dewey concluded the essay ominously: "if the atomic splitting by science and its technological application in the bomb fail to teach us that we live in a world of change so that our ways of organization of human interrelationships must also change, the case is well-nigh hopeless" (LW 15:202–3).

Through innovative education like the Edible Schoolyard, moral but not moralizing, teachers and learners may become better at perceiving the complex nature of problems, evoking imaginative searches for technical and communal solutions, and critiquing inherited prejudices and insensitivities that stand in the way of working democratically toward those solutions (FC, LW 13:79). This is not news to Dewey-inspired progressive educators, who have for some decades been experimenting with pedagogies that are more rooted ("place-based"), sensitive to context, interdisciplinary and integrative, and pluralistic. Such educators regard teachers and students as co-inquirers striving to refine aesthetic sensibility while disclosing relationships that can confer greater significance through our lives together.

Summary

In Dewey's view the job of modern intellectuals is to critically respond to the unrealized opportunity to humanize technological–industrial civilization. The road to reconstruction is blocked by classical laissez-faire liberals (a.k.a. doctrinaire conservatives) who have long held that our penchant for looking out for number one is due to our essential and unchanging human nature, and not (they think) due to historical and cultural conditions. Free market capitalism, they argue, is not simply an economic engine worth giving a try, but the right system ideally suited to running on the fuel of self-interested human nature. In part as a consequence of such atomistic individualism, the technologies of mass production and consumption have produced social interactions that are regimented, standardized, tight, hardened, mechanical, and hence unimaginative. Goods of human life are repressed rather than enjoyed, and difficulties are treated in isolation rather than comprehensively. In his social and political philosophy Dewey aimed to reform these entrenched conditions through a form of radicalism for grown-ups, those with the patience to secure the "democratic means to achieve our democratic ends" (LW 11:332). By "democratic means" Dewey meant above all education. His faith in democracy was, at bottom, faith in the educative capacity of experience. Whenever people have a purpose they desire to realize, they have a durable interest in moving it along. The aim of Deweyan education is lifelong growth, and he steadfastly opposed any reduction of education to a mere industrial sector whose job is to manufacture skilled labor for the workforce in a way that is maximally efficient.

Notes

1 Steven Kiernan, *Authentic Patriotism* (London: Macmillan, 2010), 271.

2 On Dewey and race, see Shannon Sullivan, *Revealing Whiteness: The Unconcious Habits of Racial Privelege* (Bloomington, IN: Indiana University Press, 2007). Cf. J. E. Tiles, *John Dewey: Political Theory and Social Practice*, vol. 2 of *John Dewey: Critical Assessments* (London: Routledge, 1992), 132ff.

3 See Charlene Haddock Seigfried, Introduction to Jane Addams' *Democracy and Social Ethics* (Urbana, IL: University of Illinois Press, 2002), xi. On the contemporary capabilities approach, see for example, Martha C. Nussbaum, *Creating Capabilities: The Human Development Approach* (Cambridge, MA: Belknap Press, 2011).

4 See Thomas M. Alexander, "John Dewey's Uncommon Faith: Understanding 'Religious Experience,'" *American Catholic Philosophical Quarterly* 87, no. 2 (2013): 347–62, at 353.

5 See Melvin Rogers's excellent introduction to *The Public and Its Problems* (University Park, PA: Pennsylvania University Press, 2012).

6 Despite Niebuhr's unsympathetic portrayal of Dewey as a universalizing "bourgeois liberal," they both agreed that perfect fulfillment is unattainable.

7 For a full picture of Dewey's hopeful, melioristic, but not naïve sense of tragedy and potential progress, see Melvin Rogers, *The Undiscovered Dewey* (New York: Columbia University Press, 2008).

8 Missing this point, a contemporaneous critic wrote that Dewey's philosophy "assumes that if things are only given the opportunity to work themselves out completely they must inevitably work themselves out well" (quoted in textual apparatus to QC, LW 4:273).

9 Cf. Ralph Ross, Introduction to *Reconstruction in Philosophy* (MW 12:xxix).

10 G. W. F. Hegel, *Phenomenology of Spirit*, Preface, trans. A. V. Miller (Delhi: Motilal Banarsidass Publishers, 1998), 45.

11 Cf. George Eliot's finale to *Middlemarch* (London: Penguin Classics, 1965 [1871–72]), 896.

12 Robert B. Westbrook, *John Dewey and American Democracy* (Ithaca, NY: Cornell University Press, 1991). For a view of Dewey as more middle-of-the-road, with less participatory emphasis, see Alan Ryan, *John Dewey and the High Tide of American Liberalism* (New York: W. W. Norton & Co., 1995).

13 Work today in positive psychology by Martin Seligman and others shows that, if it is within your power, aim for optimism over pessimism. You will be happier. James and Dewey were making a finer-tuned distinction about the sort of trust or confidence (or "faith") required to ameliorate circumstances; they were not knocking the psychological benefits of optimism.

14 1920.09.12 (04102): Dewey to Albert Barnes.

15 Jessica Ching-Sze Wang, *John Dewey in China* (Albany, NY: SUNY Press, 2007), 50.

16 Fei, in Wang, *John Dewey in China*, 50–51, italics added.

17 See Westbrook, *John Dewey and American Democracy*, 469ff., on Dewey's indictment of communism.

18 In *Human Nature and Conduct*, Dewey crisply summed up this perennial conservative line of argument that he rejected: "Wary, experienced men of the world have always ... thought to find in the doctrine of native instincts a scientific support for asserting the practical unalterability of human nature. ... Effort for the serious alteration of human institutions is utopian. As things have been so they will be. The more they change the more they remain the same" (HNC, MW 14:76).

19 See Robert D. Putnam and David E. Campbell, *American Grace: How Religion Divides and Unites Us* (New York: Simon & Schuster, 2010).

20 Dewey spilled a great deal of ink criticizing state socialism as coercive, but he can be safely categorized as a democratic socialist with regard to state ownership of utilities. For example, in "America's Public Ownership Program," a 1934 discussion of electricity, mines, oil, and natural resource conservation, Dewey wrote: "The one great question before the American public is whether ... it has the intelligence and courage to take over the basic agencies of public welfare and manage them for the welfare of all the people" (LW 9:286).

21 *Survival of the fittest* is Spencer's term, not Darwin's. However, Darwin did eventually use the phrase in the sixth edition of *On the Origin of Species*.

22 George Herbert Mead, "The Philosophies of Royce, James, and Dewey in Their American Setting," in *John Dewey: The Man and His Philosophy*, Addresses Delivered in New York in Celebration of His Seventieth Birthday (Cambridge, MA: Harvard University Press, 1930), 104–5.

23 For an exploration of equality that engages Dewey with a focus on intellectual disability, see Heather E. Keith and Kenneth D. Keith, *Intellectual Disability: Ethics, Dehumanization, and a New Moral Community* (Chichester: Wiley-Blackwell, 2013). For a discussion of moral equality in education, see Jim Garrison, *Dewey and Eros: Wisdom and Desire in the Art of Thinking* (New York: Teachers College Press, 1997).

24 The civil rights movement of the 1950s and 1960s, the women's movement of the 1970s, and the marriage equality movement today have built in part on modest Depression-era achievements in public legislation such as the Social Security Act of 1935.

25 See Jon Meacham, *Thomas Jefferson: The Art of Power* (New York: Random House, 2012).

26 Of the United States Constitution, Dewey wrote in a 1915 letter: "The American people have made a rather bad document fairly workable." 1915.07.05 (03542): John Dewey to Scudder Klyce.

27 For a genealogy of Dewey's pragmatism in a social and political context that includes Jefferson's heritage, see Robert B. Westbrook's *Democratic Hope: Pragmatism and the Politics of Truth* (Ithaca, NY: Cornell University Press, 2005).

28 1965.11.05 (21701): James T. Farrell to "whom it may concern."

29 John J. McDermott, *The Philosophy of John Dewey* (Chicago: University of Chicago Press, 1981), 421.

30 David F. Labaree, "Progressivism, Schools and Schools of Education: An American Romance," *Paedagogica Historica* 41, no. 1–2 (2005): 283–84.

31 Ellen Condliffe Lagemann, "The Plural Worlds of Educational Research," *History of Education Quarterly* 29, no. 2 (1989): 184–214, at 212.

32 See Herbert M. Kliebard, *The Struggle for the American Curriculum, 1893–1958* (London: Routledge, 1986).

33 "John Dewey, at 85, Defends Doctrines," *The Collected Works of John Dewey, 1882–1953*, Supplementary Volume 1, electronic edition, ed. Larry A. Hickman (InteLex, 1989–2013), 234.

34 1932.03.30 (07522): John Dewey to Abraham Flexner.

35 John J. McDermott, *The Drama of Possibility: Experience as Philosophy of Culture* (New York: Fordham University Press, 2007), 206.

36 Lagemann, "The Plural Worlds of Educational Research," 184–214. Cf. Stephen Tomlinson, "Edward Lee Thorndike and John Dewey on the Science of Education," *Oxford Review of Education* 23, no. 3 (1997), 365–83.

37 Labaree, "Progressivism, Schools and Schools of Education: An American Romance," 279–80.

38 Jim Garrison, private communication.

39 On Dewey, moral equality, and industrialized standards in education, see Jim Garrison, "Individuality, Equality, and Creative Democracy—The Task Before Us," *American Journal of Education* 118, no. 3 (2012): 369–79.

40 Cf. Alexander, "John Dewey's Uncommon Faith: Understanding 'Religious Experience,'" 352.

41 Cf. Fritjof Capra, "Speaking Nature's Language: Principles of Sustainability," in *Ecological Literacy*, ed. Michael K. Stone and Zenobia Barlow (Boston: Sierra Club Books, 2005), 18–29. On the Edible Schoolyard project, see: https://edibleschoolyard.org/; accessed July 17, 2014.

Further reading

Jim Garrison, *Dewey and Eros: Wisdom and Desire in the Art of Thinking* (New York: Teachers College Press, 1997). Reissued by Information Age Publishing, 2010.

Melvin Rogers, *The Undiscovered Dewey* (New York: Columbia University Press, 2008).

John J. Stuhr, "Dewey's Social and Political Philosophy," in *Reading Dewey: Interpretations for a Postmodern Generation*, ed. Larry A. Hickman (Bloomington, IN: Indiana University Press, 1998), 82–99.

Robert B. Westbrook, *John Dewey and American Democracy* (Ithaca, NY: Cornell University Press, 1991).

Six

Aesthetics and technology reconstructed

The only distinction worth drawing is not between practice and theory, but between those modes of practice that are not intelligent, not inherently and immediately enjoyable, and those which are full of enjoyed meanings. When this perception dawns, it will be a commonplace that art—the mode of activity that is charged with meanings capable of immediately enjoyed possession—is the complete culmination of nature, and that "science" is properly a handmaiden that conducts natural events to this happy issue.

(EN, LW 1:269)

The juxtaposition of aesthetics and technology in this chapter's title will strike many as counterintuitive. Yet Dewey held that the greatest problem of modern techno-industrial civilizations is the need to reconcile scientific–technological attitudes with aesthetic ones. The first sections of this chapter build on concepts and arguments examined in prior chapters to introduce Dewey's aesthetic theory and philosophy of art (taking jazz as a model), especially as set forth in Experience and Nature, "Qualitative Thought," and Art as Experience. My aim will be to explain the concept of consummatory experience as the unifying pulse of Dewey's philosophy, and I will generally avoid the temptation to explicitly engage him in twenty-first-century debates among aestheticians. Subsequent sections highlight the importance of his theory of consummatory experience for, first, his view of moral intelligence, and second, his approach to technology. I explain his instrumentalist approach to science and technology from the standpoint of his aesthetic theory, which is the qualitative standpoint from which Dewey himself interpreted science and technology: they should be conceived in the service of the aesthetic.

Consummations

If there is a single beating heart of Dewey's philosophy, it is his
belief that experience has a fundamental developmental principle.
We commonly speak of an experience in the singular, as when we
say "that was an experience!" after a hospital stay, a traffic jam, a
sporting event, a concert, an amusement park ride, a party, an
argument, an exam, a special meal, or a romantic encounter. We
speak of *an* experience when experience becomes sufficiently
demarcated from other experiences so that it has a coherent story to
tell, from commencement to culmination. "An experience has a
unity that gives it its name, *that* meal, that storm, that rupture of
friendship" (AE, LW 10:44).

Our lives do not flow evenly. Life "is a thing of histories, each
with its own plot, its own inception and movement toward its
close, each having its own particular rhythmic movement; each
with its own unrepeated quality pervading it throughout" (AE, LW
10:42–43; cf. EEL, MW 10:321–24). There is an urge to complete
our emerging "histories," though distractions, routines, and
lethargy often bring us up short. This is why we generally remember things that are unfinished or that do not have closure, as when
an unfinished job nags at us. Dewey explained this drive toward
consummation:

> We have *an* experience when the material experienced runs its
> course to fulfillment. Then and then only is it integrated within
> and demarcated in the general stream of experience from other
> experiences. A piece of work is finished in a way that is satis-
> factory; a problem receives its solution; a game is played
> through; a situation, whether that of eating a meal, playing a
> game of chess, carrying on a conversation, writing a book, or
> taking part in a political campaign, is so rounded out that its
> close is a consummation and not a cessation. Such an experi-
> ence is a whole and carries with it its own individualizing
> quality and self-sufficiency. It is *an* experience.
>
> (AE, LW 10:42)

The greatest human tragedy is the failure of experience to be
consummated and fulfilled. When we dwell on a worrisome future

or a regretful past, or are numbed by conventional routine, imagination becomes so contracted that we do not act to realize the world's creative potentialities. Dewey observed that in such experiences "one thing replaces another, but does not absorb it and carry it on. There is experience, but so slack and discursive that it is not *an* experience" (AE, LW 10:47). This is not just a private tragedy; it diminishes us all. Creative action matters.

Tragically, as revealed in the discussion of contemporary education in Chapter Five, our narrow utilitarian–industrial outlook directs our attention to activities that do not ultimately develop our experiences toward fulfillment and thereby make our lives more significant.[1] Many of the socialized canals down which our behaviors flow tend to narrow the affective horizon of immediate experience, to the detriment of meaningful, value-rich, and responsive lives.

Dewey endures today as a powerful ally in the fight against deadening efficiency, narrow means-end calculation, and "frantic exploitation" (LW 5:268; cf. UPMP:344). A stirring passage from *Experience and Nature* clarifies the real cost of a contracted industrial imagination that does not inquire into consequences of activities for quality of life:

> The existence of activities that have no immediate enjoyed intrinsic meaning is undeniable. They include much of our labors in home, factory, laboratory, and study. By no stretch of language can they be termed either artistic or esthetic. ... So we optimistically call them "useful" and let it go at that. ... If we were to ask useful for what? we should be obliged to examine their actual consequences, and when we once honestly and fully faced these consequences we should probably find ground for calling such activities detrimental rather than useful.
> (EN, LW 1:271–72)

When daily activities are divorced from a direct and moving interest in their ends or products, they become anesthetic, and whatever is best in the potential of work or leisure is frustrated and unfulfilled.

Dewey noted in his 1932 *Ethics* the truism that "things sometimes regarded as 'practical' are in truth highly impolitic and shortsighted."

But the way beyond such narrowness and shortsightedness is to engage and support the qualitative dimension of practical activities, not to condemn the practical as "low and mercenary in comparison with spiritual ideals" (1932 E, LW 7:209). We do not honor the aesthetic by denying its consummations to the vast bulk of daily life (see UPMP:344).

Stated in a general and idealized form, any experience transformed toward consummation has a beginning, middle, and conclusion just as journeys have starting points, paths traversed, and destinations. Each phase is distinct, though connected, as events develop toward fulfillment (cf. 1932 E, LW 7:168). The reader will recognize the general pattern from prior chapters. The starting point of the journey of *an* experience is an active phase of stable habits setting a dominant tone of relative equilibrium. The middle or path traversed is characterized by disrupted habit, disharmony with surroundings, and competition among habits and desires. The troubled situation becomes increasingly organized as a reflective phase of dramatic rehearsal predominates. The conclusion or destination is a consummatory phase of recovered action and reunification of desires. The conclusion takes a form that coherently expresses the tensions that initiated the journey (see HNC, MW 14:127).

Dewey married the source-path-goal structure of this temporally rich journey metaphor with that of experience as a field event. When reading Dewey on consummatory experience, it is helpful to keep both metaphors—journey and field—in mind. I introduced the notion of the "horizon" or "field" in Chapter Two to explain the term *situation*, which encompasses both the focus and the qualitative field of an experience. Alexander explains that our cultural inhabitation of nature is "a total *field* of action which has a complex structure at each and every moment and different degrees of focus, clarity, obscurity, and organization. ... Experience for Dewey is *both* process and field—a 'field-process,' if you will."[2]

As discussed in Chapter Four, Dewey highlighted that only through imagination do we creatively meet a situation's possibilities. The skilled carpenter grasps the potential of the wood; the experienced gardener grasps and cultivates the possibilities of the soil; the sculptor creatively envisions the expressive possibilities of stone, bronze, wood, or clay. Carpentry, gardening, and sculpting require us to consider "what may be, but is not yet" (DE, MW 9:153). Such imagination is fundamental to all genuine thinking—scientific, aesthetic, or moral.

If we wish to understand who we are, how we have meaningful and humdrum experiences, how we communicate with others, and indeed how we think and durably resolve problems, we must examine the immediately felt or qualitative dimension of experience. This is the aesthetic, the felt richness of life's consummations.[3] The aesthetic, for Dewey, was not a peculiar kind of emotion separate from the ordinary run of desires and feelings, nor was aesthetics as a philosophical study reducible for him solely to the philosophy of art. Dewey summarized his position: "I have tried to show ... that the esthetic is no intruder in experience from without, ... but that it is the clarified and intensified development of traits that belong to every normally complete experience" (AE, LW 10:52–53). We find consummations in writing a book, buying a house, going on a date, making a snowman, or running a double-blind experiment.

A few distinctions are essential at this point. Dewey treated inquiry (intelligent activity, thinking) as a subset of consummatory experience, uniquely important because *inquiry helps to make human fulfillments more secure and more widely shared*. Many of life's consummations in love, art, family, friendship, and nature are not outcomes of inquiry, and many are. Whether or not the consummation is an outcome of inquiry, it follows the same generic pattern of development toward *an* experience. Art was Dewey's prototype for this pattern of development. Dewey rejected attempts to drive a sharp wedge between art and inquiry. He sometimes spoke of art in terms of inquiry, but he more commonly spoke of the various forms of inquiry as arts—for example, operative arts and fine arts. To whatever extent artistic production and appreciation involve inquiry, it is a very distinctive *sort* of inquiry, one in which the most noteworthy outcome is aesthetic experience rather than knowledge or practical action.

It is because Dewey took art as the prototype for *an* experience that he preferred to speak of inquiry as an art. Inquiry is quite literally an art in the *broad* sense that it is an operative intellectual tool, just as an equation in physics is a tool. But Dewey also understood inquiry *as* art, and here it will help to see this as a rich metaphor— that is, inquiry for Dewey is both literally and metaphorically art.

Distinguishing this metaphorical sense best conveys how Dewey highlighted two features of inquiry at its best: (1) the way in which inquiry follows the generic pattern of development toward consummation, and (2) the way in which inquiry can be valued and enjoyed for itself.

To bring these abstractions down to earth, consider your own best, and worst, writing experiences. When our stabs at writing are incomplete and underdeveloped, the quality of the product generally suffers. Such experiences tend to be relatively shallow and narrow, and the expressive object (e.g., an essay) is too loosely organized to give coherent form to *relevant* (quantity is insignificant) connections and relationships. A well-developed writing experience, *like any form of inquiry*, concludes with provisional resolution of discordance, or more precisely it involves thousands of resolutions—such as your felt sense for the right word—bound together as parts of an overarching experience. In your search for the right word, conflicting tendencies in the writing situation create a tension, evoking an affective phase in which emotions come to the fore. This spurs imaginative rehearsal to resolve the tension. Imagination shuttles back and forth between alternative words and the immediate context that needs to be mediated. Emotions climax as a choice is made that at least tentatively completes the search. This emotional quality merges with others that have pervaded the writing process, stamping the experience with its distinctive felt quality as *that* memorable experience.

Dewey distinguished feelings from emotions. Consider the difference between being suddenly startled and being scared. The former is an initial disruption that triggers limbic system responses. This is a feeling. The latter, in Dewey's jargon, is an emotion. As you quickly try to identify what startled you, your feeling may dissipate or (depending on what happens next) it may resolve into any number of emotions which will bind the experience together into a coherent whole. Recall an interview, or a rejection letter, or a long-ago break-up. They are likely remembered as emotion-steeped wholes, even if in their initial occurrences they were largely verbal. Or recall a special place you have visited, a memorable concert, an autumn hike, a film, a painting. An emotional quality unifies these experiences, giving them a coherent identity.

In *Art as Experience*, Dewey returned to his vivid metaphor of the mind's "tentacles" (see Chapter Two) to suggest the way emotions keep our attention alert to subject matter that can be integrated in an experience. "An emotion," he wrote, "is more effective than any deliberate challenging sentinel could be. It reaches out tentacles for that which is cognate, for things which feed it and carry it to completion" (AE, LW 10:73). Consider the way an ordinary job interview is aesthetically guided. The interviewers project the interviewee "imaginatively into the work to be done," and they judge her fit with the job by "the way in which the elements of the scene assemble and either clash or fit together. ... Such factors as these, inherently esthetic in quality, are the forces that carry the varied elements of the interview to a decisive issue" (AE, LW 10:50). Unseemly as it may be, for Dewey we cannot keep our emotional tentacles to ourselves.

Consider a mathematician wrapping up a difficult proof. The resolution of the proof has an emotional dimension, which is present in even the most subtle and sophisticated forms of symbol-mediated inquiry. From a mathematical proof to buying a car, an experience *as lived* is "neither emotional, practical, nor intellectual." But reflection may find that "one property rather than another was sufficiently dominant so that it characterizes the experience as a whole" (AE, LW 10:44). Upon reflection we rightly call buying a car a practical experience, while we call finishing a proof an intellectual one, but in their "actual occurrence" they were "emotional as well" (AE, LW 10:44, 80). A painting, sculpture, or poem is distinctively aesthetic in its production and enjoyment, but both the artist and the physicist are engaged in experimental inquiry.

Most importantly, for Dewey, the physicist produces the equation through the same general developmental process that characterizes the artist's production of the painting. The scientific–intellectual and the aesthetic are distinct as lived experiences, but they are continuous with each other. Scientific–intellectual life and emotional life do not stand aloof from each other as inherently isolated kinds of psychological experience.

Nor is there anything inherent in practical occupations of work, home, business, and school that justifies our isolation of such daily behavior from "direct consummation and fulfillment" (UPMP:344). Of course any sociological report on prevailing conditions will be disturbingly accurate when it describes how anaesthetizing practical occupations can be, but this is not due to any inevitable and hence unchangeable separation between the practical and aesthetic (UPMP:343–45). Perpetual bliss in daily life is a fantasy, but a richer happiness for all is an ideal worth striving for, so that we may achieve together what is possible instead of starting with untested and indeed unrealistic assumptions about the inherent stick-and-carrot nature of work and human motivation.

Experience in its integrity

True to his postulate of continuity (see Chapter Two), Dewey strove in *Art as Experience* "to connect the higher and ideal things of experience with basic vital roots" (AE, LW 10:26). The fragrance, color, and delicacy of roses can be *appreciated* when they are cut and placed in a vase. But the botanist cannot *understand* them except as rooted in complex interactions between pollinators, sun, soil, water, and air (AE, LW 10:10). We should expect equal attention to rootedness and context from a philosopher who theorizes about art. Yet this expectation challenges aestheticians such as Clive Bell, who in his influential book *Art* (1914) celebrated rare spirits who are able to scale the "cold, white peaks of art" to experience an eternal and austere emotion cut off from ordinary experience and the "gross herd."[4] In Dewey's view, artistic creation and aesthetic experiences are indeed peak experiences, but any geologist knows that the peaks of a mountain "do not float unsupported; they do not even just rest upon the earth. They *are* the earth in one of its manifest operations" (AE, LW 10:9). We should expect no less naturalism of the aesthetician studying art than of the geologist studying mountains. For Dewey, as Alexander observes, "works of art do not belong to a separate realm; they are realizations of this one."[5]

In McDermott's words, art arises from "the aesthetic drama of the ordinary." At the close of "The Live Creature," the first chapter of *Art as Experience*, Dewey explored this aesthetic drama through our continuity with other animals:

> To grasp the sources of esthetic experience it is, therefore, necessary to have recourse to animal life below the human scale.

> The activities of the fox, the dog, and the thrush may at least
> stand as reminders and symbols of that unity of experience
> which we so fractionize when work is labor, and thought with-
> draws us from the world. The live animal is fully present, all
> there, in all of its actions: in its wary glances, its sharp sniffings,
> its abrupt cocking of ears. All senses are equally on the qui vive.
>
> (AE, LW 10:24)

The sniffing of animals is a surprising starting point for a book on
aesthetics, particularly for the reader who is used to tracing the origins of aesthetic experience to art galleries and performance venues.

If Dewey locates the vital living *roots* of the aesthetic in life's everyday consummations, then what are its most visible *fruits* in human
experience? Central to Dewey's aesthetic theory is the claim that "art
is the most direct and complete manifestation there is of experience
as experience" (AE, LW 10:301). "To esthetic experience, then,
the philosopher must go to understand what experience is" (AE, LW
10:278). Inquiry into artistic and aesthetic experience is revelatory of
the nature of any complete experience because "esthetic experience
is experience in its integrity" (AE, LW 10:278).

Art narrowly construed—and here Dewey alternates between
wide and narrow senses of art—directly celebrates the creative
development of an experience toward consummation for the sake of
immediately enjoying that development. One might even say art and
aesthetic experience are "pure," in the sense that their instrumental
value is their enjoyed significance rather than being principally a
means to some further end.

Distinctively intellectual endeavors—intellectual arts in the broad
sense of the denotative method—such as science, mathematics, and
philosophy are equally endeavors with qualitatively rich consummations. This is, in part, why we pursue such inquiries and
how we "keep them honest." The aesthetic stamp is also essential
to rounding out any intellectual activity as *an* experience (AE, LW
10:45). The mathematician, scientist, or philosopher intentionally
uses signs and symbols to map terrain, and he or she does this to a
degree that makes intellectual activity distinctive. The art (broadly
construed) of intellectual inquiry is aesthetic insofar as it serves
the immediate fulfillments found in new lines of questioning,

experimentation, mistakes, and discoveries. Still, such emphatically intellectual activity is characterized by signs and symbols working toward remote ends, whereas the artist's thought is "immediately embodied in the object" (AE, LW 10:45; EN, LW 1:269).

To say the scientist's ends are remote simply emphasizes that science maps targeted parts of the social, physical, and cultural terrain of our existence, which we can use to better manage our interactions and nourish the quality of our lives. That is, what is ultimately most valuable in scientific inquiry (and some technologies) is the way in which it potentially makes our immediate lives more significant. This of course includes the immediate enjoyment of the inquiry itself.

Artistic production and aesthetic experience (narrowly construed), meanwhile, zoom in on immediately charged meanings in a way that is comparatively uncluttered with aims external to or remote from the sensuous medium of activity. Consequently, by investigating the preeminently "pure" or "uncluttered" events of artistic expression and aesthetic experience we may learn something valuable about the capacity of other human experiences to develop toward consummation. "All the elements of our being that are displayed in special emphases and partial realizations in other experiences are merged in esthetic experience" (AE, LW 10:278). This is the gist of why Dewey preferred to speak of all inquiry as an art, despite the equal truth that artistry involves inquiry. By understanding the contours of art as experience, we can better envision how to establish the conditions through which other experiences may fulfill their potential as art.

The imaginative social communication and culturally refined skills of the arts at any rate offer a reminder of consummatory potential. In sum, Dewey asserted that artistic production (narrowly construed) and aesthetic experience reveal human experience in its full developmental potential, so they serve as model and inspiration for the rest of experience to become more aesthetically complete. Most of our interactions with each other and with the rest of nature fail as art. They involve cessations or mere terminations and not consummations. Some of this is unavoidable, but much is due to the conditions of life and to our ignorance and insensitivity, hence it is changeable. That is, many of our intellectual, moral, and everyday experiences could be as fully developed as those peak experiences which we justly celebrate in the fine arts.

The work of art and generative form

Art, Dewey declared with a penchant for erotic metaphors, "is the impregnation of sensuous material with imaginative values" (AE, LW 10:297). When he speaks of art in the narrowest sense, does Dewey mean the "fine arts," such as a painting by Matisse? Does he include useful and technological productions such as rugs, furniture, clothing, dishes, and weapons? The answer is "it depends." These are all arts in the broad sense, and there is nothing inherent in works of art themselves that distinguish them as either useful or fine (AE, LW 10:33; cf. EN, LW 1:271–72). A tea cup or a chair may be made and perceived with a far greater "degree of completeness in living" than a painting; it is to that degree a fine or aesthetic object (AE, LW 10:34). Notably, although the "artwork" is popularly identified with physical products that stand apart from experience, Dewey emphasized the activity of artistic production and enjoyment over its tangible products. The real work of art, he argued, "is what the product does with and in experience" (AE, LW 10:9).

The issue of what is genuinely useful in art highlights a political dimension of Dewey's democratized aesthetics. "That many, perhaps most, of the articles and utensils made at present for use are not genuinely esthetic happens, unfortunately, to be true. ... Wherever conditions are such as to prevent the act of production from being an experience in which the whole creature is alive and in which he possesses his living through enjoyment, the product will lack something of being esthetic" (AE, LW 10:34). Counterexamples readily come to mind: for example, the fact that garments or shoes were produced in a sweatshop does not necessarily make them aesthetic failures for the consumer. Such items are useful for specific ends, and they may come to have great aesthetic value for the end-user. On one level, Dewey could simply respond that aesthetically complete production generally leads to objects with greater aesthetic richness. But this is not all he was saying. When an object—shoes, a computer, a steak—is produced through a process that fails miserably to contribute "directly and liberally to an expanding and enriched life" for many involved in producing it, only a subjectivized notion of the aesthetic, an atomistic notion of form, and a narrow notion of imagination would be compatible with forgetting and obscuring the connections and relationships that inhere in that object. The form of the object includes the relationships that are woven into it, and through imagination we can aesthetically perceive and artistically respond to the object in light of these relationships. Dewey lamented: "The story of the severance and final sharp opposition of the useful and the fine is the history of that industrial development through which so much of production has become a form of postponed living and so much of consumption a superimposed enjoyment of the fruits of the labor of others" (AE, LW 10:34).

In Dewey's view, a philosopher's aesthetic theory is not just a test of whether he or she is capable of the heightened experience under study. It is also "a test of the capacity of the system he puts forth to grasp the nature of experience itself" (AE, LW 10:278). Dewey's aim was to dignify both art and ordinary experience. Even in the thick of troubles, regret, and anxiety, or amid ordinary problem-solving that short-changes the present to some remote end, art and aesthetic experiences offer a store of memories and resources "by which to move confidently forward" (AE, LW 10:23, 278).

Experiences that are intensified, refined, and clarified in the arts reveal the potential of experience to grow and be fulfilled. This stands in opposition to frequent identification of art and aesthetic experience in popular culture with what is pretty or pleasant or tasty, or of art as stress relief for desperate, hyper-individuals sealed in their private jars. As Dewey pointedly observed, art is not "the beauty parlor of civilization" (AE, LW 10:346), and "there are few intense esthetic experiences that are wholly gleeful" (AE, LW 10:48). As Alexander observes, a transformative encounter with good art may forever haunt us. The haiku master Issa, pained by the death of his toddler daughter, gave form to this tragedy when he wrote:

This world of dew
is just a world of dew
and yet ... and yet ... [6]

When we take in Issa's haiku we renew and contribute to its form through our own vital, if painful, reconstructive encounter.

In Dewey's idiom, the *artistic* "refers primarily to the act of production" while the *aesthetic* refers to acts of "perception and enjoyment" (AE, LW10:53). Consider a collaborative medium such as an orchestra, choir, band, or play. (While considering this, take Dewey at his word: through reflection on art he intended to explore the prototypical contours of *any* consummatory experience. The general contours should apply as readily to a fully developed event in sports, science, or romance.) We need both artistic creation and aesthetic perception simultaneously, Dewey asserted, or experiences are limited. All active artistry in life is funded by aesthetic perceptiveness, and experiences need a balance between the two if they are to be aesthetically complete. In a collaborative medium such as a band, experiences that overreach due to hyperactive impulsiveness, obsessive urges, or other sorts of self-centered steamrolling by some members of the group, will distract focus and distort the work. Here there is production (the *potentially* artistic) with too little perception (the aesthetic). Or members of the group may listen and appreciate without individually contributing much through their own voices, instruments, or gestures. Here there is receptivity with too little artistry. Similarly, potential artistic-aesthetic experiences that overemphasize emotions by wallowing in sentimentality fail to balance activity with receptivity (AE, LW 10:51). "Unbalance on either side blurs the perception of relations and leaves the experience partial and distorted, with scant or false meaning" (AE, LW 10:51). These experiences fall short of *art* in the honorific sense. In *good* art, makings and perceptions, executions and sensitivities, are "reciprocally, cumulatively, and continuously instrumental to each other" (AE, LW 10:56–57).

As a reader, viewer, or listener I am simultaneously an artist. I configure experiences and extend the form—and indeed the world—of the original product. When my own artistry is imaginatively flat, little is achieved by way of growth and heightened vitality. Most of the beauty and power of art is revealed only after sympathetic perception, what American philosopher Jonathan Edwards called a "sense of heart." When I (inevitably) lack such perception, I do not fulfill the capacity for aesthetic experience to be more than mere consumption. Aesthetic experience can overspill the narrow banks of egoistic preference and flow into a wider and deeper current.

To take an example of Dewey's own occasional lack of sympathetic perception, he implied that jazz music is analogous to vulgar tabloids (AE, LW 10:12). He said the same of movies. This raises a red flag about possible classist biases, yet his aesthetic theory is on the whole refreshingly antielitist without being populist. He followed up his comments on jazz and movies with penetrating cultural criticism. Many popular art forms are sought out, he claimed, because of an aesthetic vacuum in our culture. Dewey regularly visited and supported museums, but the more the products of fine art are held up as museum pieces and pricy markers of wealth and status, the more remote they seem from ordinary experience. As a result of this *museum concept of art*, the necessity for aesthetic outlets is too often filled by reckless pandering and sentimentalism.

Not all art is good art. Much art fails to cohere as a qualitative whole in which parts reinforce each other. For example, much entertainment is a by-product of our consumer demand for killing time, or for distractedly taking our minds offline, or a response to our craving for simulated worlds that temporarily transport us from monotony and return us unchanged. We are just passing through. The interval during which we are withdrawn is extraneous to the ordinary conditions of life, so it calls forth no new adjustment, no reckoning with tensions, no expansion or enrichment of experience, no growth. Dewey was not wagging his finger at this. "Such pleasures are not to be despised in a world full of pain" (AE, LW 10:23). But neither are they sources for deep-seated fulfillment that reverberates through life. They do not offer much in the way of a repository, resource, or standard, nor a reminder and hope.

In his comments about jazz, Dewey accepted a then-common stereotype of jazz improvisation as *haphazardly* unrehearsed, improvised in the sense of offhand. Even Duke Ellington was ambivalent in the 1930s about the *word* jazz. Improvisational music played into Dewey's worries about "hasty improvisation" in progressive education (EE, LW 13:109; LW 17:53). Whether in art or education, the absence of forethought or discipline yields results that are disjointed. At the opposite extreme we find cultural rigidity, conformity, and dogmatism, spawning grounds for propaganda art and doctrine-thumping. Both extremes, he observed, have a deadening rather than a liberating effect on imagination.

Dewey's nuanced aesthetic perceptions of painting—he even befriended Matisse, who made charcoal portraits of him in the early 1930s—and literature were not matched by any facility with music.[7] Despite this, his approach to artistic–aesthetic experiences can be summarized using jazz as a model.

The tight structure and aesthetic richness of jazz are well suited to Dewey's philosophy, particularly given his emphasis on refined empathy and collective imaginative rehearsal. The musical instrument—voice, trumpet, piano—is "instrumental" to the immediate significance of the playing. It is not primarily instrumental to some extraneous end. The musician enjoys the work in a way that is configured in the performance, which consequently expands the immediate enjoyments of fellow musicians and audience. This enjoyment is not merely subjective. Self-absorbed prima donnas tend to obstruct or damage the aesthetic quality of the work and world, and that is an objective result. Both good musicians and good listeners are fully alert to the developing rhythmic event. Their sensations and emotions, far from being shut up and privately withdrawn, are vital and active participants in what is happening.[8]

Moreover, as with any vital artistic production, the "form" of the jazz composition is not static, final, complete, eternal. No such Platonism. The form is generative, not stagnant. It evolves because it is constituted and reconstituted through interaction. The form is reconfigured as a new achievement in all subsequent vital experiences of the work. This is manifest in jazz, but it is equally true of a symphonic composition or of our appreciative interactions with an ancient sculpture or a Renaissance painting. Form is never static in a moving world in which the live creature's experience and his or her environment are in a continuous feedback loop.

The aesthetics of moral life

It is now possible to weave in the final strands of Dewey's reconstruction of ethics. To recap, art involves operative intelligence or inquiry, and aesthetic experiences are continuous with (though distinct from) scientific inquiries. Because Dewey held up artistic creation and enjoyment as exemplars or prototypes of consummatory experience, he had a strong predilection for art metaphors. Art shares in inquiry, and inquiry at its best attains to art. In Dewey's view all forms of inquiry follow a pattern of artistic development whenever they spread their wings completely, so we can intelligibly speak of the art of scientific inquiry, the art of democratic deliberation, and moral artistry.

As discussed, this idea that art is paradigmatic of *all* experience is at odds with the compartmentalization of the aesthetic and the intellectual as autonomous spheres. Dewey treated the aesthetic and intellectual as "dominantly different" traits that nonetheless have the same experiential origin and seat. This raises a suspicious eyebrow for dualists who worry that Dewey has subjectivized intellectual life. The situation looks even worse when Dewey approaches moral conduct from the standpoint of aesthetic experience. This boundary-jumping transgression, duplicated in the structure of the chapter you are reading, appears to radically subjectivize moral reflection. Our Enlightenment heritage has tutored us to see moral reasoning as discontinuous from imaginative artistic-aesthetic experiences. A rationalistic moral system may partially satisfy "the demands of impartial and far-sighted thought," Dewey countered, but it fails to offer any fruitful channel for "the urgencies of desire" (1932 E, LW 7:191). In their quest for rational impartiality, moral philosophies that invalidate our driving urgencies and interests cultivate what Eliot pointedly describes as "that bird's-eye reasonableness which soars to avoid preference and loses all sense of quality."[9]

"One great defect in what passes as morality," Dewey urged, "is its anesthetic quality. Instead of exemplifying wholehearted action, it takes the form of grudging piecemeal concessions to the demands of duty" (AE, LW 10:46). This is a recipe for moral sterility, fragmentation, and alienation. When moral reflection is not immediately experienced as significant, it too often has little instrumental worth. That is, it does not help us to achieve our best ends. Anesthetic experience lacks any revelatory or generative sense of a situation's possibilities, so foresight and critical appraisal fall back on the inertia of reactive habits.

Consider the pregnant sense in which playing a musical instrument has worth, as with the prior discussion of jazz. The musician is inspired in part or in whole by goods internal to the act of playing, not external to it, and the instrument is quite literally instrumental to these goods. Analogously, when we recognize a familiar instance to be lumped under a predetermined set of ends or duties, in Dewey's terms we intellectually *recognize* that things are at stake, but we may not richly *perceive*. That is, we recognize attributes of the situation but may not perceive the relational whole (AE, LW 10:30). As discussed in Chapter Four, critically examined principles and rules can help us to be more perceptive so long as our carefully argued diagnoses and prescriptions are in support of, rather than substituting for, imaginative engagement. But in the main, we have focused so much on frozen moral criteria that we tend to anesthetize imagination.

We do not gain long-range, widely distributed foresight by neglecting the quality of immediate experience. The opposite is true: we *cannot* respond to what we do not perceive, and we will not respond to perceptions unless they have some emotional traction. Dewey opposed *overreliance* on the still-dominant utilitarian model of moral deliberation as cold, calculative cost-benefit analysis. His concerns would likely have extended to the now-current assumption in some quarters that the *prototypical* moral problem, its poster child, is a prisoner's or trolley dilemma.[10] Instead, he highlighted the aesthetics of moral life.

Wise moral deliberation is not primarily a matter of good utilitarian bookkeeping, toiling industriously over calculations of a distant greater good. Actual men and women take their enjoyment "at as short range as possible" (EN, LW 1:69). This fact is behind familiar and very real conflicts between desires and duties, but we do not preserve the sanctity of reason by separating it from emotional life. Our felt urge for fulfillment is something we must thoughtfully direct rather than flee. Democratic education, experimental intelligence, aesthetic virtues of sensitivity and perception, and moral imagination are among our resources to direct our desires toward consummations that rejuvenate and enrich immediate experience.

A fine-tuned imagination is not a panacea for the sort of aesthetic insensitivity that leads us, again in George Eliot's words, to "walk about well wadded with stupidity."[11] But there is no substitute, and we need all the help we can get. When we simulate connections and alternatives in imagination, we immediately feel their tendencies. What results is a unifying felt quality that marks an experience with its distinctive character, as that reproductive choice or this decision to break off a romance. This quality funds concerted moral action. This felt character is an integral part of moral experience, not something opposed to good decision-making. It is a necessary ingredient for perceptively and artistically negotiating the conflicts between ends, goods, responsibilities, rights, and duties that we daily face in moral life (see Chapter Four), including hard choices about which consummatory fulfillments to prioritize. In social interactions, as exemplified in cooperative arts such as jazz, we must respond empathetically to each other instead of imposing insular designs, and we must rigorously imagine how others will respond to our actions. Such perception and responsibility does not follow on the heels of anesthetized reflection.

Qualitative thought

Dewey's watershed essay "Qualitative Thought" (1930) has become a treasure trove for ongoing scholarly research. I will borrow Plato's notion of "the ancient quarrel between philosophy and poetry" to introduce a few key insights from Dewey's dense, technical essay. Imagine the quarrel as one between *poeisis* (the Greek origin of "poetry") and *logos* (the origin of "logic").

The opening lines of "Qualitative Thought" are among Dewey's most quote-worthy: "The world in which we immediately live, that in which we strive, succeed, and are defeated is preeminently a qualitative world. What we act for, suffer, and enjoy are things in their qualitative determinations" (LW 5:243).[12] The immediate quality of an experience, which Dewey identifies with the aesthetic, is as much a part of natural existence as scientific objects. It evokes or accompanies experimental inquiry when a situation is problematic, but in experiences we call "aesthetic" the quality of primary experience does not ask to be a means to some extrinsic end. It is valued for itself.

The modernist tradition that we typically trace back to Descartes assumed that human experience is essentially about *knowing*, which is set over and against qualitative *feeling*. This has been canvassed in prior chapters, but it bears repeating that Dewey consistently rejected as obsolete and obstructive the "doctrine of the supremacy of the cognitive experience" and the presumption that noncognitive experiences must be relegated to second class.[13] Along the same dualistic lines as the split between knowing and feeling, logic and rational inquiry are widely understood in opposition to artistic production and aesthetic experience. Think of the stereotyped contrast between the imaginative warmth of artists and the cool reason of scientists. Poetic emotion is set against scientific inquiry and philosophical analysis, *poeisis* against *logos*. Plato's "ancient quarrel" lingers: Does human experience peak in cognition directed at scientific objects? Or does it peak in immediately felt, noncognitive receptiveness? The reader is by now familiar with the dualisms, such as reason *versus* imagination, thinking *versus* feeling.

The *logos* (intellectualist) camp and *poeisis* camp share a misconception and a fallacy. The misconception is that each assumes that the experiences that generate scientific knowledge are essentially different in kind from artistic and aesthetic experiences, and the fallacy is the fallacy of hypostatization (see Chapter Two). Science and philosophy, it is widely thought, are the province of dispassionate, rule-governed reason, while art is the province of an imagination that swerves with unruly passions. Accordingly, the *logos* camp approaches the world primarily as an object to be known, while the *poeisis* camp approaches it as an object to be felt. Science or art: One is accorded the seat of honor, and the other a footstool.

In Dewey's opposing view, the matrix of *all* experience is tonal, and logic no less than art grows out of a qualitative background. He simultaneously de-subjectivized the aesthetic and de-objectivized understanding. "The gist of the matter is that the immediate existence of quality, and of dominant and pervasive quality, is the background, the point of departure, and the regulative principle of all thinking" (LW 5:262). He elaborated the felt horizon of experience as a pervasive, "underlying qualitative character that constitutes a situation." All meaning, whether linguistic or affective, is dependent upon this qualitative field, which suffuses and differentiates experience (LW 5:248).

To recap, the *poeisis* camp contends that rational thought falls short where aesthetic feeling prevails, while the *logos* camp argues the reverse. But they misconceive the situation. *All thought is qualitative, and artistic-aesthetic experience is suffused with thought.* In generative works of art that are "genuine intellectual and logical whole[s]," Dewey wrote, "the underlying quality that defines the work, that circumscribes it externally and integrates it internally, controls the thinking of the artist; his logic is the logic of what I have called qualitative thinking" (LW 5:252). In other words, qualitative thought pervades and regulates both artistic construction *and* logic.

Consequently, art does not inhabit a realm of genius separate from logic. It is sometimes said, quite rightly, that art is ineffable (i.e., that its meaning exceeds what can be expressed through language). But this is not because art outstrips *thought*. To the extent that language falls short of art, it is because artistic (or any) thought is itself richly qualitative. As discussed in Chapter Two, thought requires "language, the tool of tools," but thought is not identical or reducible to language (EN, LW 1:134; see EN, LW 1:132–61). Many philosophers may find this statement jarring, or they may wonder if Dewey is suddenly, despite his professed naturalism, positing some gaseous extralinguistic "thought." Yet the notion that there is a qualitative dimension to all thinking has been suggested in all discussions of inquiry throughout this book. Dewey argued: "Language fails not because thought fails, but because no verbal symbols can do justice to the fullness and richness of thought" (LW 5:250). Religious life is analogous. Language is inadequate to the reach of religious attitudes not because thought is inadequate, and certainly not because spiritual life touches an ethereal realm, but because thought is so qualitatively nuanced.

Art, science, and instrumentalism

Speaking to a Japanese audience at Tokyo University in 1919, Dewey argued that the foremost global philosophical challenge is the reconciliation of contemplative–aesthetic attitudes with scientific–experimental attitudes. He urged that such philosophical reconciliation would promote cross-cultural cooperation and fertilization between East and West. He made early steps in the direction of a global philosophical outlook by promoting a fusion of the contemplative refinements of Asia with Euro-American experimentalism. In this cross-cultural context, Dewey made explicit that his aim was to set forth the possibility and method by which the scientific and aesthetic might be reconciled in order to humanize techno-industrial civilization. Without the methods of science, he urged, we drift at the mercy of natural forces. But without lives rich in aesthetic consummations, he anticipated with foreboding, we "might become a race of economic monsters, restlessly driving hard bargains with nature and with one another, bored with leisure or capable of putting it to use only in ostentatious display and extravagant dissipation" (RP, MW 12:152).

Perhaps the most common interpretive error among both admirers and critics of Dewey has been to read him principally as a trumpeter of science. This will, and should, lead to head-scratching for a reader now steeped in Dewey's reflections on the primacy of the qualitative. As discussed in Chapters Two and Three regarding the "intellectualist's fallacy" that reduces all experiencing to knowing, art discloses nature's emergent potential. "Art" in the broad sense includes the intellectual art we call science, but it is not limited to science, so the "real" or "nature" cannot be boiled down to the distinct objects of scientific study alone. If science is taken broadly to encompass all of the predominantly intellectual endeavors engaged in the "denotative method" of inquiry (see Chapters Two and Three), then for Dewey science is an operative art whose proper role is to serve aesthetic enjoyments (EN, LW 1:269).

When we ask which scientific questions are most worthy of investigation, and which technologies are most worthy of development, we broach questions about our highest ideals. Ultimately, what is our science, technology, and information defensibly a means toward? In response, as has been shown, Dewey emphasized the immediately possessed meanings and enjoyments that characterize all well-developed experiences. Science broadly construed is a central art that is "auxiliary to the generation and utilization of other arts" (AE, LW 10:33). In a footnote to *Art as Experience*, Dewey cross-referenced the quote from *Experience and Nature* that serves as the epigraph to this chapter, doing the scholarship for us to ensure we do not mistake his meaning: taking "science" broadly, it is the servant of the aesthetic (AE, LW 10:33; EN, LW 1:269).

Critics of Dewey's instrumentalist theory of inquiry nonetheless often mistake it as an attack on intrinsic value or as an attempt to collapse the value of means into the value of ends. They write as though Dewey might at any moment grab a violinist by the lapels and demand to know "What are you doing that for?" To repeat, there is indeed a "point" to playing the violin. It is to enhance this immediate (often shared) experience. The violin is "instrumental" to just that, the playing and listening, whatever other value it may have by way of garnering a livelihood, showcasing talent, or establishing a reputation. This is what Dewey's instrumentalism boils down to, as he says in *Art as Experience*:

> What is intimated to my mind, is, that in both production and enjoyed perception of works of art, knowledge is transformed; it becomes something more than knowledge because it is merged with non-intellectual elements to form an experience worth while as an experience. I have from time to time set forth a conception of knowledge as being "instrumental." Strange meanings have been imputed by critics to this conception. Its actual content is simple: *Knowledge is instrumental to the enrichment of immediate experience through the control over action that it exercises.*
> (AE, LW 10:294, emphasis added)[14]

Does technology corrupt?

"The solution to any problem from technology isn't less technology but more technology," said the cofounder of *Wired* magazine.[15] Dewey's likely response to this bald assertion depends on the meaning of technology. Under the economic and cultural conditions in which industrial technology currently operates, this blanket endorsement is misguided. Dewey was a potent critic of blind and ill-considered "technology *as it operates under existing political-economic-cultural conditions*" (LW 15:190). But despite current narrow usage, technology is of course not a recent thing. The word derives from the Greek *technē*, meaning art, craft, or control. All tool- or knowledge-based mediation of our environments is in a broad sense technological.[16] Technology in this inclusive sense "signifies all the intelligent techniques by which the energies of nature and man are directed ... ; it cannot be limited to a few outer and comparatively mechanical forms" (LW 5:270). This broad sense of technology suggests a way to reclaim and affirm technology on behalf of living more fulfilling lives.

In *Agrarianism in American Literature*, Thomas Inge expresses a widely held view: technology corrupts while nature redeems.[17] This dualistically sets technology in opposition to nature. But must we conceive technology in this antagonistic way? Dewey's alternative approach was to reclaim technology as *part* of our cultural inhabitation of nature. He suggests a way to extol science and its technological applications, at least in *the abstract*, as essential to actualizing our most humane ideals. For in Dewey's view, the defensible aim of science and technology is to help make our lives more significant. By the 1940s Dewey even favored the word technology—if taken in a very broad sense—over instrumentalism to convey his operational view of scientific knowledge (LW 15:89). So taken, instead of calling a referendum on technology, we can strive to alter the current conditions in education, government, and industry in which technology is currently developed and deployed.

Dewey's robust philosophy of technology is receiving a new round of scholarly attention due to recovery of the "lost" book (see UPMP:203–51), but it is still common for writers to cherry-pick statements that depict Dewey as an excessive technocrat. *Reconstruction in Philosophy* and *The Quest for Certainty* contain the best cherries to pick. A twenty-first-century nose catches occasional whiffs of Francis Bacon's seventeenth-century vision of an "empire over nature." Dewey at times overindulged in admiration for the industrial revolution and its progressive actualization of Bacon's watchword: "knowledge is power." His 1920s confidence in the humanizing arts of technological control can at times strain twenty-first-century eyes fatigued by resource depletion, oil wars, climate change, and American swagger.[18]

Bertrand Russell even presented Dewey as a "power" philosopher promoting a socialized and technologically enhanced version of Nietzsche's will-to-power.[19] Once again Russell's pronouncements, though influential, did not reflect any serious attempt to understand Dewey's positions. Through the work of philosophical reconstruction, Dewey sought to "permit the Baconian aspirations to come to a free and unhindered expression" (RP, MW 12:108).[20] Dewey did share Bacon's commitment to advancing human welfare through scientific knowledge, but he *rejected* Baconian philosophy. It was entangled in a deeply flawed view of human intelligence as "an exaggeratedly self-sufficient Ego" (RP, MW 12:108). Bacon conceived human experience as dualistically set over and against nature, which must be conquered and subjugated. Bacon valued and obeyed nature only inasmuch as this was necessary to extract secrets for humane ends.

In Dewey's opposing view, experimental intelligence can indeed transform the world and reshape "those phases of nature and life that obstruct social well-being" (RP, MW 12:108), but we thwart our own best aims when we fail to understand that *human initiative, inventiveness, and labor are themselves natural events. They do not descend from the heavens or from a psychical inner realm separated from our bodies and cultures.* Sidney Hook summed up this humane spirit of Dewey's philosophy: "He has shown with patient detail that intelligence is at home in the natural world and not a mysterious intruder bringing its own standards from a realm beyond the skies."[21]

Martin Heidegger, whose philosophy of technology is often cited as a contrast to Dewey, contended that means–end reasoning inevitably overreaches because it puts us in a controlling and "calculative" mode that hides aspects of the world.[22] Albert Borgmann helpfully develops Heidegger's insights to explore the way our lives become dominated by efficient devices.[23] For example, most of us pay bills to run a furnace, replacing the seasonal rhythms that centered on the hearth. Some devices have improved our quality of life, but we have also lost meaning-making "focal practices" that brought coherence, significance, and a sense of place. In his reconstruction of an early nineteenth-century boy's diary, *Diary of an Early American Boy*, Eric Sloane observes: "Few of us today would think of wood splitting as anything but a tedious chore, but when one learns to do it well, there is a certain joy involved. Striking your axe in an exact spot, watching a log divide miraculously into segments and squares with single blows, or even learning to stack a simple pile of wood correctly, gives pleasure to the art of woodsmanship."[24]

We should conserve things, ideas, and practices that are functioning well. If the aesthetic richness we directly experience as fulfilling in the course of daily occupations—for example, splitting wood and building a fire—is reduced by a proposed technological device, then that device may be a dysfunctional means to our most valuable ends. (Recall from Chapter Three the separation of means from ends revealed in the "discovery" of roast pig.) Quality of life is sometimes eroded by pursuit of mechanical efficiency, and there are generally more effective, inclusive, and enduring means to secure consummations than fixating on new and ever-more-efficient devices.

More generally, Dewey argued in *Unmodern Philosophy and Modern Philosophy* that the greater part of those techno-industrial and vocational activities which we narrowly regard as instrumental actually reduce "to a very minimum the esthetic aspect of experiences had in the course of the daily occupation" (UPMP:344). We enjoy the anticipation of getting paid, but the way we make our living is "isolated from direct consummation and fulfillment" (UPMP:344). To respond that this is "just the nature of work" is a sign of neither practical realism nor wisdom.

Dewey argued that criticism of means–end or technological reasoning—such as the claim that it is invariably exploitative—does nothing "to free experience from routine and from caprice" (MW 10:45). He sought to liberate human activities from an anesthetizing status quo in part by advancing an educational ideal of forward-looking, aesthetically funded intelligence that imaginatively projects new ends. Ends fixed in advance, such as the twentieth- and twenty-first-century worship of efficiency, can impoverish the art of inquiry.[25] Through imaginative engagement we see extant conditions in light of novel possibilities and guide the world's transformation. This is Dewey's picture of instrumental intelligence that has intrinsic worth, that is, in which means are valued and aesthetically enjoyed for themselves (MW 10:45).

In other words, our problem is not instrumental intelligence, but mechanically instrumental activity. Hickman engages Dewey to criticize the latter as a narrowing product of "straight-line" instrumentalism that "works toward fixed goals, heedless of the collateral problems and opportunities that arise during the thick of deliberation."[26] What goes by the name of progress is too often purchased by sacrificing the very goods this "progress" is defensibly a means toward.

Summary

All complete experiences—whether they are directed toward knowledge, practical action, or emotional fulfillment—follow the same general pattern of development, a pattern Dewey described as an experience. Civilization's high water mark, aesthetic experience, is not a merely subjective episode encased in a free-willing mind cut off from nature. Aesthetic experience, Dewey asserted, is "the culminating event of nature as well as the climax of experience" (AE, LW 10:8). He investigated the uprootedness, dislocation, and unrealized potential wrapped up in a museum concept of art that displays the aesthetic refinements of cultural existence chopped off from our natural history as imaginative living creatures. For Dewey inquiry at its best is an art that has the enrichment of immediate experience as its principal charge. When experience attains to art, it does not sacrifice the present to the industrial gospel of efficiency or calculated promises of future yields. Technology can be art in precisely this sense, but under current economic conditions it too often falls tragically short of its potential to support life's fulfillments.

Notes

1 By "narrowly utilitarian" I intend "utilitarian" in a colloquial sense, akin to my criticisms in this volume of "narrow pragmatism." I indicate in the text whenever I am speaking of utilitarianism as a philosophical position. On fulfillment, cf. Thomas M. Alexander, "The Art of Life: Dewey's Aesthetics," in *Reading Dewey: Interpretations for a Postmodern Generation*, ed. Larry A. Hickman, 1–22 (Bloomington, IN: Indiana University Press, 1998), 3.

2 Thomas M. Alexander, *John Dewey's Theory of Art, Experience, and Nature* (Albany, NY: SUNY Press, 1987), 128. Cf. Alexander, *The Human Eros: Eco-ontology and the Aesthetics of Existence* (New York: Fordham University Press, 2013), 1.

3 For a critique of Dewey's notion of aesthetic experience as essentialistic (i.e., as striving to capture an essence of the aesthetic as a set of necessary and sufficient conditions), see Richard Shusterman, *Pragmatist Aesthetics: Living Beauty, Rethinking Art*, 2nd ed. (Lanham, MD: Rowman & Littlefield, 2000).

4 Clive Bell, *Art* (London: Chatto & Windus, 1914), 12, 14.

5 Thomas M. Alexander, "John Dewey's Uncommon Faith: Understanding 'Religious Experience,'" *American Catholic Philosophical Quarterly* 87, no. 2 (2013): 347–62, at 352.

6 I am grateful to Thomas M. Alexander (personal communication) for this example of the capacity of art to "haunt." Issa's haiku runs: "Tsuyu no yo wa/ tsuyu no yo nagara/sari nagara." The translation is inspired by Donald Keene's popular version. Cf. Alexander, *The Human Eros*, 351.

7 Herbert Schneider writes: "At a concert in Carnegie Hall, to which Dewey had invited a few of us, I noticed that he took little interest in the concert. He told me that he regretted being tone deaf and being unable to enjoy music. And he added that the only arts that were really of serious concern to him were

painting and poetry." 1973.02.13 (22053): Herbert W. Schneider to H. S. Thayer.

8 For a detailed analysis of social intercourse as jazz, see my *John Dewey and Moral Imagination* (Bloomington, IN: Indiana University Press, 2003), 92–96; on moral artistry more generally, see chs. 6–7.

9 George Eliot, *Daniel Deronda* (New York: Random House, 2002 [1876]), 677.

10 Although it is shortsighted to see trolley dilemmas as paradigmatic instances or poster children of ordinary moral life, this in no way implies a lack of pragmatic worth in this emerging area of ethics. For an entertaining and thoughtful introduction to what is now called "trolleyology," see David Edmonds, *Would You Kill the Fat Man?: The Trolley Problem and What Your Answer Tells Us about Right and Wrong* (Princeton, NJ: Princeton University Press, 2014). See especially the material on US drone strikes to see the pragmatic relevance for contemporary policy decisions.

11 George Eliot, *Middlemarch* (London: Penguin Books, 1965 [1871–72]), 226.

12 For contemporary cognitive research on the centrality of emotions in thinking that draws on Dewey's "Qualitative Thought," see, for example, Mark Johnson, *The Meaning of the Body* (Chicago: University of Chicago Press, 2007). For research in neuroscience on the feeling brain, see for example Antonio R. Damasio, *Descartes' Error: Emotion, Reason, and the Human Brain* (New York: Avon Books, 1994), and *The Feeling of What Happens: Body and Emotion in the Making of Consciousness* (Fort Worth, TX: Harcourt Brace, 1999).

13 "Dewey's Reply," in *The Philosophy of John Dewey*, ed. Paul Arthur Schilpp and Lewis Edwin Hahn (Chicago: Open Court, 1989), 525. This is another statement of the "intellectualist's fallacy" (QC, LW 4:232).

14 Dewey explained the relationship between art and science a bit more cautiously in "Time and Individuality": "Art is the complement of science. Science as I have said is concerned wholly with relations, not with individuals. Art, on the other hand, is not only the disclosure of the individuality of the artist but also a manifestation of individuality as creative of the future, in an unprecedented response to conditions as they were in the past" (LW 14:113).

15 Kevin Kelly in "Marketplace," *National Public Radio*, October 19, 2010 http://www.marketplace.org/shows/marketplace/marketplace-october-19-2010; accessed August 25, 2014.

16 Larry Hickman emphasizes technological management, not control, and he argues that for Dewey technology was a way of engaging the world through the tools of inquiry. See, for example, Hickman's "Nature as Culture: John Dewey's Pragmatic Naturalism," in *Environmental Pragmatism*, ed. Andrew Light and Eric Katz (London: Routledge, 1996).

17 M. Thomas Inge, *Agrarianism in American Literature* (New York: Odysseus Press, 1969). In Paul Thompson, *The Agrarian Vision* (Lexington: University Press of Kentucky, 2012), 7.

18 In his historical overview of the modern mechanical worldview in *Reconstruction in Philosophy*, Dewey's critique of hypostatization is mixed with naïve celebration of some technologies that would eventually present new problems for

investigation. For example: "When chemical fertilizers can be used in place of animal manures, when improved grain and cattle can be purposefully bred from inferior animals and grasses, when mechanical energy can be converted into heat and electricity into mechanical energy, man gains power to manipulate nature" (RP, MW 12:120).

19 Russell suggests that this is related to Dewey's Hegelian roots. On this controversy, see Thomas Burke, *Dewey's New Logic: A Reply to Russell* (Chicago: University of Chicago Press, 1998), 21ff.

20 Bacon's operative and active inductive method of the 1620s heralded the empiricism of the eighteenth century and, eventually, the experimental methods that gradually took hold in the nineteenth century. It was no mistake, in Dewey's view, to banish Aristotelian final causes from nature and to shift discussion about purposes to "factors in human minds capable of reshaping existence" (RP, MW 12:120). He baldly stated in *Reconstruction in Philosophy* that "A natural world that does not subsist for the sake of realizing a fixed set of ends is relatively malleable and plastic; it may be used for this end or that" (RP, MW 12:120).

21 Sidney Hook, *John Dewey: An Intellectual Portrait* (New York: John Day Co., 1939), 3.

22 For example, see Rorty's comparison of Heidegger and Dewey on the latter's treatment of "philosophies as if they were means to the enhancement of human life" (Richard Rorty, *Consequences of Pragmatism* [Minneapolis, MN: University of Minnesota Press, 1982], 50). In contrast with Heidegger (on a standard interpretation), Dewey did not relegate engagement with practical human problems to second-class status. He criticized all holdovers of the medieval *vita contemplativa* as aristocratic philosophies that maintain "institutionalized class interest" (LW 15:191).

23 On Borgmannn's critique, see Paul B. Thompson, *The Agrarian Vision* (Lexington, KY: University Press of Kentucky, 2010), ch. 5, "Farming as Focal Practice." For a critique of Borgmannn and Heidegger from the standpoint of Dewey's philosophy of technology, see Larry A. Hickman, *Pragmatism as Post-Postmodernism: Lessons from John Dewey* (New York: Fordham University Press, 2007), 92–111.

24 Eric Sloane, *Diary of an Early American Boy* (Mineola, NY: Courier Dover Publications, 2008), 31.

25 On inquiry as art, see Jim Garrison, *Dewey and Eros: Wisdom and Desire in the Art of Thinking* (New York: Teachers College Press, 1997).

26 Hickman, "Nature as Culture: John Dewey's Pragmatic Naturalism," 50. Other relevant works by Hickman include *Philosophical Tools for Technological Culture: Putting Pragmatism to Work* (Bloomington, IN: Indiana University Press, 2001); "Dewey's Theory of Inquiry," in *Reading Dewey: Interpretations for a Postmodern Generation*, ed. Larry A. Hickman (Bloomington, IN: Indiana University Press, 1998); and his earlier defense of a pragmatic view of technology in *John Dewey's Pragmatic Technology* (Bloomington, IN: Indiana University Press, 1990), 13ff. In contrast with Hickman's reading, Robert Brandom presents Dewey as a materialist whose instrumentalism pivots on subjective satisfaction of desires. See Robert B. Brandom, *Perspectives on Pragmatism* (Cambridge, MA: Harvard University Press, 2011), 42, 51–51, 72–77. Brandom's reading differs from my own.

Further reading

Thomas M. Alexander, *John Dewey's Theory of Art, Experience, and Nature: The Horizons of Feeling* (Albany, NY: SUNY Press, 1987).

Larry A. Hickman, *John Dewey's Pragmatic Technology* (Bloomington, IN: Indiana University Press, 1990).

Larry A. Hickman, *Philosophical Tools for Technological Culture: Putting Pragmatism to Work* (Bloomington, IN: Indiana University Press, 2001).

Philip W. Jackson, *John Dewey and the Lessons of Art* (New Haven, CT: Yale University Press, 1999).

Richard Shusterman, *Pragmatist Aesthetics: Living Beauty, Rethinking Art*, 2nd ed. (Lanham, MD: Rowman & Littlefield, 2000).

Seven

Religious philosophy reconstructed

A Common Faith was not addressed to those who are content with traditions in which "metaphysical" is substantially identical with "supernatural." It was addressed to those who have abandoned supernaturalism, and who on that account are reproached by traditionalists for having turned their backs on everything religious. The book was an attempt to show such persons that they still have within their experience all the elements which give the religious attitude its value.

(LW 14:80)

This chapter introduces Dewey's naturalistic reconstruction of religious attitudes and emotions. Two emphases bind his reflections on religious life with Chapter Six on aesthetics: the human drive toward meaningful consummations, and the necessity of breaking down the tall barriers that keep these consummations from becoming more widely available. Dewey's reconstruction of religious life must be understood in this context. It was a moral, aesthetic, and social-political critique. He did not expect it to be an entirely welcome one.

Doctrinal religion vs. the religious attitude

A few days after September 11, 2001, biologist Richard Dawkins wrote an essay for the *Guardian* in which he compared the religious conditioning of the 9/11 hijackers with B. F. Skinner's Second World War research on pigeon-guided missiles. The challenge, Dawkins wrote, is to

> develop a biological guidance system with the compliance and dispensability of a pigeon but with a man's resourcefulness and ability to infiltrate plausibly. ... As luck would have it, we have

just the thing to hand: a ready-made system of mind-control which has been honed over centuries, handed down through generations. Millions of people have been brought up in it. It is called religion and, for reasons which one day we may understand, most people fall for it.[1]

Dawkins's disdain for dogmatic religion that operates as mere belief-programming is shared by many modern practitioners and scholars of religion, but most traditional religionists persist in wrapping their outlook up with faith in a spring for human values external to terrestrial life. As Dewey noted, "faith" in the old and still dominant sense means "adherence to a creed consisting of set articles," such as the Apostle's Creed recited weekly in Christian churches. The acceptance of this checklist of propositions is "based upon authority—preferably that of revelation from on high" (LW 5:267). But there is also a newer, pragmatic notion of faith: faith as inspirational belief where doubt is still plausible. As William James famously perceived, often our active contribution is a necessary ingredient for bringing about a valued outcome, from getting a date to making a democracy work. We act because we believe in the possibility despite the absence of any guarantee. This is Dewey's melioristic sense of faith, which looks only to natural and human interactions for its "sole ultimate authority" (LW 5:267).

Dewey observed in *A Common Faith* (1934) that values pretending to be not-of-this-world are quarantined from critical scrutiny. The old dogmatic and otherworldly notion of faith is "common" only in the sense that it is widespread. But it is exactly opposite to a faith that could be shared across boundaries of sects and creeds. A discourse that culls the damned and the heretic inevitably frames salvation in terms of exclusive commitments not open to public questioning. Religious dogmatism implies access to unchanging and authoritative truths that were once upon a time revealed to a credentialed and privileged few through priestly vocation or spiritual attunement (see MW 4:173). Such a closed and limited faith, particularly when combined with nationalism, ethnocentrism, and defense of the economic establishment, is not a promising resource for greater responsibility, public dialogue, restoration of trust, or reconciliation. It *is* a resource for oppression, rage, and fanaticism.

In his *Candle in the Dark*, Irwin Edman wrote on the eve of the Second World War: "Men in the nineteenth century were sad that they could no longer believe in God; they are more deeply saddened now by the fact that they can no longer believe in man."[2] Dewey sought in *A Common Faith* to fill this hole with a secular and human-centered democratic faith "that shall not be confined to sect, class, or race" (ACF, LW 9:58). Most philosophers had by the 1930s left behind the supernatural metaphysics, natural rights perspective, and belief in nature's benevolent intentions that had inspired Jefferson. These views no longer had much traction. Dewey aimed to marry the devotion of the Jeffersonian democratic ideal with the intellectual integrity of an experimentalist and naturalist. The weaker our cultural faith in divinely ordained natural laws and natural rights, he declared in *Freedom and Culture*, "the more urgent is the need for a faith based on ideas that are now intellectually credible ... , which will inspire and direct action with something of the ardor once attached to things religious" (FC, LW 13:179). To be more than a utopian pipe dream, he held, such a faith needs to be already implicit in our emotional lives and our ordinary social interactions.

Dewey was a scathing critic of doctrinaire religion and a signatory to the *Humanist Manifesto* (1933).[3] But he strenuously rejected humanism as a name for his philosophy, except when "prefixed to naturalism" as naturalistic humanism. Regarding humanism as a philosophical stance on religion, he accepted the word's use for his own views solely in the special case of "opposition to supernaturalism." It was thus a "secondary aspect" of his philosophy, and he bristled at attempts by would-be disciples to limit his philosophy's scope to mere rejection of supernaturalism.[4] In fact, he seemed genuinely puzzled at why so many people found their own private rejection of an obsolete form of supernaturalism to be worthy of professional philosophical attention.

Dewey's writings on religion and religiosity appeared over a decade after he had lived for two-and-a-half years in East Asia. Though a critic of hierarchical collectivism in the Confucian model, Dewey had also imbibed what Roger Ames calls the human-centered religiousness that stands in relief against Western transcendental religion.[5] To appreciate this perspective, imagine a Western theologian giving a lecture in China or Japan on the subject "Does God Exist?" The mostly empty room might trouble someone living in a geographic bubble, until a realization finally dawns that the question of a supernatural being's existence is not essential philosophical terrain of universal import.

Dewey derided militant forms of atheism that are "impious toward nature" and that contemptuously fail to take seriously the qualitative, psychologically adjustive dimension of religious experience. He did not pen *A Common Faith* to urge the faithful to rethink the meagerness of their stated convictions. He wrote it to challenge naturalists to take seriously the function of religious attitudes, which he understood as an outgrowth of consummatory experience (e.g., AE, LW 10:23). He also aimed to defend the naturalist from traditionalists who claim that jettisoning supernaturalism leaves human experience flat and incomplete.[6] The mere fact that individuals have left behind the religion on which they were weaned does not entail that they have no "attitudes in themselves that if they came to fruition would be genuinely religious" (ACF, LW 9:8; cf. LW 14:80).

Dewey directed his intellectual energy toward social problems rather than religious questions (LW 5:154). Many who take religion and religious life to be essential philosophical territory tend also, he suggested, to be motivated more by partisanship for a particular worldview than by a general interest in understanding religious experience (LW 5:154). He nonetheless had an abiding, albeit highly qualified, respect for religious life "wherever religion is not hopelessly at the mercy of a Frankenstein philosophy which it originally called into being to be its own slave" (MW 4:142). His tendency was to write as though doctrinal religion is always irreconcilably at war with whatever is best and most humane in religious attitudes. If only we would heuristically examine religious attitudes in distinction from doctrinal religions we would finally find ourselves standing on essential philosophical terrain.

The relative value and import of *A Common Faith* within Dewey's corpus is disputed by scholars.[7] Sidney Hook, for example, shrugged it off as one of Dewey's minor works.[8] This dispute stems mostly from Dewey's use of religious language such as "faith," "the religious," and optionally even "God" (absent any hypostatized supernatural referent).

By *religious* Dewey did not mean religious experience in the popular sense. He described "the religious" as a "quality of experience," but this language continues to confuse readers who get hung up on colloquial meanings of the words quality and experience (see Chapter Two). He did not have in mind a subjective mental quality that marks a rare and peculiar type of experience that we popularly call "religious." That is, as Alexander observes, he was not zooming in on the subject matter of James's *Varieties of Religious Experience*. What Dewey had in mind instead was a general existential attitude adjustment, an active reorientation toward life's entire conditions (see ACF, LW 9:11–12).[9]

The use of the adjective *religious* was less of a stretch to Dewey's original audience—for example, it was used repeatedly in the first *Humanist Manifesto*. Dewey did not insist upon the word, only upon the profound importance of this attitude as an indigenous experiential function. It is all too common to dismiss the function along with the word. The experimentalist rejects foregone ecclesiastic conclusions and immediate knowledge, and the naturalist rejects supernatural explanations. One could readily sidestep Dewey's sparing religious terminology on these grounds. But he controversially held that there is equally little point in denying such usage as a reconstructive option.

Dewey's sense of the religious as a "mode or attitude of *existence*"[10] was presaged by George Eliot in her novel *Felix Holt*. Eliot's heroine Esther, a clergyman's daughter who is temporarily separated by tragic events from her politically strident friend Felix,

> had been so long used to hear the formulas of her father's belief without feeling or understanding them, that they had lost all power to touch her. The first religious experience of her life—the first self-questioning, the first voluntary subjection, the first longing to acquire the strength of greater motives and obey the more strenuous rule—had come to her through Felix Holt. No wonder that she felt as if the loss of him were inevitable backsliding.[11]

Take any significant event that reoriented your attitude toward living in a way that lent you "deep and enduring support" (ACF, LW 9:12) for your endeavors and that put you on a more secure and less irksome footing, from which you might at times "backslide."

In the language of *A Common Faith*, this reorientation in your attitude can be characterized as having a religious quality.

Dewey was acutely aware of the fact that many existential adjustments of a "religious" sort are primed by orthodoxies. Orthodoxies are only contented after a member of the flock arrives safely at a foregone conclusion that is then declared an epiphany.[12] Pressed for evidence to back up cherished intuitions, metaphysical idealists of all stripes tend to nod knowingly to religious experience. Yet these experiences, as Peirce observed, do not come prepackaged with their own interpretations. The way we interpret a religious event, Dewey noted, "is not inherent in the experience itself. It is derived from the culture with which a particular person has been imbued" (ACF, LW 9:10).

Dewey's relentless criticisms of monotheistic orthodoxies resonate today with devotees of popular countercultural spiritual movements, and with those who have rejected doctrinal religion while retaining a traditional metaphysical map. But his metaphysics and epistemology may offer them few footholds. For example, participants in "New Age" spiritualism, new offshoots of shamanism, contemporary paganism, and some (not all) forms of mysticism tend to affirm what philosophers call panpsychism, a belief that all is soul. Panpsychism shares the old Cartesian assumption that we must choose one of two substances (*res extensa* or *res cogitans*, body or mind) as the "fundamental and superior" one (LW 5:268). The panpsychist agrees with Dewey that Descartes was wrong about mind-body dualism, but then says Descartes' mistake was to separate matter from the one truly encompassing substance, a gaseous mind or spirit.

Compared to knowledge claims authorized by churches, synagogues, mosques, and temples, from Dewey's angle the most redeeming cultural feature in the many forms of New Age spiritualism is a relative lack of institutional respectability and sedentary dogma. They are blessedly not (yet) part of the establishment. Their least redeeming feature, however, is a pronounced tendency to believe in immediate knowledge: a mind directly tuned in to the fixed frequencies of the cosmos. A mental/physical dualism controls any magical outlook that seeks direct mental access to the way of things. Scientists, meanwhile, labor along the educational slowpoke route, mediating material inquiries by controlled techniques and scrutiny of physical evidence.

In Dewey's view, magical thinking is as much a flight from experience and a product of hypostatization as any other quest for extraempirical succor, singular purpose, and guaranteed security.

Eager claimants to immediate knowledge (see Chapter Three) feel that it dishonors an experience to politely observe that the experience does not on its own support a particular set of convictions. Inquiry might reveal many prospects for expansion and growth opened up by a religious experience, but partisans trade this growth in for a feeling of exceptionalism. They gain partisan security, and perhaps a compensatory sense that, again in Eliot's words, they are in "secure alliance with the unseen but supreme rule of a world in which their own visible part was small."[13] This possession, however much it reconciles people with their lot, is bought by conflating the religious quality of a complex and varied experience with the specific doctrines of a packaged religion.

Democracy as community and communion

When in pain, near death, Einstein was asked "Is everything all right?" "Everything is all right," he replied, "but I am not."[14] Most believe, with Einstein, that there is a relational attunement in the universe that can ultimately be affirmed as good, beautiful, and purposive. It is held that, in our greatest contemplative moments, this congenial attunement can be fathomed as a singular and benevolent unity. The only alternative most Westerners see is the cold, mechanistic, intellectualistic, and defiant one that Dewey joined others in reacting against. Neither alternative is at home in our emerging world. Dewey used Wordsworth's term "natural piety" (see Chapter Two) to characterize the possibility for wholehearted responsiveness to nature, a sensibility that ideally stays with us throughout our lives.[15]

Setting aside idle speculations about their piety toward nature, modern confrontational atheists such as Richard Dawkins and Daniel Dennett can be criticized on Dewey's grounds for failing to see the baby of reorienting experience in the bathwater of doctrinaire religion. Although Dawkins and Dennett do not fit neatly into Dewey's cross hairs, there are two familiar philosophical assumptions at the root of aggressive atheism, both rejected by Dewey. First, militant atheists single out knowing as the quintessential human activity, hence they commit the intellectualist's fallacy. Second, they labor under a spectator theory of knowing-without-acting and a conception of belief and meaning as propositional states. In this way they funnel the entire qualitative dimension of religious attitudes—that which inspires fulfilling actions—into a checklist of the set doctrines to which traditional religionists assent. On the militant atheist view, religious attitudes are significant only insofar as they are translatable into literally true propositions. In contrast, for Dewey as for other classical pragmatists, beliefs are interpreted and evaluated as dispositions to act one way rather than another, and the enriching and generative possibilities of human existence go unrealized except through action.

That said, insofar as traditional religionists themselves shrink-wrap the meaning of their own varied experiences into truth assertions about existence, militant atheists and Dewey are allied in opposition to them. As Kitcher observes, Dewey disparaged sophisticated religious apologists who "provide cover for fanatics" through their unwillingness to publicly declare which commitments must be jettisoned.[16]

Nonetheless, intense and evocative experiences, distinguishable from sectarian baggage, may reach deep into our attitudes toward existence and effectively reorient our lives. Such events may open up new possibilities for growth and social communion. They may help us to meet each situation in a way that expresses what is best in our whole characters, checking us from falling back on reactive habits. They may heal our traditional dualistic antagonism toward and estrangement from nature. They may transform behaviors, change fundamental attitudes toward living, and even affect the way shared activities and enjoyments are coordinated within an entire social system. In Dewey's view, such qualitatively rich, adjustive experiences are the fundamental constituents of religious life, while doctrines are secondary accretions. Against all odds, such reorienting events persist among many religious practitioners despite being hijacked by doctrine.

If such events are "religious," then they may at least potentially gain richness through texts, cultural symbols, and traditions. As Kitcher observes, militant atheists can plausibly argue here, in opposition to Dewey, that religious experiences are rooted in promulgated doctrines, and that the psychology of religious experiences grows out of these more fundamental beliefs.[17] If so, then Dewey's argument is shaky, as the religious attitude cannot in that case be meaningfully distinguished from its subjugation to the overreaching of partisan religious institutions.

However, as discussed in Chapter Two, Dewey argued that this is only half of the story. The map is not the journey. Doctrinal accretions are abstractions that inevitably cycle back to shape primary experiences, but they can be inspected, reconstructed, or shed altogether as communities mature and grow. The aggressive atheist, hand-in-hand with the fundamentalist, conflates the secondary doctrinal products of religion with primary religious experiences, and so plays a zero-sum game that ignores change and growth. The historical evidence for doctrinal reconstruction is unambiguous. "I have enough faith in the depth of the religious tendencies of men," Dewey rather hopefully concluded, "to believe that they will adapt themselves to any required intellectual change, and that it is futile (and likely to be dishonest) to forecast prematurely just what forms the religious interest will take as a final consequence of the great intellectual transformation that is going on" (LW 5:153). What remains is to liberate historic religions from "zombie" ideas and methods (see Introduction).

When religion plants the oak of human faith in a flowerpot of sedimented beliefs, doctrines, or fixed ends, the constrictive pot should be rejected. Dewey held that there is no "essence" of religion such that it is essentially either a toxin or a blessing, but in *A Common Faith* he consistently identified religion with sectarian dogma: "The opposition between religious values as I conceive them and religions is not to be bridged. Just because the release of these values is so important, their identification with the creeds and cults of religions must be dissolved" (ACF, LW 9:36).

Dewey was not sanguine that religion's tendency to shunt experience down exclusive channels would ever do more than divert and narrow whatever is good in humanity's socially transformative religious attitudes. But he focused his criticisms only on the *intellectual* tendency to identify human religious attitudes with narrowing partisan set articles. Historically, religious attitudes have been lived out through the stories, symbols, and practices of historic religions, and Dewey conceived it as a possibility—however dim—that religions might finally grow out of their trappings to support "the better adjustment in life and its conditions" (ACF, LW 9:11).

One doctrine Dewey thought especially ill-suited to our common welfare is the trivializing proposition that Earthly happenings are secondary to an ontologically superior realm. Plotinus, Augustine, and their twenty-first-century descendants would cringe at the degeneracy and disorderliness of Dewey's fundamental love and orientation toward the natural and humane. They would judge his existential attitude "fallen," because he asserted that we can best learn to listen, relate, and love without recourse to a fixed anchorage in a realm of spirit. John Calvin took the Christian notion that we should be "in, but not of" the world to a troubling extreme: "If Heaven is our country, what is the Earth but a place of exile?" Limiting the sacred to encounters with a supernatural Being sidelines the sacredness of the everyday and humane, which seemed to Dewey the proper center of gravity for a rich religious discourse.

At the same time, taken pragmatically, God as love reinforces some of our best ideals, while God as truth blocks the road of inquiry. Unlike Dawkins, Dewey held that the evolution of religious practices, moral images, and communal narratives holds potential personal and public value for transforming relationships to "create a vital sense of the solidarity of human interests and inspire action to make that sense a reality" (LW 5:273–74). Although a common faith need not await such a hopeful turn of events, religions could help to direct human emotions in a way that enhances and expresses faith in the possibilities of our cultural existence. If institutions that are nominally religious evolve through open critical inquiry, they might "become useful allies of a conception of life that is in harmony with knowledge and social needs" (LW 5:274).

Communal religious narratives are not simply reducible to mind control. Faith communities may offer resources to see beyond sectarian ties so that their rites and symbols open new possibilities for public inquiry and humane solidarity. But the fact that a community cherishes a set of values—say, the Ten Commandments or sharia law—does not on its own justify which values ought to be socially consecrated. So there is need for the arbitration of a wider outlook to separate the recyclables from the refuse. The outlook Dewey proposed, of course, is experimental intelligence attached to a democratic faith. This offers a direction for religious emotions that restores intellectual integrity while contributing to greater responsibility. "One of the few experiments in the attachment of emotion to ends that mankind has not tried," Dewey urged, "is that of devotion, so intense as to be religious, to intelligence as a force in social action" (ACF, LW 9:53).

Is the word "God" rubbish? Dewey argued throughout *Experience and Nature* that no unifying superordinate-level substance like mind or soul or God is logically or practically required for experience to cohere, value to emerge, and criticism to reconstruct. He wrote in *A Common Faith* that God is "a unification of ideal values" that we have hypostatized into "an antecedent reality" (ACF, LW 9:29–30). At best, a supernatural God is superfluous for Dewey, and in theories of personal identity (selfhood) a foundational substance like "soul" or "mind" is redundant. At worst, traditional substance-thinking hearkens to a metaphysical map of dependency on and servility to a cosmic monarchy in which biological organisms are split from a perfected realm of timeless truths and law. The metaphysical monarchist may belittle human neural anatomy as a pale imitation of a completed Mind whose sovereign guidance is required to live the best life. From that perspective it is no wonder that little trust is placed in human inquiry to solve widely shared problems. The actual result is that conclusions are dictated by whichever conceptual framework currently wields authority. Dewey regarded this deeply entrenched outlook as one of our chief intellectual obstacles to moral, social-political, and scientific wisdom.

In Dewey's account, the jealous God of traditional theism as an exclusive object of worship has been disintegrated by experimental methods. Many will miss Him. But underneath this notion of a personal divine author there exists something real that was long ago hypostatized "into a single objective existence, a God" (ACF, LW 9:35). The undeniable fact operating behind the noun God is that people experience "a multitude of factors and forces" as furthering human goods, and they regard these as worth cherishing (LW 9:221). These goods are various, but they operate as a force in cultural existence whenever people unite their actions with their most esteemed ideals.

This "working union of the ideal and actual" has been densely concentrated into the concept "God" in a way that intensifies emotions. Dewey held that "intelligent and honest persons will differ among themselves as to the desirability of carrying over the term, God" (LW 9:221). Some will avoid such "hypostatic concentration," choosing instead to distribute their devotion and affection to a variety of objects. Dewey regarded this as the saner course, less given to the excesses that have marked theism. He insisted that those who choose to distribute their devotions, rather than concentrate them in a God, can enjoy within the "normal processes of living and human relationships all the goods which the theist, no matter how liberal, is still striving to confine to special types of experience and to particular objects and systems of objects" (LW 9:222).

Summary

Eager claimants to immediate knowledge conflate the religious quality of a complex and varied experience with the specific doctrines and foregone conclusions of a packaged religion. Nonetheless, Dewey did not write A Common Faith to urge the faithful to rethink the meagerness of their convictions. He wrote it to challenge those who have rejected supernaturalism to take seriously the function of religious attitudes. Dewey derided militant forms of atheism that are "impious toward nature" and that contemptuously shrug off the qualitative, psychologically adjustive function of religious experience. He argued that experimental intelligence attached to a democratic faith offers a direction for religious emotions that restores intellectual integrity, responsibility, and joy.

Notes

1 Richard Dawkins, "Religion's Misguided Missiles," The Guardian, September 15, 2001, http://www.theguardian.com/world/2001/sep/15/september11.politicsphilosophyandsociety1; accessed September 26, 2014.

2 Irwin Edman, Candle in the Dark: A Postscript to Despair (New York: Viking Press, 1939), 10.

3 Dewey wrote: "I signed the humanistic manifesto precisely because of the point to which you seem to object, namely because it had a religious context, and my signature was a sign of sympathy on that score, and not a commitment to every clause in it." 1940.09.06 (13667): Dewey to Corliss Lamont. Notwithstanding Dewey's rejection of the term humanism, his legacy through Paul Kurtz (1925–2012), who in 1973 drafted Humanist Manifesto II,

was far-reaching. See Kurtz's obituary at http://www.prometheusbooks.com/public/PKAnnouncement.html; accessed June 12, 2014.

4 He wrote to Lamont: "I note that you prefer the word Humanism as a name for my philosophy. I do not, and have definite objection to it save as an adjective prefixed to Naturalism." 1940.09.14 (13677): Dewey to Corliss Lamont, typos silently corrected.

5 See Roger T. Ames, *Confucian Role Ethics: A Vocabulary* (Honolulu, HI: University of Hawai'i Press, 2011).

6 Looking back to Dewey's Terry Lectures (i.e., *A Common Faith*) for inspiration, Philip Kitcher offered a fresh defense of secular humanism in his 2013 Terry Lectures, recently expanded and published as *Life after Faith: The Case for Secular Humanism* (New Haven, CT: Yale University Press, 2014). Kitcher's main line of argument is a response to the old accusation that rejecting supernaturalism leaves experience flat and incomplete.

7 See Thomas M. Alexander, "John Dewey's Uncommon Faith: Understanding 'Religious Experience,'" *American Catholic Philosophical Quarterly* 87, no. 2 (2013): 347–62, at 347–48.

8 See Sidney Hook, *John Dewey: An Intellectual Portrait* (New York: John Day Co., 1939), ch. 11.

9 See Alexander, "John Dewey's Uncommon Faith: Understanding 'Religious Experience,'" 351.

10 Alexander, "John Dewey's Uncommon Faith: Understanding 'Religious Experience,'" 357.

11 George Eliot, *Felix Holt: The Radical* (London: Penguin Books, 1995 [1866]), 254. See AE, LW 10:289 for a direct reference by Dewey to Eliot's novel, though not in the context of religious attitudes.

12 For a thoughtful autobiographical critique of orthodox religious attitudes, see Stephen Batchelor, *Confession of a Buddhist Atheist* (New York: Random House, 2010).

13 Eliot, *Felix Holt*, 48.

14 Walter Isaacson, *Einstein* (New York: Simon & Schuster, 2007), 541.

15 See Alexander, "John Dewey's Uncommon Faith: Understanding 'Religious Experience,'" 356–57.

16 Philip Kitcher, *Preludes to Pragmatism: Toward a Reconstruction of Philosophy* (Oxford: Oxford University Press, 2012), 289.

17 Kitcher, *Preludes to Pragmatism*, 291.

Further reading

Thomas M. Alexander, "John Dewey's Uncommon Faith: Understanding 'Religious Experience,'" *American Catholic Philosophical Quarterly* 87, no. 2 (2013): 347–62.

Philip Kitcher, *Life after Faith: The Case for Secular Humanism* (New Haven, CT: Yale University Press, 2014).

Steven C. Rockefeller, *John Dewey: Religious Faith and Democratic Humanism* (New York: Columbia University Press, 1991).

Eight
Influence and legacy

In considering a system of philosophy in its relation to national factors it is necessary to keep in mind not only the aspects of life which are incorporated in the system, but also the aspects against which the system is a protest. There never was a philosopher who has merited the name for the simple reason that he glorified the tendencies and characteristics of his social environment; just as it is also true that there never has been a philosopher who has not seized upon certain aspects of the life of his time and idealized them.

(LW 2:6)

It made ready sense to philosophical popularizer Will Durant's 1926 audience that his best-selling *The Story of Philosophy* began with Plato and ended with Dewey, who "has given philosophic form to the realistic and democratic temper of his people."[1] As a cultural icon Dewey's star remained high until some years after his death. In *The Atlantic*'s December 2006 list of "the 100 most influential Americans of all time," Dewey, James, and philosophical social scientist W. E. B. DuBois were the only academic philosophers to rank. *Life* magazine, for its part, hailed Dewey in 1990 as one of the "100 most important Americans of the 20th century."[2] The US Postal Service honored Dewey in 1968 with a postage stamp as part of its Prominent Americans series.[3] Astronaut Story Musgrave even took a copy of Dewey's *Art as Experience* with him on a 1991 space shuttle mission as a reminder to enjoy the aesthetic experience of space flight and not get lost in mechanical tasks.[4]

Philosophers build houses of theory. The dimensions, room locations, and finishing touches are our own, but the overall floor designs and general layouts juxtapose the architectural labors of other philosophers. There are few master philosophical architects of the twentieth century whose constructions became archetypes for thousands of others and whose influence is still expanding. By these criteria, John Dewey must be included on any short list.

Dewey's heyday among professional philosophers, as distinct from his status as a cultural icon, arguably fell roughly between the 1916 publication of *Democracy and Education* and his seventieth birthday celebration, attended by thousands in 1929.[5] As the Anglo-American "analytic" tradition began to shape academic philosophy in the United States in the 1930s and 1940s, Dewey's direct influence waned among professional philosophers (see Introduction). As Edman observed in 1955, analytic philosophers found Dewey "too large and vague," postwar existentialists found him "too hopeful," theologians and metaphysical idealists found him "too earthbound and secular," and doctrinaire conservatives did not "find in him fixed dogmas."[6]

In the academy he remained a dominant figure primarily among theorists housed in university schools of education and education departments. He identified himself above all as a philosopher who conceives the problems of education as philosophy's best medium, and his influence among scholars of education in the United States—at least on rhetoric if not practice (see Chapter Five)—has never flagged. Of course Dewey's influence on education extended far beyond his writings. An editorial written to mark his eightieth birthday rightly noted his far-reaching national and international influence as an educational reformer: "there are countless school children today and yesterday whose lives have been influenced in a constructive way by this one man who never shouted, and whose formally stated philosophy often is a stiff dose for more subtle minds."[7]

Since the 1980s, professional philosophical interest in Dewey has grown exponentially, both within and outside traditional philosophy departments. This renascence is due in part to professional organization in the early 1970s by philosophers working to advance the classical American tradition, giving birth to the Society for the Advancement of American Philosophy.[8] Another catalyst for the growing professional interest in Dewey has been the language-oriented "neopragmatist" movement generally associated with philosophers such as Rorty, Putnam, and Richard Brandom.[9]

Dewey's renascence has also been fueled by publication of the critical edition of his works under the editorship of Jo Ann Boydston, along with publication of his correspondence under the editorship of Larry Hickman. Over the past twenty years, centers for Dewey studies have opened in China, Italy, Germany, Poland, Hungary, Japan, Turkey, Argentina, and Spain, in addition to the original Center for Dewey Studies in Carbondale, Illinois.[10]

The resurgence of interest in Dewey in the 1980s and 1990s was most pronounced in epistemology with comparatively scant attention to other areas, but this has changed. To sample the diversity of research, consider the dissertations of newly minted philosophy PhDs. From 2000 to 2009 there were 65 PhD dissertations in philosophy in the United States that had Dewey as a primary focus. About one-third of these were general studies of Dewey or comparative studies with another major philosopher. The rest ran the gamut of subject areas, including philosophy of education (11 dissertations), ethics (8), social-political philosophy (9), Chinese comparative philosophy (7), philosophy of religion (5), and aesthetics (3). Each of these areas is discussed in prior chapters.

For the sake of a manageable scope that nonetheless presents a representative slice of the variety of ongoing research, I will introduce a small sampling of contemporary Dewey-inspired developments in social-political philosophy and ethics. As discussed in Chapter Five, Dewey argued for a democratic way of life that incorporates different voices instead of sacrificing them on the altar of myopic preconceptions. Contemporary movements such as pragmatist feminism, pragmatist bioethics, legal pragmatism, prophetic pragmatism, and environmental pragmatism are among the many legacies of Dewey's pluralistic and democratic approach to value inquiry. Without any intimation of relative importance, the first section will explore one of these movements, environmental pragmatism. The subsequent section will offer snapshots of Dewey's far-reaching and increasing influence in current social-political philosophy and ethics.

Environmental pragmatism

Contemporary environmental pragmatism is part of the legacy of Dewey's pluralistic, democratic approach to situations that involve conflicting values. Environmental pragmatism is an orientation toward environmental philosophy that grew out of frustration with the dominant trend in twentieth-century environmental thought, which was the search for a single coherent and defensible paradigm—Dewey would say *conceptual framework* (e.g., see LTI, LW 12:46, 76)—for understanding the appropriate relationship between human beings and the rest of nature.[11] The prevailing view had been that we cannot solve our environmental problems with anything short of a revolutionary cultural paradigm shift away from anthropocentrism (human-centeredness) and toward ecocentrism (ecosystem-centeredness).

Environmental pragmatists such as Bryan Norton, Andrew Light, and Anthony Weston reject this attempt to find a single paradigm with which we must align ourselves. Another leading environmental pragmatist, Paul Thompson, is additionally a principal voice in agricultural philosophy and the ethics of biotechnology, who has uncovered American pragmatism's agrarian roots.[12]

In their edited volume *Environmental Pragmatism* (1996), which helped to solidify this movement, Andrew Light and Eric Katz define environmental pragmatism as "the open-ended inquiry into specific real-life problems of humanity's relationship with the environment."[13] Bryan Norton's *Toward Unity among Environmentalists* (1991), one of the most influential books by an environmental pragmatist, argues that when almost all who take a problem seriously agree that the status quo is ethically unacceptable, yet disagree about why, we must prioritize a deliberative process to agree upon actions and policies rather than insisting upon fundamental agreement about justifications. In this way we can grapple with problems that involve competing value frameworks, emphasizing convergence on solutions (or at least a way forward) rather than simply advocating for one's preferred framework.[14]

Norton's and Light's respective versions of pragmatic pluralism differ somewhat from those developed by ethicists who work more directly and explicitly in the classical American philosophical tradition that included Dewey. Hugh McDonald's edited volume *Pragmatism and Environmentalism* (2012) offers a good representation.[15] Classically oriented environmental pragmatists agree with Norton and Light that an emphasis on convergence is salutary. But as illustrated in Chapter Four, classical pragmatists more explicitly approach environmental philosophy using tools honed through the pragmatist tradition to highlight relevant situational factors hidden by dominant monistic conceptual frameworks. For example, the emerging movement of animal pragmatism has been well informed by classical sources, as seen in Erin McKenna and Andrew Light's edited volume *Animal Pragmatism: Rethinking Human–Nonhuman Relationships* (2004) and McKenna's *Pets, People, and Pragmatism* (2013).

In the field of environmental philosophy more generally, Dewey's legacy is still very much being written, but some baselines from his map can be noted here. The classic idea of harmonious nature, married to the persistent (anti-Darwinian) Aristotelian doctrine that nature does nothing in vain, fed a nineteenth-century romantic backlash against the modern Cartesian schism of values from nature. In the United States, romantic tendencies toward the revalorization of nature shone through the great transcendentalists Emerson and Thoreau and found an environmental champion in John Muir's view of nature as a sympathetic home that ultimately requires little adaptation or transformation.[16] On the romantic "preservationist" view, things are ultimately what they ought to be, which is a pleasant thought until we remember with Dewey that we have intellectually fashioned a harmonious and complete Nature in the image of our own greatly magnified and hypostatized ideals. It is easier to serve and accommodate, without reshaping, a natural world that we believe has a final order, a single ultimate purpose, and an infinite store of goodness. Our world, however, is a moving world.

We did not begin "playing God" with the advent of nuclear technology or genetic modification. If playing God means elevating humans above nature, then our tradition has cast human minds and human knowledge in this troublesome transcendental role all along. Since the seventeenth century, philosophers have increasingly downplayed or rejected the old supernaturalism, retained the damaging sense of separateness from nature, and played up the antagonism that pits us against nature. These intellectual habits have outlived whatever usefulness they once had. Dewey's existential attitude of "natural piety" in *A Common Faith* was an attempt to reconcile what is best in our romanticism with our scientific outlooks toward nature.

As the visible and invisible shock waves of our sciences and technologies spread irrevocably deeper into nature, one of the greatest challenges of the twenty-first century is to cultivate habits of ecological imagination that enable us, when guided by the consequences of past decisions, to mediate shared problems while also reconciling our scientific and aesthetic attitudes. Dewey's view supports and strengthens the ecological habit of forecasting the way this act here will tug at proximal and distant others, in the absence of which we make whatever end we are defensibly pursuing less secure. The destabilizing effect of our ecological myopia is magnified by a global economic milieu in which a sense of blameless innocence among consumers and corporations is purchased by ignorance of the hazards posed by our business-as-usual behaviors.

Dewey in contemporary social-political philosophy and ethics

Dewey's work has been a powerful resource for philosophers who are framing a theory of moral imagination that is compatible with contemporary cognitive research, such as Mark Johnson's *Morality for Humans: Ethical Understanding from the Perspective of Cognitive Science* (2014).[17] Contemporary sciences of mind have far surpassed Dewey in technical sophistication and detailed experiment, but they lack his philosophical sophistication. Of course he did not know that dramatic rehearsal—like any sort of attentive planning or decision-making—activates the prefrontal cortex, or that imagining an alternative scenario for action simulates a physical encounter that strengthens synaptic connections in the same neural region that would be involved in a direct physical encounter.[18]

Dewey analyzed experiences in terms of diverse functions and phases in the absence of much knowledge about *how* such processing occurs and how it is structured, but cognitive scientists are benefiting from his trailblazing insights into imagination and qualitative thought as they map the territory of projective mental habits like metaphors, images, semantic frames, symbols, and narratives.[19] Dewey anticipated that the way our imaginative habits develop along definite lines through our embodied interactions is no more (or less) mysterious than any other neurally instantiated, emergent habit. And he anticipated the most important practical upshot: the capacity for fine-grained imaginative simulation can be nurtured by education.

Dewey's influence in ethics continues rapidly to gain momentum. In *Pragmatic Bioethics* (2003), for example, Glenn McGee brings together a venerable team of Dewey-inspired philosophers to respond with perception and empathy to the vexing details of complex bioethical questions in the absence of any "simple ethics machine or a bucket of solutions that can be dumped on any emergent fire."[20] In *Community as Healing: Pragmatist Ethics in Medical Encounters* (2001), Micah Hester draws from Dewey to incisively criticize principle-based bioethics and inhumane atomistic views of patients. Instead, he advocates communities of healing that help us to negotiate perplexing decisions with families and clinicians. In *Intellectual Disability: Ethics, Dehumanization, and a New Moral Community* (2013), Heather Keith and Kenneth Keith draw from the social ethics of Dewey and Addams, and from Dewey's theory of intelligence as a function rather than an entity, as they chart an empathetic course beyond the notion that our rational grappling power is the essential defining trait of our humanity.

Dewey's legacy in social and political philosophy continues to grow, perhaps most visibly through the prism of African-American identity, from Cornel West's "prophetic pragmatism" in *The American Evasion of Philosophy: A Genealogy of Pragmatism* (1989) to Eddie Glaude Jr.'s more recent engagement with Dewey's rich sense of tragedy *In a Shade of Blue: Pragmatism and the Politics of Black America* (2007).[21] In another vital area of contemporary research, philosophers such as Kwame Anthony Appiah and Leonard Harris place Dewey and fellow classical pragmatists in conversation with their African-American contemporaries such as W. E. B. DuBois and Alain Locke, as part of an effort to articulate a more inclusive and durable democratic ethics and politics.[22]

Scores of scholars have produced books and articles articulating a visionary pragmatist feminism that incorporates and critiques Dewey's philosophy while also recovering voices of the pragmatist tradition's founding mothers, most notably Jane Addams.[23] Charlene Seigfried's now classic *Feminism and Pragmatism: Reweaving the Social Fabric* (1996) was the principal book that gave coherence to this orientation. Maurice Hamington and Celia Bardwell-Jones's *Contemporary Feminist Pragmatism* (2012) is a more recent volume that thoroughly engages Dewey. In *Deep Democracy* (1999) and *Pragmatism and Social Hope* (2008), Judith Green draws from fellow feminist pragmatists as well as Dewey, Royce, and Alain Locke to deepen democratic community life.[24] Nel Noddings, Shannon Sullivan, Erin McKenna, Lisa Heldke, and Heather Keith are among the many pragmatist feminist philosophers who demonstrate the truth of Dewey's statement on feminist philosophy in "What I Believe" (1930):

> The codes which still nominally prevail are the result of one-sided and restricted conditions. Present ideas of love, marriage, and the family are almost exclusively masculine constructions. Like all idealizations of human interests that express a dominantly one-sided experience, they are romantic in theory and prosaic in operation. ... The growing freedom of women can hardly have any other outcome than the production of more realistic and more human morals.
>
> (LW 5:276)

In another burgeoning field, legal pragmatism, United States Circuit Judge Richard Posner defends existing democratic legal institutions from Dewey's more progressive, participatory vision of democracy.[25] In a work that better fathoms Dewey's social and political moves, Michael Sullivan in *Legal Pragmatism* (2007) draws from Dewey to develop a pragmatist defense of rights based on individual growth. He criticizes the late legal philosopher Ronald Dworkin, who had developed a dismissive, straw-man view of pragmatism's approach to rights. Dewey's democratic ideal, Sullivan argues, supports the construction of laws as social tools and the use of the legal system to uphold rights against majority opinions.[26]

Dewey in dialogue

There are many general affinities between ongoing scholarly work engaging Dewey, and scholarly work in other philosophical traditions. His philosophy is today playing a vital role in cross-cultural and emerging cultural dialogue. Many scholars are pursuing comparative projects, especially American–Continental, American–East Asian, and North American–Latin American. In addition to comparative work, Dewey's philosophy is being actively discussed in an emerging global philosophical culture that is continuing to grow beyond—or at least more aware of—philosophy's inherent provincialism. As above, I will limit the scope to a very small but hopefully representative sampling of cross-cultural developments in social-political philosophy broadly construed, hoping to offer just enough to whet appetites.

Just as he had hoped, Dewey's emphases on contextual sensitivity and the felt qualities of all human experience continue to hold great promise for facilitating East–West dialogue that is mutually transformative rather than unidirectionally assimilative. The literature on Dewey and East Asia is extensive, and it is growing rapidly due in part to the nearly completed Chinese translation of the thirty-seven-volume *Collected Works* at Fudan University in Shanghai. If we simplify matters by focusing only on Dewey and Chinese philosophy, some key titles include Roger Ames's *Confucian Role Ethics: A Vocabulary* (2011), Roger Ames and David L. Hall's *Democracy of the Dead: Dewey, Confucius, and the Hope for Democracy in China* (1999), Jessica Ching-Sze Wang's *John Dewey in China: To Teach and to Learn* (2007), and Joseph Grange's *John Dewey, Confucius, and Global Philosophy* (2004).[27] Much of this work aims at understanding and developing the networks of social and natural relationships in which our lives are embedded and grow. As discussed, Dewey held that such cross-cultural dialogue is desperately needed to rejuvenate us all from tendencies in techno-industrial societies toward anesthetization and irresponsibility.

Scholarly inquiry on the meaning of "American" in "American philosophy" has produced many books and articles exploring the roots and fruits of the American tradition in which Dewey worked. In *Pragmatism in the Americas* (2011), Gregory Pappas breaks new ground for inter-American collaboration by bringing together essays by Latin American, North American, and Spanish philosophers to undermine United States exclusivity regarding its intellectual borders and to challenge the notion that there are two Americas not crossed by any philosophical bridge. Like jazz, Dewey's pragmatism was North American in its historical origin, Pappas observes. But both jazz and pragmatism continue to evolve outside the United

States, and what is called the Hispanic world is a vital cultural participant within the United States, no less in our growing intellectual life than in jazz. In part as a result of this important volume, a 2012 conference in Mexico City explored the reception and enduring significance of Dewey's visits to Mexico on American/Latin American philosophy.

Further undermining exclusionary biases regarding what is "American" in pragmatism, in *Native Pragmatism: Rethinking the Roots of American Philosophy* (2002) Scott Pratt hypothesizes potential lines of influence by indigenous Americans on the eventual development of Dewey's pragmatic pluralism. Thomas Alexander, in *The Human Eros* (2013), explores metaphors of "cooperative action and experimental discovery" in Native American wisdom traditions and in Dewey's philosophy of experience, and he develops a contrast between the earthward native orientation toward the sacred and the traditional skyward Western orientation.[28]

At this writing there are three European journals dedicated to American philosophy, each of which attends carefully to Dewey. For example, a special issue of the *European Journal of Pragmatism and American Philosophy* entitled *Language or Experience: Charting Pragmatism's Course for the 21st Century* (2014) extends Dewey's legacy by advancing the debate between classically steeped pragmatism and language-focused neopragmatism.[29] Dozens of books also explore Dewey in relation to Continental philosophy, including Paul Fairfield's edited volume on *John Dewey and Continental Philosophy* (2010) and Mitchell Aboulafia, Myra Bookman, and Cathy Kemp's *Habermas and Pragmatism* (2002).[30]

Richard Bernstein of the New School for Social Research carried the torch for Dewey in dialogue with Continental philosophy even while Dewey's star was low among professional philosophers. Bernstein's clear and insightful *The Pragmatic Turn* (2010) is a culminating scholarly work placing Dewey, James, and Peirce in dialogue with Hegel, Habermas, Putnam, Rorty, and others. He recently responded to younger critics in Judith Green's edited volume *Richard J. Bernstein and the Pragmatist Turn in Contemporary Philosophy: Rekindling Pragmatism's Fire* (2014).[31]

Victor Kestenbaum's *The Phenomenological Sense of John Dewey* (1977) was among the first to pursue a comparative analysis of Dewey with French phenomenologist Merleau-Ponty, a study furthered by

Shannon Sullivan in *Living across and through Skins: Transactional Bodies, Pragmatism, and Feminism* (2001).[32] In a series of recent books that includes *Pragmatism Ascendent* (2012), Joseph Margolis applauds the hybridization of Dewey's naturalism with contemporary Continental and analytic philosophy and advances "a future pragmatism no longer parochially bound to its American provenance but unwilling to deny its genealogical engine."[33] And as we struggle in international affairs to chart a course toward a more democratic future, Molly Cochran's essay in *The Cambridge Companion to Dewey* (2010) urges reconsideration and rehabilitation of Dewey as an international political philosopher.[34]

Appraised against the backdrop of twentieth-century European philosophy, Dewey is sometimes conceived as too modern, still caught up in completing the Enlightenment project. He is too trusting of "makers" for Julia Kristeva, too "calculative" for Heidegger. In Hook's view, Dewey is in an odd sense the culmination of the Enlightenment project which sought to liberate knowledge from the shackles of dogma and to liberate humanity from its cacophony.[35] Dewey exemplified the courageous spirit of the Enlightenment by shattering its own assumptions.

It is true that Dewey was not satisfied with deconstruction alone. But he was acutely aware that he was constructing (see Chapters Two and Three). He still had the audacity to engage in philosophical reconstruction work with some shrewd Yankee earnestness, not with Rorty's carefree irony or Michel Foucault's omnipresent suspicion of all constructive projects.[36] Philosophy after Auschwitz is rightly suspicious of overweening confidence, and scholars such as John McDermott argue persuasively that Dewey did not have a theory of evil adequate to the atrocities of the Holocaust (in LW 11: xxxii). Yet Dewey's philosophy is "postmodern" in many relevant respects, without becoming a hall of mirrors.[37] It is a plea for concerted, yet tempered and self-aware, intelligence. Given the insistent problems of our own day, it is mature and realistic, not a philosophical analgesic, to renew an energizing and self-testing trust in human possibility. Dewey wrote early in the 1930s:

> The possession of constructive ideals is taken to be an admission that one is living in a realm of fantasy. We have lost confidence in reason because we have learned that man is chiefly a

creature of habit and emotion. The notion that habit and impulse can themselves be rendered intelligent on any large and social scale is felt to be only another illusion. Because the hopes and expectations of the past have been discredited, there is cynicism as to all far-reaching plans and policies. That the very knowledge which enables us to detect the illusory character of past hopes and aspirations—a knowledge denied those who held them—may enable us to form purposes and expectations that are better grounded, is overlooked.

(LW 5:276–77)

Conclusion

Life mocks the relentless deductions of doctrinal systems. To the extent that Dewey's naturalistic empiricism or cultural naturalism was a system, it was at any rate not a closed system to safeguard. It was a map to journey with, revise, and improve. His work is not the possession of modern-day disciples.

Irwin Edman wrote in 1955 that "Dewey in a deep sense is the voice of a persistent central hard core of practical sense and humane hope and courage in this country." The alternatives to rigorous intelligence and engaged imagination, Edman added, are "fanaticism, nihilism, sentimentalism, triviality or despair."[38] Even amid rising global awareness of the unplanned systemic effects that radiate from our actions—such as alienated work, resource depletion, climate change, and institutionalized discrimination—it has become increasingly difficult for ordinary citizens to give coherent and positive meaning to the relationships that twine us up with each other and with natural systems.[39] We must nevertheless negotiate the complex systems in which our relationships inhere, in our private choices and through our laws, governing institutions, international institutions, and educational systems. And we must make the journey in the absence of the familiar landmarks that once guided us and gave us an unwarranted sense of assured security. We are much in need of courageous young intellectuals who are intent on engaging these problems with fresh hypotheses.[40]

Dewey's philosophy has become a global resource for regenerating our social and natural interconnections while avoiding moralistic or authoritarian education that freezes growth. He understood that an education focused exclusively on technological training and transmission of discrete knowledge will do little to ameliorate our problems. Ideally we will educate in a way that will bring meaning and a renewed sense of responsibility to what would otherwise be no more than the "flickering inconsequential acts of separate selves" (HNC, MW 14:227).

Summary

Dewey's reputation as a cultural icon continued to be strong well after his leadership among philosophers in the United States had faded. Dewey and other classical pragmatists were by the 1960s dismissed by the majority of mainstream professional philosophers as crude figures whose positive achievements had been fully assimilated by the more exacting style and methods of the Anglo-American or "analytic" philosophers who replaced them. But since the 1980s interest in Dewey's work has grown exponentially among professional philosophers, and this growth is ongoing. In addition to work in international relations, a representative sample of current scholarship in social-political philosophy and ethics, for example, would include pragmatist feminism, pragmatist bioethics, legal pragmatism, prophetic pragmatism, and environmental pragmatism among the many legacies of Dewey's pluralistic and democratic approach.

Notes

1 Will Durant, *The Story of Philosophy* (New York: Simon & Schuster, 1926), 576.
2 "Influence," The Center for Dewey Studies at Southern Illinois University Carbondale, http://deweycenter.siu.edu/about_influence.html; accessed August 25, 2014.
3 Excepting the constitutional framers and Ralph Waldo Emerson, Dewey, Addams, and DuBois are the only philosophers to date to be honored with US postage stamps.
4 See John Yemma, "The Astronaut Who Learned How to See," *The Christian Science Monitor*, Editor's Blog, http://www.csmonitor.com/Commentary/editors-blog/2011/0516/The-astronaut-who-learned-how-to-see; accessed August 25, 2014.
5 Details of the narrative of Dewey's "eclipse" among professional philosophers by analytic philosophy are contested. Certainly Dewey's decline among academic

philosophers began well before the mid-twentieth century, contrary to a wide-spread view that his influence only lost momentum after his death. The rise of analytic philosophy completed a process that had begun earlier. Meanwhile, Dewey's influence among professional educators remained strong even as most philosophy departments were shutting their doors to the American tradition. See James Campbell, *A Thoughtful Profession: The Early Years of the American Philosophical Association* (Chicago: Open Court, 2006). Also see the discussion of Campbell's book in *The Transactions of the Charles S. Peirce Society* 43, no. 2 (2007): 404–10.

6 Irwin Edman, *John Dewey* (New York: Bobbs-Merrill, 1955), 34.

7 Obituary of John Dewey, *The New York Times*, June 2, 1952, https://www.nytimes.com/learning/general/onthisday/bday/1020.html; accessed May 21, 2014.

8 The principal umbrella organization is the Society for the Advancement of American Philosophy: http://www.american-philosophy.org/. The website contains a history of the Society, written by Beth Singer (a founding member): http://www.american-philosophy.org/documents/BethSingersOriginsofSAAP.pdf; accessed June 10, 2014.

9 More recently, Dewey's influence has spread through the work of prominent pragmatist philosophers coming from the analytic tradition, such as Philip Kitcher and Peter Godfrey-Smith. For a comprehensive bibliographical essay on twentieth- and twenty-first-century pragmatists that includes recent figures and works and emphasizes Dewey's legacy, see John R. Shook and Tibor Solymosi, "Pragmatism: Key Resources," *Choice* 50 (April 2013): 1367–77. Also see the Pragmatism Cybrary: http://www.pragmatism.org/; accessed July 17, 2014. On neopragmatism, see David L. Hildebrand's "The Neopragmatist Turn," *Southwest Philosophy Review* 19, no. 1 (2003): 79–88, and his "Neopragmatism," encyclopedia entry for *New Catholic Encyclopedia Supplement 2012–13: Ethics and Philosophy*, ed. Robert L. Fastiggi, Joseph W. Koterski, Trevor Lipscombe, Victor Salas, and Brendan Sweetman (Washington, DC: Catholic University of America Press and Gale Cengage, 2012). On major currents within American pragmatism from the nineteenth century through the period of tension and cross-fertilization with analytic philosophy (with emphasis on Peirce as a heroic figure), see Cheryl Misak, *The American Pragmatists* (Oxford: Oxford University Press, 2013). Also see Misak's edited volume of essays on currents in contemporary pragmatism, *New Pragmatists* (Oxford: Oxford University Press, 2009).

10 The website for the Center for Dewey Studies, directed by Larry A. Hickman, is http://deweycenter.siu.edu/; accessed July 17, 2014.

11 For a more detailed description of the movement, see William Throop and Steven Fesmire, "Environmental Pragmatism," entry for *America Goes Green: An Encyclopedia of Eco-friendly Culture in the United States* (Santa Barbara, CA: ABC-Clio, 2012).

12 See Paul B. Thompson and Thomas C. Hilde, eds., *The Agrarian Roots of Pragmatism* (Nashville, TN: Vanderbilt University Press, 2000), and Paul B. Thompson, *The Agrarian Vision* (Lexington, KY: University Press of Kentucky, 2010). In many cases the agricultural extension agent in the 1930s through the 1960s was something

of an exemplar of Deweyan open inquiry in rural America. Some influence was due to the twentieth-century Jeffersonian intellectual John Brewster (1905–65), a student of Mead's at the University of Chicago who received his PhD in philosophy at Columbia University in 1938, before embarking on an agricultural career. (See Thompson, The Agrarian Roots of Pragmatism, 18.)

13 Andrew Light and Eric Katz, eds., Environmental Pragmatism (London: Routledge, 1996), 2.

14 Bryan Norton, Toward Unity among Environmentalists (Oxford: Oxford University Press, 1991).

15 Hugh P. McDonald, ed., Pragmatism and Environmentalism (Amsterdam and New York: Rodopi, 2012). Also published as Contemporary Pragmatism 9, no. 1 (2012).

16 Ralph Waldo Emerson was a friend of the James family, and he had a profound impact on Dewey, who regarded him as "the prophet and herald of any system which democracy may henceforth construct and hold by" (MW 3:191). Recognizing classical pragmatism as an outgrowth of the American philosophical tradition happily complicates any picture of Dewey as celebrating what environmental historian Donald Worster has called a "Linnaean" model of the exploitation of nature. Donald Worster, ed., Nature's Economy: A History of Ecological Ideas (Cambridge, UK: Cambridge University Press, 1994), 53ff.

17 Mark Johnson, Morality for Humans: Ethical Understanding from the Perspective of Cognitive Science (Chicago: University of Chicago Press, 2014).

18 For example, see Benjamin K. Bergen, Louder than Words: The New Science of How the Mind Makes Meaning (New York: Basic Books, 2012). For a discussion of imagination and qualitative experience that thoroughly incorporates James and Dewey, see Mark Johnson, The Meaning of the Body (Chicago: University of Chicago Press, 2007).

19 George Lakoff, The Political Mind (New York: Viking Press, 2008), 241. For a bibliography of research on imagination in cognitive science, see Lakoff and Mark Johnson, Philosophy in the Flesh (New York: Basic Books, 1998). In the jargon of Lakoff and Johnson, metaphors ferry (meta-pherein, to ferry across) content and logic from a source domain over to a target domain, structuring understanding and experience of the target. Image schemas are metaphor's scaffolding. They are prelinguistic gestalt structures that arise directly from sensorimotor interactions.

20 Glenn McGee, ed., Pragmatic Bioethics, 2nd ed. (Cambridge, MA: MIT Press, 2003).

21 Cornel West, The American Evasion of Philosophy: A Genealogy of Pragmatism (Madison, WI: University of Wisconsin Press, 1989); Eddie Glaude Jr., In a Shade of Blue: Pragmatism and the Politics of Black America (Chicago: University of Chicago Press, 2007). Also see Shannon Sullivan's Revealing Whiteness: The Unconcious Habits of Racial Privilege (Bloomington, IN: Indiana University Press, 2007).

22 See, for example, Judith M. Green, Deep Democracy (Lanham, MD: Rowman & Littlefield, 1999).

23 For example, see Maurice Hamington and Celia Bardwell-Jones, eds., Contemporary Feminist Pragmatism (London: Routledge, 2012); Charlene Haddock Seigfried, Feminism and Pragmatism: Reweaving the Social Fabric (Chicago: University of Chicago

Press, 1996); Charlene Haddock Seigfried, ed., *Feminist Interpretations of John Dewey (Re-reading the Canon)* (University Park, PA: Penn State University Press, 2001).

24 Judith M. Green, *Pragmatism and Social Hope* (New York: Columbia University Press, 2008).

25 Richard A. Posner, *Law, Pragmatism, and Democracy* (Cambridge, MA: Harvard University Press, 2005).

26 Michael Sullivan, *Legal Pragmatism: Community, Rights, and Democracy* (Bloomington, IN: Indiana University Press, 2007).

27 Roger T. Ames, *Confucian Role Ethics: A Vocabulary* (Honolulu, HI: University of Hawai'i Press, 2011); Roger Ames and David L. Hall, *Democracy of the Dead: Dewey, Confucius, and the Hope for Democracy in China* (Peru, IL: Open Court, 1999); Jessica Ching-Sze Wang, *John Dewey in China: To Teach and to Learn* (Albany, NY: SUNY Press, 2007); Joseph Grange, *John Dewey, Confucius, and Global Philosophy* (Albany, NY: SUNY Press, 2004). There are also many philosophers in the American grain working on Japanese philosophy. Books include Steve Odin's *The Social Self in Zen and American Pragmatism* (Albany, NY: SUNY Press, 1996). My own limited contributions include "Ecological Imagination in Moral Education, East and West," *Contemporary Pragmatism* 9, no. 1 (2012): 205–22.

28 Thomas M. Alexander, *The Human Eros: Eco-ontology and the Aesthetics of Existence* (New York: Fordham University Press, 2013), 20, 12.

29 David L. Hildebrand, ed., "Language or Experience: Charting Pragmatism's Course for the 21st Century," special issue, *European Journal of Pragmatism and American Philosophy* 6, no. 2 (2014).

30 Paul Fairfield, ed., *John Dewey and Continental Philosophy* (Carbondale, IL: Southern Illinois University Press, 2010); Mitchell Aboulafia, Myra Bookman, and Cathy Kemp, eds., *Habermas and Pragmatism* (London: Routledge, 2002).

31 Judith M. Green, ed., *Richard J. Bernstein and the Pragmatist Turn in Contemporary Philosophy: Rekindling Pragmatism's Fire* (Basingstoke: Palgrave Macmillan, 2014).

32 Victor Kestenbaum, *The Phenomenological Sense of John Dewey* (New York: Humanities Press, 1977); Shannon Sullivan, *Living across and through Skins: Transactional Bodies, Pragmatism, and Feminism* (Bloomington, IN: Indiana University Press, 2001).

33 Joseph Margolis, *Pragmatism Ascendent: A Yard of Narrative, a Touch of Prophecy* (Palo Alto, CA: Stanford University Press, 2012), 6.

34 Cf. the two-volume collection of Dewey's writings titled *Intelligence in the Modern World*, ed. Sidney Ratner (New York: Modern Library, 1939). Many of the essays are directly on world politics, published on the eve of the Second World War.

35 Sidney Hook, *John Dewey: An Intellectual Portrait* (New York: John Day Co., 1939), 3.

36 Randall Auxier argues that Foucault's own work on behalf of prison reform was influenced by reading Dewey and by his daily conversations with French Dewey scholar Gérard Delladale while in Tunisia in the late 1960s. Randall E. Auxier, "Foucault, Dewey, and the History of the Present," *Journal of Speculative Philosophy* 16, no. 2 (2002): 85–86.

37 See Larry A. Hickman, *Pragmatism as Post-Postmodernism: Lessons from John Dewey* (New York: Fordham University Press, 2007).

38 Edman, *John Dewey*, 34–35.

39 On this now-familiar theme, see Robert N. Bellah *et al.*, *Habits of the Heart*, 2nd ed. (Berkeley: University of California Press, 1996), and Robert D. Putnam, *Bowling Alone* (New York: Touchstone Books, 2001).

40 See Edman, *John Dewey*, 35.

Further reading

Eddie Glaude Jr., *In a Shade of Blue: Pragmatism and the Politics of Black America* (Chicago: University of Chicago Press, 2007).

Maurice Hamington and Celia Bardwell-Jones, eds., *Contemporary Feminist Pragmatism* (London: Routledge, 2012).

Mark Johnson, *Morality for Humans: Ethical Understanding from the Perspective of Cognitive Science* (Chicago: University of Chicago Press, 2014).

Andrew Light and Eric Katz, eds., *Environmental Pragmatism* (London: Routledge, 1996).

John J. McDermott, *The Drama of Possibility: Experience as Philosophy of Culture* (New York: Fordham University Press, 2007).

Charlene Haddock Seigfried, *Feminism and Pragmatism: Reweaving the Social Fabric* (Chicago: University of Chicago Press, 1996).

For a comprehensive bibliographical essay on twentieth- and twenty-first-century pragmatists that includes recent figures and works and emphasizes Dewey's legacy, see:

John R. Shook and Tibor Solymosi, "Pragmatism: Key Resources," *Choice* 50 (April 2013): 1367–77, http://www.cro3.org/content/50/08/1367.full.pdf; accessed 17 July 2014.

Glossary

Dewey often employed ordinary English words in technical ways, so it is important to explain (or eschew) his usage of familiar words. Where helpful, I use Dewey's own stated definitions.

accommodation For Dewey in *A Common Faith*, accommodation refers somewhat counterintuitively to the modification of our own attitudes to accord with particular and limited environing conditions (modifying our specific behaviors to meet recalcitrant conditions), as when "we accommodate ourselves to changes in weather" (ACF, LW 9:12). Compare to **adaptation**.

adaptation For Dewey in *A Common Faith*, adaptation refers somewhat counterintuitively to control or active manipulation of environing conditions to meet ends (modifying conditions to suit us), as when "dry soils are irrigated so that they may bear abundant crops" (ACF, LW 9:12). Compare to **accommodation**.

adjustment In the terminology of *A Common Faith*, adjustment is an active, deep-seated, and durable psychological reorientation toward life's general existential conditions (ACF, LW 9:11–13).

aims Conscious purposes or **ends-in-view**.

amelioration See **meliorism**.

an experience In the terminology of *Art as Experience*, an experience is experience in the singular that has become sufficiently demarcated from other experiences so that it has a coherent story to tell, from commencement to culmination. Also see **experience**.

consummatory experience. See **an experience**.

continuity, postulate or **principle of** "The primary postulate of a naturalistic theory of logic is continuity of the lower (less complex) and the higher (more complex) activities and forms" (LTI, LW 12:30–31). For example, the principle of continuity excludes reducing the ideal to the material (as in materialism), or the material to the ideal (as in idealism), and it precludes complete ruptures and gaps between mind and body. It also excludes "the appearance upon the scene of a totally new outside force as a cause of changes that occur" (LTI, LW 12:31).

cultural naturalism Among Dewey's names for his mature philosophy (see LTI, LW 12:28).

denotative method Experimental inquiry. An experimental method loops or spirals from immediate (primary) experience to symbolically mediated (secondary) experience and back to immediate experience (EN, LW 1:16ff.). The method is best understood as an ongoing mapping project (see Chapter Two). Also see **primary experience** and **secondary experience**.

dramatic rehearsal Our psychological capacity for imaginatively crystallizing possibilities for thinking and acting and transforming them into directive hypotheses.

dualism A distinction that has become dysfunctional. Also see **hypostatization**.

effort In Dewey's philosophy of education, effort is a demand for persistence and "continuity in the face of difficulties" (MW 7:175).

empathy See **sympathy**.

empirical naturalism Among Dewey's names for his philosophy, especially in *Experience and Nature*.

empiricism Traditionally defined as the view that all knowledge comes from experience, but it may be pragmatically defined as habituation toward exposing ideas to experience as test for their viability.

ends Ideally synonymous with consummations or fulfillments, but in Dewey's terminology an end may also be a mere terminus or cessation.

ends-in-view Consciously anticipated results. Synonymous with present **aims**, deliberate purposes.

environment Dewey noted the kinship of his usage with the French *milieu*, which, unlike the English word environment, wraps in cultural as well as physical conditions and suggests an inter-active medium rather than external surroundings.

experience Nature that has become conscious through human culture. For British empiricists the word meant inner receptivity to sensory impressions—the mind as moviegoer. But in Dewey's idiom the term designates not just the subject side of an encounter with the world, but experiencing and experimenting as a transactive whole.

experimental method. See **interaction** and **denotative method.**

faith In the old and still dominant sense, faith means "adherence to a creed consisting of set articles." The acceptance of this checklist of propositions is "based upon authority—preferably that of revelation from on high" (LW 5:267). But James and Dewey contributed to a pragmatic and melioristic notion that faith is inspirational belief where doubt is still plausible.

fallibilism Peirce's principle that doubt can never be completely purged from our assertions. The term was born of Peirce's disgust with the doctrine of papal infallibility, defined by the First Vatican Council in 1870. In Dewey's interpretation, Peirce's principle is the epistemological companion of the metaphysical principle of continuity. "It signifies that as our knowledge swims in a continuum of indeterminacy, so things themselves swim in continua; there are no exact breaks and divisions such as would make exact knowledge possible" (LW 6:275).

foundationalism Belief in an immovable bedrock for securing knowledge claims.

habit Dewey used the everyday word habit to broadly capture the propulsive power of latent recurring tendencies: "We need a word to express that kind of human activity which is influenced by prior activity and in that sense acquired; which contains within itself a certain ordering or systematization of minor elements of action; which is projective, dynamic in quality, ready for overt manifestation; and which is operative in some subdued subordinate form even when not obviously dominating activity" (HNC, MW 14:31).

horizon Synonymous with context. Dewey's emphasis on context-sensitivity enabled him to develop one of the overriding themes of his philosophy: Immediate (primary) experiences are pervaded with a quality that we feel rather than know. See **situation.**

humanism Dewey strenuously rejected *humanism* as a stand-alone name for his constructive philosophy, except in the simple and philosophically uninteresting sense of opposition to supernaturalism. He occasionally used the word as a modifier for naturalism, as in naturalistic humanism or humanistic naturalism.

humanistic naturalism Among Dewey's names for his philosophy. See **humanism**.

hypostatization, fallacy of (a.k.a. *the philosophical fallacy*) Dewey defined this fallacy of reification as "conversion of eventual functions into antecedent existence" (EN, LW 1:34). The image is of medical hypostasis, a blockage that slows the flow of blood. We block the "flow" of inquiry when we abstractly configure a substance, like Plato's forms or God or soul, out of the flow of processes, events, or concepts, and then treat "it" as a self-existing basic entity. We thereby forget that "it" originated through abstract analysis. When we read useful abstractions like "mind" or "object" back into the world as though they were preexisting features that we happened upon, and then convert what was selectively taken from a situation into the whole of what may be found there, we end up with dysfunctional **dualisms** and pseudo-problems.

idealism In its modern technical sense, which Dewey was targeting, idealism is "the complete resolution of everything into psychical existence" (MW 7:227) so that mind is "the sole monopolistic existence." Dewey regarded such idealism as incompatible with the evolutionary evidence that mind "is itself an expression of life, and the means by which life secures its most effective control of the environment in the furtherance of its own active processes" (MW 7:228).

imagination Our capacity for "realizing what is not present" to the senses (LW 17:242). Also see **dramatic rehearsal**.

immediate experience See **primary experience**.

inquiry Reflective thinking, ideally in accord with an **experimental method**. Active reflection occupies an intermediate position between an unstable situation and a temporarily controlled one. See especially Chapter Two on inquiry as mapping. Also see **intelligence**.

instrumentalism The aspect of Dewey's theory of experience that emphasized cognitive experiences of knowing and thinking.

intellectualism (a.k.a. the "intellectualist's fallacy" [QC, LW 4:232])
"The great vice of philosophy," intellectualism is "the theory that
all experiencing is a mode of knowing, and that all subject-matter,
all nature, is, in principle, to be reduced and transformed till it is
defined in terms identical with the characteristics presented by
refined objects of science as such" (EN, LW 1:28).

intelligence Humanity's experimental instrument for dealing with
perplexing situations. In Dewey's terminology intelligence
replaces the old notion of a universal Reason that transcends
culture, historical context, social relations, embodiment, and
emotion. Dewey's own examples highlighted *combined individual
efforts*, as with the joint development of maps and other navigational technologies.

interaction The unity of organism and environment as experiential
factors. In simple physical interactions, air, food, and ground are
incorporated into breathing, eating, and walking through interaction with lungs, stomach, and legs (EN, LW 1:19; HNC, MW
14:15). For Dewey the term interaction "assigns equal rights to
both factors in experience—objective and internal conditions.
Any normal experience is an interplay of these two sets of conditions. Taken together, or in their interaction, they form what
we call a *situation*" (EE, LW 13:24). Also see **situation**.

interactivity Among Dewey's terms marking the unity of the psychical and physical as well as the organism and environment. In
chapters 7–10 of the "new" book *Unmodern Philosophy and Modern
Philosophy*, written during Dewey's early 1940s shift to the term
transaction, the term *interactivity* is used for cases in which "one of
the partakers in the transaction has been analyzed out" (for
example, "I" as a subject or "pond" as an object). Dewey first
described this usage to Bentley in 1942.10.06 (15243): Dewey to
Arthur Bentley. Cf. EN, LW 1:222. Also see **interaction**.

interest The "identification of mind with the material and methods
of a developing activity" (MW 7:197). In Dewey's philosophy
of education, interest "depends upon the proper balance of the
old and the new in experience. ... [A] certain degree of difficulty, a certain amount of obstacle to be overcome, enough to
set the problem of a readjustment of habit, is necessary for
sustained interest" (MW 7:253–54).

judgment In the technical terminology of Dewey's logic, "Judgment may be identified as the settled outcome of inquiry. It is concerned with the concluding objects that emerge from inquiry in their status of being conclusive. Judgment in this sense is distinguished from *propositions*. The content of the latter is intermediate and representative and is carried by symbols; while judgment, as finally made, has *direct* existential import" (LTI, LW 12:123).

meliorism Steering between Pollyanna optimism and gloomy pessimism, meliorism "holds to the reality of evil as a genuine fact, but emphasizes the possibility, through good will and intelligently directed effort, of a progressive amelioration. It is essentially a doctrine of progress" (MW 7:297).

monism The opposite of **pluralism** in metaphysics and ethics. In ethics, monism denotes the search for a single principle or unifying concept to explain and direct moral life. Dewey argued that moral philosophers have generally abstracted some factor of moral experience as central and uppermost, hypostatized it, then treated this factor as the self-sufficient starting point for moral inquiry and the foundational bedrock for all moral justification.

natural piety Dewey used Wordsworth's term to characterize the possibility for wholehearted responsiveness to nature, a sensibility that ideally stays with us throughout our lives.

naturalism The analysis of art, science, values, mind, and religious life as among nature's possibilities and thus continuous with nonconscious physical interactions. Dewey's naturalism extended beyond epistemology to characterize the way we inhabit nature as cultural beings, so it should be distinguished from the much narrower meaning of naturalism in contemporary philosophy of science. But his naturalism shares with this newer movement a rejection of foundationalism, which in the specific terminology of analytic philosophy of science refers to any theory that tries to provide epistemology with a "pure" starting point free of any assumptions about the validity of prior scientific work.

naturalistic empiricism Among Dewey's names for his philosophy, from 1909 through his revision of *Experience and Nature*.

naturalistic humanism Among Dewey's names for his philosophy, mostly limited to *Experience and Nature*.

philosophical fallacy See **hypostatization**.

pluralism In metaphysics, the "theory according to which there are a number of independent ultimate principles of reality or real beings" (MW 7:324). In ethics, affirmation of multiple "independent variables in moral action" (LW 5:280). The opposite of **monism**.

pragmatism The critical attempt to replace received beliefs with inquiry, interpreting and evaluating beliefs as dispositions to *act* one way rather than another. Dewey held that the enriching and generative possibilities of human existence go unrealized except through action (Greek *pragma*). He expanded and rigorously systematized Peirce's and James's pragmatism as a means for regenerating philosophy and intelligently redirecting culture to meet life's evolving difficulties. In opposition to a popular sense of the word pragmatism, Dewey's writings ring with criticisms of shallow American practicality and acquisitiveness. He wrote in a 1940 letter: "The word 'pragmatism' I have used very little, and then with reserves" (1940.09.06 [13667]: Dewey to Corliss Lamont).

precariousness Synonymous in Dewey's metaphysics with instability. Empirical scrutiny through the sciences and ordinary experience reveals an existential mix of precariousness and stability, chance and regularity, struggle and safety.

primary experience Dewey made a functional distinction (a distinction for purposes of analysis) between primary and secondary phases or levels of an experience. The primary phase is immediately given. It is primal and raw, or only minimally and incidentally refined by reflection. It is viscerally *had* but not intellectually *known*, and it is the pretheoretical origin of our secondary cognitive or linguistic "take" on any matter. See also **secondary experience**.

problematic situation or **problematic character of experience** Reflective thought is occasioned by situations that are "disturbed, troubled, ambiguous, confused, full of conflicting tendencies, obscure, etc." (LTI, LW 12:109). In this way, problematic situations destabilize, engage, intensify, and stimulate deliberate readjustment to meet the surprises of a moving world. See **situation, inquiry,** and **intelligence.**

secondary experience. Secondary experience selectively discloses features of **primary experience.** It is mediated or cooked by our symbolic-conceptual frameworks. In Dewey's denotative (experimental) method, in order to operate as intelligent guides, such symbolic conceptions must be derived and refined with systematic rigor, and then traced back to the primary context from which they emerged *and* which they nourish and expand (EN, LW 1:39). See especially the discussion of inquiry as mapping in Chapter Two.

situation The whole biosociocultural context and focus of this or that experience. The term encompasses both internal and objective conditions—for example, the kissers, the kiss, and the entire setup of circumstances. If Dewey could be said to have a theory of substance even remotely analogous to traditional metaphysics, then it was encompassed in his idea of the situation as basic. Situation refers to any experience at hand, from its brilliant focus—conspicuous and apparent—to its horizonal field or background, the obscured, concealed, enveloping, and felt context (EEL, MW 10:323). Also see **interaction.**

subjectivism In epistemology, the notion that knowledge is merely a matter of private mental activity. Dewey attributed subjectivism to the fallacy of hypostatization.

sympathy Sympathy is "entering by imagination into the situations of others" and taking up their attitudes (1908 E, MW 5:150). This usage by Dewey and Mead fits the term **empathy** in contemporary feminist ethics.

technology Technology "signifies all the intelligent techniques by which the energies of nature and man are directed and used in satisfaction of human needs; it cannot be limited to a few outer and comparatively mechanical forms" (LW 5:270).

transaction From 1942 Dewey agreed with Arthur Bentley's contention that the word interaction retained a dualistic connotation inadequate to the thoroughgoing organic-environmental standpoint of primary experience. The terminological shift to *transaction* is most evident in their 1949 *Knowing and the Known* (LW 16). Due to the narrow contemporary connotation of transaction as a commercial deal, I have for better or worse preferred the word interaction in this volume. See **interaction** and **interactivity**.

truth Contemporary theories of truth are typically divided into three categories: correspondence, coherence, and pragmatic. Dewey is the chief twentieth-century exponent of the pragmatic theory of truth. He did not jettison truth understood as a function of inquiry. Instead, he rejected the *word* truth due to its cultural baggage: the word inclines us to picture a cocksure symbolizing knower standing outside of states of affairs that are known. He aimed to incorporate the *function* of truth within the concept of **warranted assertibility**.

warranted assertibility The provisional terminus of inquiry. The term *warranted assertion* sidesteps the popular sense of the words knowledge and truth as infallible ideas to which we commit ourselves irrevocably. To say an assertion is warranted is to affirm that it can be trusted, relied upon. When we act on the assertion things will (provisionally) go as anticipated. See especially the discussion of inquiry as mapping in Chapter Two. See also **truth**.

Index

Please note that page numbers relating to Notes will contain the letter "n" followed by note number.